JAILS AND JUSTICE

All materials appearing in this volume are regarded as appropriate expressions of ideas worthy of thought but should not be considered as an endorsement by the United States Bureau of Prisons.

JAILS AND JUSTICE

Edited by

PAUL F. CROMWELL, JR.

*Professor of Criminology
San Antonio College
San Antonio, Texas*

In Collaboration with

JOSEPH H. SCHRYVER

United States Bureau of Prisons

With a Foreword by

U.S. District Judge JOHN H. WOOD, JR.
Western District of Texas

CHARLES C THOMAS • PUBLISHER
Springfield • Illinois • U.S.A.

Published and Distributed Throughout the World by
CHARLES C THOMAS • PUBLISHER
BANNERSTONE HOUSE
301-327 East Lawrence Avenue, Springfield, Illinois, U.S.A.

This book is protected by copyright. No part of it may be produced in any manner without written permission from the publisher.

© 1975, by CHARLES C THOMAS • PUBLISHER
ISBN 0-398-03144-4 (cloth)
ISBN 0-398-03145-2 (paper)
Library of Congress Catalog Card Number: 74 1337

With THOMAS BOOKS careful attention is given to all details of manufacturing and design. It is the Publisher's desire to present books that are satisfactory as to their physical qualities and artistic possibilities and appropriate for their particular use. THOMAS BOOKS will be true to those laws of quality that assure a good name and good will.

Library of Congress Cataloging in Publication Data
Cromwell, Paul F comp.
   Jails and justice.
   Bibliography: p. 299
   1. Prisons—United States—Addresses, essays, lectures. 2. Corrections—United States—Addresses, essays, lectures. 3. Prisoners—Legal status, laws, etc.—United States—Addresses, essays, lectures.
   I. Schryver, Joseph H., joint comp. II. Title.
HV9471.C76   365'.973   74-1337
ISBN 0-398-03144-4
ISBN 0-398-03145-2 (pbk.)

Printed in the United States of America
A-2

Every graduate student remembers one professor who was both an unrelenting taskmaster and an inspirational mentor. Mine was Dr. Hazel M. Kerper. This book is for her.

CONTRIBUTORS

ROBERT M. CARTER, Director, Center for the Administration of Justice, University of Southern California, Los Angeles, California.

JOHN D. CASE, Warden, Bucks County Prison, Doylestown, Pennsylvania.

PAUL F. CROMWELL, JR., United States Probation and Parole Officer, Western District of Texas, and Professor of Criminology, San Antonio College.

VERNON FOX, Professor, Department of Criminology, Florida State University, Tallahassee, Florida.

JOHN H. GAGNON, Senior Resident Sociologist, Institute for Sex Research, Indiana University.

SARAH T. HUGHES, United States District Judge, Northern District of Texas.

SYLVIA MCCOLLUM, Education Research Specialist, United States Bureau of Prisons, Washington, D.C.

RICHARD A. MCGEE, President, American Justice Institute, Sacramento, California.

MIKE PLACE

MARK S. RICHMOND, Assistant Director (retired), United States Bureau of Prisons, Washington, D.C.

EARL RUBINGTON, Professor of Sociology, Center for Alcohol Studies, Rutgers, The State University, New Jersey.

DAVID A. SANDS

RICHARD TATHAM, Chief, Office of Alcoholism and Drug Addiction Program Development, District of Columbia Department of Public Health.

JOHN H. WOOD, United States District Judge, Western District of Texas.

FOREWORD

LIKE MANY OF OUR governmental institutions, the penal system of this country is under re-examination and attack. Between the covers of this book, the author, Paul Cromwell, presents useful information about the various phases of this system. His purpose was to compile a broad collection of varying viewpoints—some conservative and some liberal—with which you may or may not agree.

Professor Cromwell's experience in the correctional field includes employment at the Texas Department of Corrections, and as both a juvenile probation officer for the State of Texas and as a federal probation and parole officer for the United States District Court of the Western District of Texas. He is currently a professor of Criminology and Police Science at San Antonio College in San Antonio, Texas. He has acted as a police training consultant for the San Antonio Police Department and conducted training schools for police instructors pursuant to their certification by the state of Texas.

This is the fourth anthology in the general area of corrections which Professor Cromwell has prepared. He is also responsible for one other anthology in the general field of sociology as well as various articles in professional journals in the field of corrections, probation, parole, and police training. This current effort, *Jails and Justice,* is designed for use as either a beginning textbook, as a supplement to more advanced courses, or as an in-service training manual. This work is divided into four general sections. Section One, titled "The Problem," gives the reader a general view of the kinds of conditions and problems that do exist in our jails today. It is important to note that by the term "jail," reference is not made to federal or state penal institutions but generally to the local jail. Richard A. McGee, the author of the article, "Our Sick Jails," found in Section One, quotes Richard W. Veld as follows:

> Jails are festering sores in the criminal justice system. There are no model jails anywhere; we know, we tried to find them. Almost nowhere are there rehabilitative programs operated in conjunction with jails. It's harsh to say, but the truth is that jail personnel are the most uneducated, untrained and poorly paid of all personnel in the criminal justice system—and furthermore, there aren't enough of them.
> The result is what you would expect, only worse. Jails are, without question, brutal, filthy, cesspools of crime—institutions which serve to brutalize and embitter men to prevent them from returning to a useful life in society.

This is a rather startling statement and doubtless an exaggeration, but it is thought-provoking and does point up the basic problem. There are too few jails, too ill-equipped with too little room and too few trained personnel. If rehabilitation is truly to be one of the goals of jails and the incarceration of the criminal, something very definitely has to be done. As Professor Cromwell points out in his article, "Jails: 200 Years of Progress?," "The present problems of the jail today reflect the relatively low priority given it in the overall correctional continuum, yet this institution affects the vast majority of all persons who enter the process."

Section Two of this literature, "Jail Management and Administration," presents for the reader the overall problems of prisoner management and control. It deals generally with jail management procedures, with the custody of the prisoner, and the security of the institution. It is important to stress here that anyone who would enter the field of jail management must have foremost in his mind and basic in his education an understanding of the society into which he is placing himself: a society of incarcerated individuals whom society in general has for the time rejected. It is a society with its own social caste, its own set of rules, and its own set of values. The jail administrator must keep in mind this fact when he sets about his task of managing this society. His is the very difficult task of securing the integrity of the institution, while insuring the dignity of the individual confined therein.

Section Three of the anthology, "Dilemmas and Alternatives," points out, among other things, that there are almost as many different methods of rehabilitating an individual as there are individuals to be rehabilitated. For example, should the alcoholic repeatedly picked up for being drunk be once more thrown into the drunk tank, thereby placing a burden on the jail system, or should some other kind of program be developed that will actually aid the individual and help prevent the situation from recurring? Of what real value are work release programs and community work programs? In this regard, I highly recommend for the reader the article entitled, "Community Work: An Alternative to Imprisonment." The typical community work program allows selected prisoners to leave the institution for employment at a regular job on a daily basis. Nonworking hours are then spent back in confinement at the institution. This system, by no means a substitute for probation or parole, is a tool in helping the offender make a reasonable adjustment to the society to which he must return. It is also a system of punishment and reward, a sort of "carrot and stick" approach. Another article of particular interest in Section Three is one entitled "Why Prisoners Riot" by Vernon Fox. With the current resurgence of prison riots, a study of this article is particularly timely and helpful. In concluding this article, Doctor Fox makes the following very reasonable observation:

> ... Raising the educational level of the prison staff, especially the correctional officers, would reduce the predisposing causes. Their better understanding of personality development and social problems would provide them with the capacity for discretion that would, in turn, reduce the precipitating causes. Prison riots can be eliminated when upward and downward communication, combined with discretionary use of authority, reduces the probability of serious confrontation that should not have to occur in a democratic society.

Section Four of the anthology is titled "Legal Rights of Inmates." As a member of the federal judiciary, I highly recommend a thorough perusal of this section for anyone who would enter the field of jail administration. Rather than make a lengthy comment at this point, I would simply point out that in many instances the intervention of the federal courts system into the area of jail management and administration could most probably have been prevented had more jail administrators read this book and thoughtfully considered the problems it points out.

In conclusion, I would say that the hope and goal of any good jail administrator should be that he attain as successfully as possible the rehabilitation of his charges during the period of their incarceration and segregation from society, for when the unrehabilitated prisoner is sent back into society he often becomes a recidivist whose ultimate return to the institution is inevitable. As Professor Cromwell observes, this anthology is not meant to criticize. It offers, rather, to laymen, students and professional penologists alike a sound and useful reservoir of background information in all phases of this complex area. It is a challenge, a teacher, an exposé, and most certainly it offers some plausible and responsive answers to the problems. The reader will find himself agreeing and disagreeing, at times casually and at others resoundingly.

Succinctly stated, this book is a thought-provoking contribution to the field of penology and penal administration, and an experience in documented reality which I believe those concerned with this monumental and controversial subject will find constructive and useful.

JOHN H. WOOD, JR., JUDGE
UNITED STATES DISTRICT COURT
WESTERN DISTRICT OF TEXAS

PREFACE

THE LOCAL JAIL is the oldest of all institutions used for the detention of persons charged with violations of the law. It is the first step in the handling of the arrested offender and in it he receives his first impression of the correctional process. His experience in the jail is a potent force, molding his attitude toward law enforcement, the correctional system, and the community itself.[1] Yet, American jails, in the main, have failed to keep abreast of developments in other areas of correctional practice.

The President's Commission on Law Enforcement and the Administration of Justice stated, "No part of corrections is weaker than the local facilities that handle people awaiting trial and serving short sentences."

The Commission noted that in the vast majority of city and county jails, no significant progress has been made in the past fifty years.

The Commission reported 3,473 local jails with a projected daily population of 178,000 by 1975. The part the jail serves in the correctional process cannot be overestimated; yet, this is the last institution to be seriously studied, analyzed, and reformed. Whether for good or evil, nearly every criminal that is apprehended is subject to its influence.

Jails and Justice is a compendium speaking to the problems of the jail; to reform; to alternatives; and to the emerging role of the judiciary in the administration of the jail. The contributors are criminologists, jail administrators, attorneys, judges, law professors and the Task Force on Corrections of the National Advisory Commission on Criminal Justice Standards and Goals.

Section One sets the stage by reviewing the problems of American jails. The problem is seen as one hundreds of years old, yet still unresolved.

---
[1]American Correctional Association, *Manual of Correctional Standards* (1966), p. 43.

Section Two deals with practical considerations in administration and management. Contributors include The National Advisory Commission on Criminal Justice Standards and Goals, a former Assistant Director of the U.S. Bureau of Prisons, and the Manual of Correctional Standards.

Section Three consists of selections from many of the finest and most progressive criminologists in America. Alternative solutions to jail dilemmas are offered and the "community corrections" concept is analyzed in depth.

Section Four analyzes the death of "the hands-off doctrine" and the evolution of judicial involvement in the affairs of jail management. Prisoner legal rights are discussed and developed.

The Appendix presents model jail standards from the U.S. Bureau of Prisons, the State of Illinois and a table of cases in jail litigation.

The editor wishes to acknowledge the technical expertise and collaboration of Mr. Joseph H. Schryver, Community Programs Officer of the United States Bureau of Prisons, the encouragement of Mr. Ron Cunningham of the Bureau of Prisons, the tutelage of Dr. George G. Killinger and Dr. Hazel Kerper of the Institute of Contemporary Corrections at Sam Houston State University in Huntsville, Texas, and the generous authors and publishers who allowed the inclusion of their work in this volume.

This is not a volume of criticism, rather a presentation of the situation of the American jail and an effort to develop alternatives and solutions. It is designed as a guide for the practitioner and for the student of corrections.

PAUL F. CROMWELL, JR.
San Antonio, Texas

CONTENTS

	Page
Contributors	vii
Foreword — John H. Wood, Jr.	ix
Preface	xiii

Section One
THE PROBLEM

Chapter
1. OUR SICK JAILS — Richard A. McGee 5
2. JAILS: 200 YEARS OF PROGRESS? — Paul F. Cromwell, Jr. ... 19
3. INCARCERATING THE INNOCENT: PRETRIAL DETENTION IN OUR NATION'S JAILS — Mike Place and David A. Sands ... 29

Section Two
MANAGEMENT AND ADMINISTRATION

4. LOCAL ADULT INSTITUTIONS 47
5. PRISONER MANAGEMENT AND CONTROL — Mark S. Richmond 61
6. CUSTODY AND SECURITY 95
7. DISCIPLINE 121

Section Three
DILEMMAS AND ALTERNATIVES

8. THE DIVERSION OF OFFENDERS — Robert M. Carter 151
9. "DOING TIME" IN THE COMMUNITY — John D. Case 163
10. COMMUNITY WORK — AN ALTERNATIVE TO IMPRISONMENT . 181
11. NEW DESIGN FOR CORRECTIONAL EDUCATION AND TRAINING PROGRAMS — Sylvia G. McCollum 197

Chapter	Page
12. THE JAIL OMBUDSMAN — Paul F. Cromwell, Jr.	211
13. DETOXIFICATION CENTER: A PUBLIC HEALTH ALTERNATIVE FOR THE "DRUNK TANK" — Richard J. Tatham	216
14. WHY PRISONERS RIOT — Vernon Fox	223

Section Four
LEGAL RIGHTS OF PRISONERS AND MINIMUM JAIL STANDARDS

15. THE EVOLUTION OF JUDICIAL INVOLVEMENT — Mike Place and David A. Sands	237
16. STANDARDS AND GOALS FOR LOCAL CORRECTIONAL FACILITIES	252
17. RIGHTS OF OFFENDERS	267
18. TAYLOR V. STERRETT — Sarah T. Hughes	278
Bibliography	299
Appendix A	303
Appendix B	316
Appendix C	319

JAILS AND JUSTICE

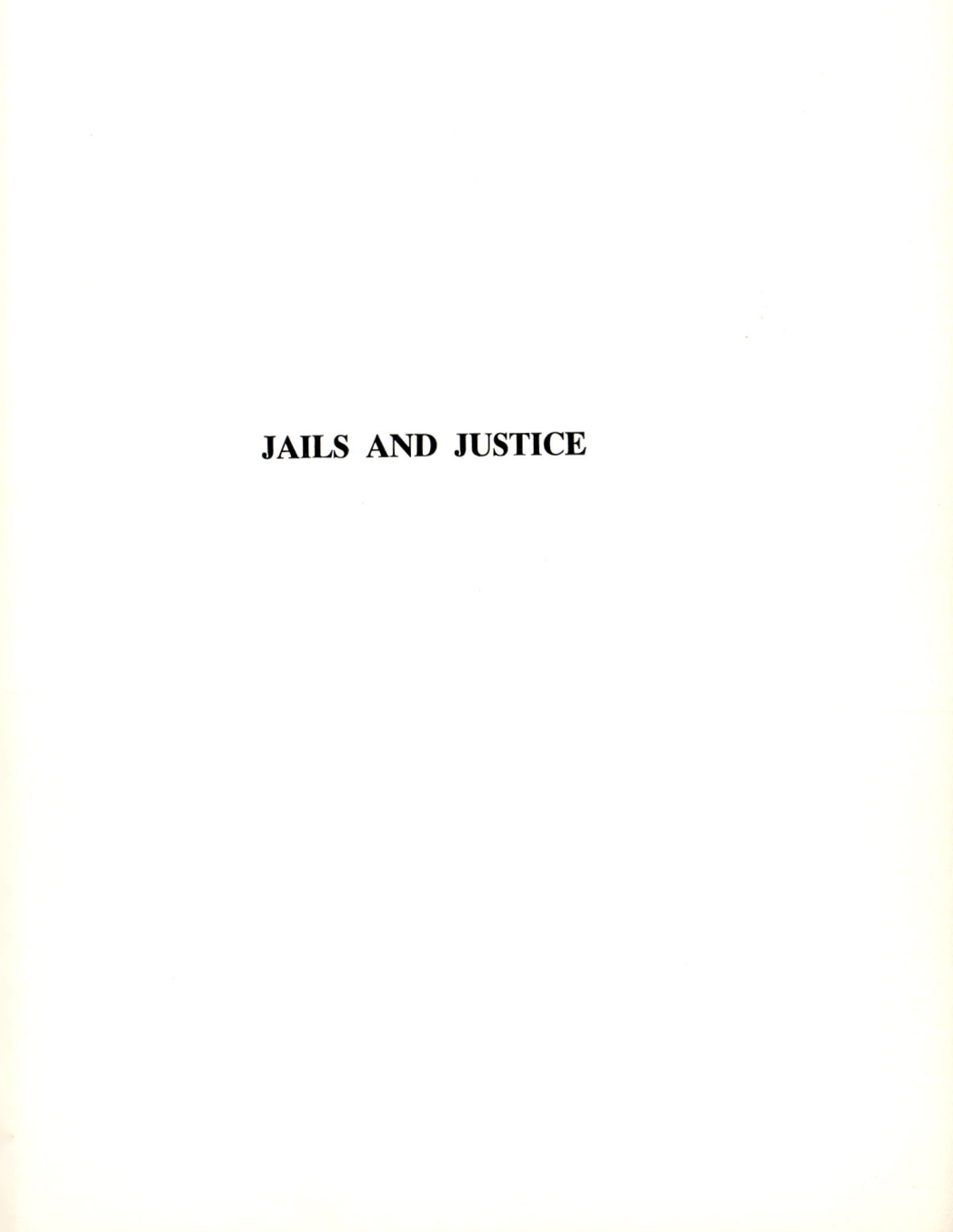

SECTION ONE

THE PROBLEM

CHAPTER 1

OUR SICK JAILS

RICHARD A. MCGEE*

THOUGHTFUL PRACTITIONERS and scholars alike have condemned this old derelict of local government for decades on end, but the common jail lives on with pathetically little change. Even when a new one comes into being, smelling of fresh paint and civic righteousness, it usually gets worse and worse until it also joins the ranks of what President Nixon's Task Force on Prisoner Rehabilitation calls "the most glaringly inadequate institution on the American correctional scene."[1]

Nearly 50 years ago, Fishman called these institutions "Crucibles of Crime."[2]

President Johnson's Commission on Law Enforcement and Criminal Justice, in its report on *Corrections*,[3] points out with commendable diligence a bare handful of "Programs of Promise" out of 3,473 local jails in the country.

Richard W. Velde, associate administrator of the Law Enforcement Assistance Administration of the U.S. Department of Justice, made this statement recently:

> Jails are festering sores in the criminal justice system. There are no model jails anywhere; we know, we tried to find them. Almost nowhere are there rehabilitative programs operated in conjunction with jails. It's harsh to say, but the truth is that jail personnel are the most uneducated, untrained and poorly paid of all personnel in

---
*Reprinted from *Federal Probation,* March, 1971.

the criminal justice system—and furthermore, there aren't enough of them.

The result is what you would expect, only worse. Jails are, without question, brutal, filthy, cesspools of crime—institutions which serve to brutalize and embitter men to prevent them from returning to a useful role in society.[4]

Sheriff Michael H. Canlis, president of the National Sheriffs' Association, said as recently as October, 1970:

It has been said that most (jails) are only human warehouses. We must ask ourselves, is merely keeping our prisoners secure, enough?

If we content ourselves with maintaining nothing more than a human warehouse, we are not only perpetuating the so-called failure of an element in the system of criminal justice, but we might, to some degree, be responsible for a contribution for some of the increases in crime.[5]

I personally opened the Rikers Island Penitentiary in New York City as its first warden, and later, as deputy commissioner and for a time acting commissioner of the New York City Department of Correction, was responsible for the administration of all of New York City's local lockups, detention prisons, and misdemeanant institutions. Since then I have inspected scores of local jails.

Only a few months ago, at the request of the San Francisco Crime Committee, I visited the jails of that proud city. The committee has made its report and I shall not add to it here, except to say that some of the conditions observed in San Francisco's new Hall of Justice Jail were shocking even to so jaded an eye as mine.

In fairness, however, it must be added that in San Francisco, as in numerous other jurisdictions, it is virtually impossible to fix responsibility for the glaring and obvious inadequacies because control of the resources of the local government are so fragmented that when the chips are down the "buck" is usually on someone else's desk. Then when the heat is off, the "buck" gets lost and nothing much happens until the next scandal hits the headlines.

But let us set aside the scandals, the instances of mismanagement and local political Indian-wrestling. Surely we don't need another century of indictments to convince us that the local city and county jails as now organized and managed simply must be replaced by a more rational system.

So, what can be done?

MANAGEMENT OF LAW OFFENDERS AFTER ARREST

First, let us discuss the larger problem, of which the jail is only the most visible part—visible because it is a physical place peopled by public offenders and public employees. The total problem is not the jail alone, but the whole agglomeration of public services involved in the *management* of *law offenders* after *arrest*.

The management problem involves all the parts of the criminal justice system—police, courts, prosecutors, defense attorneys, detention jails, probation services, and parole at the local level. Then there is the state government's correctional system, and overlapping these the federal system. The total so-called "system" must deal with the whole gamut of illegal acts, from minor traffic infractions to the most heinous of felonious crimes. The persons who commit the offenses include every imaginable kind of human being in the society—murderers, drunk drivers, prostitutes, thieves, forgers, mental cases, alcoholics, drug addicts, muggers, juveniles out of control, rioters, beggars—everybody is eligible if he gives cause to be arrested.

As a practical matter, however, we find the local jail being occupied principally by drunks, addicts, and petty thieves. And as for the women, if the prostitutes were eliminated from the jail populations, most of the women's quarters would be virtually empty most of the time.

Based on a very rough estimate, about 7 percent of the 3 million persons, more or less, who pass through these jails each year are charged with or convicted of felonies, and 93 percent are misdemeanants. It can be seen readily enough that the problem of jail administration, aside from holding a few felons awaiting disposition by the courts, is that of managing a miscellaneous array of persons charged with or convicted of offenses of a relatively minor nature. Only a very few of these are incarcerated for periods of six months to one year. A study of two large counties in California revealed that about one-third of the sentenced prisoners on a given day were serving terms of thirty days or less, one-third one month to three months, and one-third over ninety days up to and including one year.[6]

The question is often posed, what can be accomplished toward treating, managing, or rehabilitating persons who receive sentences of thirty days or less. As has been pointed out, this only accounts for about one-third of misdemeanants who are sentenced. The same question might be asked about those who receive sentences of thirty to ninety days, who constitute another one-third. The group that we might well be most concerned about is the third that receives sentences of three months to one year. What, also, of the substantial number of untried defendants presumed innocent under our law who may wait in jail for periods of three months to a year or more while the judicial machinery unwinds, leading to the day when the judge can finally render his decision? In some metropolitan jurisdictions 60 percent or more of the daily jail population is made up of persons who are unsentenced. The warehousing practice is bad enough for the unsentenced, but it has no validity whatsoever for those serving sentences. One month in jail may not seem long either to the judge or the sheriff, but to the prisoner it may be the longest 720 hours in his life, and just one of those hours could include the most damaging experience in his lifetime. Contrariwise, short stays in jail are a way of life for thousands of deteriorated middle-aged alcoholics and petty offenders. A 1963 study of some 7,000 inmates in five New York county penitentiaries showed that over 20 percent were serving a term which was their tenth or more.

SOME REMEDIES

The remedies for the deficiencies and abuses of the common jail are many. Some are relatively easy to find and can be applied by simple shifts in procedures. Others will require substantial changes in law and administrative organization.

Among the procedural changes which are available, some of which are already in use in many jurisdictions, are included:

1. The use of citations instead of jail booking for selected cases at the time of apprehension.

2. Release on "own recognizance" by the court at the time of arraignment by many of those unable to post money bail as a guaranty of appearance in court when ordered to do so.

3. Adoption of policy by the courts of giving priority in court

disposition to those in jail as opposed to those awaiting trial while out on bail.

4. The use of short form or "quicky" presentence probation reports in misdemeanor cases, so that the judge may have information about each defendant which might have relevance to his decision to choose among such alternative dispositions as suspended sentence, supervised probation, fine, and length and type of jail sentence.

5. Provision for payment of fines on the installment plan in cases wherein the defendant is employed but does not have enough ready cash on the day when sentence is pronounced.

6. The use of work-furlough releases for employable and reasonably reliable jail inmates.

7. The use of parole and postinstitutional supervision for most jail inmates and especially for men with families who receive jail sentences of more than sixty days.

8. Development of detoxification and rehabilitation programs outside the jail system for chronic alcoholics.

There is nothing either startling or new or illegal in the above list of procedural practices. What is really startling to any taxpayer who is concerned about the effectiveness of his dollar is that the number of jurisdictions which exploit *all* of these practices to the fullest are almost nonexistent.

Assuming the same number of officers and the same degree of police vigilance and efficiency now existing, and assuming that the above practices were fully utilized, it is probable that the *daily populations of the nation's local jails could be cut by as much as 50 percent without risk to the public safety.* Then, it is fair to ask, why isn't it being done?

The reasons are not difficult to find. Some are so obvious they need only to be mentioned without elaboration. Others are more elusive.

Administrative Problems

The most apparent reason for inefficiency and ineptitude in jail management lies in the governmental organizational structure in which the jails are embedded. According to the President's Commission on Law Enforcement and Administration of Justice, there were at the last count (1965), 3,473 local jails in this country. These were projected to have by 1975 an average daily population of 178,000. If this population were evenly distributed, each jail would have each day only fifty-one inmates. The fact, of course, is that hundreds of jails are mere lockups for a dozen or so and many of these are completely empty part of the time. In addition to the city and county jails there are thousands of police lockups in our towns and hamlets which are little more than cages. On the opposite end of the size distribution, we see great metropolitan facilities like those in Chicago, Los Angeles, and New York City, which number their inmates in the thousands. They are uniformly overcrowded, impersonal, undermanned and underprogrammed.

Seven hundred sixty-two, or 22 percent of all local jails, are a part of city government, and with rare exceptions these are operated by the municipal police. Except for inertia and vested interest, there is no logical reason for the municipal police to run any jail where offenders are confined for more than forty-eight to seventy-two hours to permit delivery in court and transfer to a county or regional jail. This is especially obvious in a place like Sacramento, California, where the county detention jail and the police jail are located on the same city block, or in San Francisco, where the sheriff's jail and the city police jail are on the sixth and fifth floors respectively of the Hall of Justice.

The most common practice is for local jails to be a part of county government and to be operated by the county sheriff. Twenty-five hundred and forty-seven, or 73.3 percent of all local jails, are so managed. A few jurisdictions, like New York City and Denver, Colorado, have city-county governments, with the jails operated by an administrator appointed by the mayor or the board of supervisors. At the 1965 count, there were 149 such jails or city prisons, and only 15 were operated by state governments.

A revealing survey of the jails of Illinois was made recently by the Center for Studies in Criminal Justice, the Law School, University of Chicago.[7] Of the 160 jails studied, 101 were county-operated, and fifty-nine were city jails. Even worse, of the thirteen very large jails, four were city and nine county. In California, as of September

26, 1968, there were 27,325 prisoners in local jails and camps. Of these, 2,151, or about 8½ percent, were in city-operated facilities. This percentage had dropped from about 22 percent in 1960.

Municipal police forces have trouble enough enforcing the law and keeping the peace in the cities without expecting them also to be either expert or very much interested in managing local jails with all the challenges presented by their diverse inhabitants and the ever-present potentialities for crisis and scandal inherent even in the best of them.

It appears, then, that there is substantial movement away from the practice of placing the jail management function under the city police. This begins to tidy up the administrative picture somewhat, but moves only a short step toward more rational and efficient systems of preadjudication, detention and correctional programs provided by local government.

There is no real agreement in concept or practice at this time as to how services for corrections at the local levels of government are best organized and managed. In Vermont and Connecticut the jails are under state jurisdiction. In New York City, with its "Home Rule" Charter, there is no county sheriff, and the city's detention jails and institutions for sentenced misdemeanants are administered by a Department of Correction headed by a Commissioner appointed by the mayor. In San Diego County, California, the sheriff runs the jail for pretrial detention and a separate Department of County Camps, headed by an administrator appointed by the County Board of Supervisors, operates the facilities for most of the sentenced misdemeanants.

Other patterns involve regional jail districts comprised of two or more counties, or contractual relations between adjoining jurisdictions, in which one county serves another for some kinds of prisoners on a cost reimbursement basis.

Most of these joint operations are fraught with very real problems of transportation, funding for building construction, and petty political friction.

In the preceding discussion of local jails, we have been speaking exclusively about such institutions for the care and confinement of adult men and women. These appear to have developed historically largely as unwanted appendages of agencies charged with the jurisdiction's police power. However, with the movement of population to the cities, county sheriffs have been losing more and more of their direct enforcement functions to the city police. As a result, the county jails have tended to become a larger share of each sheriff's patronage empire, and hence a function he is less willing to relinquish. The prison systems of the state governments have been used traditionally mostly for the more serious and more persistent convicted felons. In some states they may also accept sentenced misdemeanants of certain classes, especially women. But even with nearly 200,000 prisoners in state prisons, the lion's share of the day-to-day prisoner traffic is still in the local jails.

A Different Pattern for Juveniles

Parallel with this development in the adult offender field, we have seen different patterns in the delivery systems of services for juvenile offenders. Just as confinement and treatment programs for adults have tended to grow out of the police function, the juvenile services have emerged from the judicial function. This is because probation services originated in the courts. Detention halls and probation supervision for wards of the juvenile courts are more often than not adjuncts of the judicial rather than the executive branch of local government.

In spite of the division of the management of detention facilities for adults and juveniles between the sheriffs and the probation departments in most counties, probation services for both adult and juvenile offenders are combined in the local probation department in most jurisdictions. Here, again, we find every conceivable kind of variation of organization, or policy development of control over employees, and of financial support.

A few examples support this point. In California, each county has a probation department within the court system, serving both juveniles and adults, except in two counties. In Los Angeles County, the head of this largest county probation department in the state is appointed by and reports to the board of supervisors, not to the courts. Stranger still, in some counties he is appointed by the judge of the juvenile court, even though there are usually more adults than juveniles in the total caseload. In Wisconsin, probation and parole services are in the State Division of Corrections except in Milwaukee. In Washington State, adult probation is combined with the state parole system and is under the State Division of Institutions, but juvenile probation is under the juvenile courts, with some state financial aid provided. New York State has just created a unified state department of probation, but with typical illogic, has separated it from the State Department of Correction.

Viewed by anyone outside the correctional field who is possessed of the most elementary sense of administrative order and common logic, the ways in which we in this country organize our resources to deal with millions of lawbreakers, from the point of arrest on, must look as if it were designed by a madman with the advice of Public Enemy No. 1.

What Needs To Be Done

The time must come soon for concerned and responsible public officials to review this organizational "weed patch" with a view of making some sense out of it—sense to the taxpayer, even if not to all vested interests, ideological hangups, traditions, and political bickering over power and sources of money.

That so little movement has taken place in the last century might make the problem seem hopeless if it were not for some contemporary developments. Without elaboration out of scale with the scope of this article, some of these are worth mentioning.

The first is a growing concern about the nation's unbalanced tax structure. We argue that crime and the treatment of offenders are essentially a local problem, but the tax bases of the cities and counties grow weaker and weaker in comparison with those of state governments and the Federal Government. We must either find ways to feed state and federal moneys back to the local units of government or the higher levels of government must assume more of the burden for rendering direct services. "Correctional" services have always been at the end of the parade—behind health, hospitals, welfare, transportation, and education in these fiscal adjustments. Weak though recent efforts toward state subsidies and federal aid in this field have been, there are encouraging signs that our political leaders are beginning to recognize the problem.

Another hopeful sign is the increasing number of states which are developing stronger state departments of corrections, headed by competent administrators. This, coupled with stronger career services and better educated professionals at the journeyman and middle-management levels, cannot help but bring more pressure from within toward sounder organization and better performance.

It is also encouraging to note the interest shown last year by President Nixon in the appointment of a White House Task Force on Prisoner Rehabilitation, the statements of concern by Chief Justice Warren E. Burger, and the American Bar Association's recent establishment of a Commission on Correctional Facilities and Services.

The anxiety of the average citizen about the crime and delinquency problem generally must inevitably put the whole system on its mettle. All the participants in the administration of criminal justice are creatures of government. They must begin to produce, or perish.

If we would attempt to think logically about some portions of the "Justice System," such as the jails, we ought to come to some conclusions as to how to divide the total task among mutually supportive entities in the system without doing violence to our constitutional law and our established form of government.

We must start out, then, by calling to mind our doctrine of the separation of powers among the judicial, executive and legislative branches. First, let us consider the role of the judiciary with particular reference to developments in the supervision of convicted persons placed on probation. It seemed sensible enough for the trial court judge in a one-man court with one or two probation officers, to appoint these persons as functionaries of his office to make presentence investigations and to report to him from time to time on how a handful of probationers were doing. But now, with most of our population concentrated in great metropolitan complexes, this arrangement is as archaic as a one-cow dairy. In Los Angeles County, for example, the Probation Department has some 4,000 employees, administers an annual budget of $53 million, runs thirty detention facilities for juveniles, and supervises a caseload of adults and juveniles of 41,000 persons.

The decision to grant or revoke probation is, and should no doubt continue to be, a judicial function, but the operation of the probation department is as clearly an executive function as is the city police department or the operation of the state prison system. Accordingly, except in those rural counties with one-man courts, we must conclude that the administration of probation should be an executive function and a unit of state or county government. Except for the historical development of the services, there is no more logic in having the judge administer the probation service than there is for him to run the jails and prisons to which he commits defendants. If it is logical for the courts to administer large correctional (probation) programs, why then should we not suggest that the jails for adult offenders are as rational a component of court administration as detention halls for juveniles?

Looking at the question in another way, one might inquire why the sheriff or other police official should not administer the probation services with just as much logic as supports the notion that he is best fitted to manage the jails. If we persist in mixing the judicial roles of the courts with functions which are clearly executive, we may be running the risk of raising constitutional questions of jurisdiction.

The President's Commission on Law Enforcement and Administration of Justice, commenting on this issue, says:

> Most jails continue to be operated by law enforcement officials. The basic police mission of apprehending offenders usually leaves little time, commitment or expertise for the development of rehabilitative programs, although notable exceptions demonstrate that jails can indeed be settings for correctional treatment. Many law enforcement officials, particularly those administering large and professionalized forces, have advocated transfer of jails to correctional control.
>
> The most compelling reason for making this change is the opportunity it offers to integrate the jails with the total corrections network, to upgrade them, and to use them in close coordination with both institution and community-based correctional services. As long as jails are operated by law enforcement officials, no matter how enlightened, it will be more difficult to transform them into correctional centers. As a major step toward reform, jails should be placed under the control of correctional authorities who are able to

develop the needed program services. The trend should be away from the isolated jail and toward an integrated but diversified system of correctional facilities.[8]

A dispassionate view of the best possible way to organize the criminal justice system cannot but lead to the conclusion that there are three major groups of functions, each requiring different emphasis, different attitudes, and different professional training and occupational skills. In skeletal outline, they are as follows:

The Police
    Direct prevention and peace keeping
    Detection and apprehension

The Courts, including prosecution and defense
    Application of the law
    Judgmental disposition

The Correctional Agencies
    Presentence investigation and community supervision of probationers and parolees

    Management and control of defendants awaiting adjudication (jails and juvenile halls)

    Management of residential facilities and programs for all committed offenders (jails, prisons, correctional schools, and halfway houses)

If the above is a rational division of functions, it is clear that each political jurisdiction, be it a state or a county or a regional district within a state, should establish the equivalent of a department of corrections, which would be responsible for the management of all offenders under its jurisdiction, whether accused or convicted, and whether incarcerated or under community supervision.

This would mean: First, that the courts should relinquish administrative direction of probation services.

Second, that jails and camps for adult offenders must be removed from the administrative direction of police agencies.

Third, that in jurisdictions (usually counties) with too small a population to operate efficiently, they must either combine into regional districts or turn the functions over to state government.

Fourth, that the unrealistic administrative dichotomy between youth and adult correctional programs existing in many local jurisdictions be discontinued.

Fifth, that to encourage these changes and to ensure equality of treatment throughout the system, both the state governments and the federal government must provide financial assistance based upon adherence to decent standards.

"Equal Justice Under Law" are noble words engraved in marble over the entrance to the Supreme Court of the United States in the Nation's Capital. If we really believe in this great democratic concept, we can hardly continue to tolerate the spectacle of a mental case charged with disorderly conduct sitting naked on the concrete floor of a bare isolation cell in a local jail while in another jurisdiction he would be in a hospital.

It is equally incongruous for a minion of organized crime charged with felonious assault to be walking the streets free on bail while scores of minor but indigent offenders sit idly in overcrowded jails awaiting court disposition.

Finally, it is not enough to say that the local jail as we know it is a failure—it is a scandal! All the palliatives and all the uncoordinated efforts at patching up the present system will continue to fail. Basic reorganization of the whole structure for managing offenders at the local levels of government is required. Nothing less will do!

REFERENCES

1. "The Criminal Offender—What Should be Done?" Report of the President's Task Force on Prisoner Rehabilitation, April 1970.
2. *Crucibles of Crime:* A Shocking Story of American Jails. By Joseph F. Fishman. New York: Cosmopolis Press, 1923. Reprinted 1969 in "Series on Criminology, Law Enforcement and Social Problems," No. 35, *Jails,* Patterson-Smith, Publishers.
3. *Task Force Report: Corrections,* The President's Commission on Law Enforcement and Administration of Justice, 1967, p. 53.
4. From *The Correctional Trainer,* Newsletter for Illinois Correctional Staff Training, Fall 1970, p. 109.
5. *The National Sheriff,* publication of the National Sheriffs' Association, October-November 1970.
6. *Task Force Report: Corrections.* The President's Commission on Law Enforcement and Administration of Justice, chapter 7, pp. 71-81.

7. *Illinois Jails, Challenge and Opportunity for the 1970's.* A Summary of a 400-page Report by Hans W. Mattick and Ronald P. Sweet, based on *The Illinois Jails Survey* of 1967-68, conducted by the Center for Studies in Criminal Justice, The Law School, University of Chicago.
8. *Task Force Report: Corrections,* President's Commission on Law Enforcement and Administration of Justice, 1967, p. 79.

CHAPTER 2

JAILS: 200 Years of Progress?

PAUL F. CROMWELL, JR.

THE PRESIDENT'S COMMISSION on Law Enforcement and Administration of Justice, appointed by President Johnson in 1965 to study every facet of crime and law enforcement in America, presented the following indictment concerning existing problems in local jails and misdemeanant institutions:

> No part of corrections is weaker than the local facilities that handle persons awaiting trial and serving short sentences. Because their inmates do not seem to present a clear danger to society, the response to their needs has usually been one of indifference. Because their crimes are considered petty and the sentences they serve are relatively short, the corrections system gives them low status. Many local jails and misdemeanant institutions are administered by the police or country sheriffs, authorities whose experience and main concern are in other fields. Most facilities lack well-developed recreational and counseling programs, sometimes even medical services. The first offender, the innocent awaiting trial, sometimes juveniles, and women are imprisoned with confirmed criminals, drunks, and the mentally disturbed or retarded.[1]

The Commission reported that in the vast majority of city and county jails, no significant progress had been made in the past fifty years.[2] This indictment is extremely serious, yet a cursory reading of the literature of correctional history reveals that penologists were establishing standards for jail management almost 200 years ago, however:

In hundreds of jails in America today, conditions exist which were prevalent in European pest-hole prisons before the American Revolution. Penal Reformer John Howard*, in 1777 developed "correct principles" for humane jails which have not, as yet, been implemented in many "modern" American jails.

Howard brought to the attention of the world the barbarous conditions of jails throughout England and Europe with the publication of *State of Prisons*. In this classic of penology he formulated policies and recommendations for improvement of conditions and the development of humane institutions of confinement.

A comparison of the principles promulgated by Howard in 1777 and the recommendations and orders of two United States District Judges in 1971 and 1972 regarding conditions in two metropolitan jails, reveals startling similarities. Two hundred years after Howard it has become necessary for the courts, in many cases, to enforce minimum standards of humane custody of prisoners. This in the age of "enlightened corrections." Among Howard's "correct principles" were

> . . . Every prison should be built on a spot that is *airy,* and if possible near a *river,* or brook. I have commonly found prisons situated near a river the cleanest and most healthy . . . by their nearness to running water . . . is prevented . . . the stench of sewers.

In June, 1971, 194 years later, U.S. District Judge Garnett Eisele of the Eastern District of Arkansas described the Pulaski County (Little Rock), Arkansas, jail as follows:

> When the Court first inspected the jail, at the request of the parties, it came away with the impression that the cell areas were dark, dirty, very unsanitary, poorly ventilated, overcrowded, smelly, and overall, unhealthy and depressing places.[3]

Judge Eisele further observed: "Most of the toilets are of the old niche, recessed type. The plumbing is bad and requires constant attention. The washing and showering facilities are completely inadequate."[4]

In 1777 Howard recommended:

> Every court should be paved with flags or flat stones for the more

---

*All references to John Howard and his "Of Correct Principles" are found in *State of Prisons,* 1777.

convenient washing it, and have a good pump, or water laid in: both, if possible . . . In a room or shed near the pump or pipe, there should be a commodious *bath,* with steps . . . to wash prisoners that come in dirty, and to induce them afterwards to the frequent use of it. It should be filled every morning, and let off in the evening through the sewers into the drains. There should also be a copper in the shed, to heat a quantity of water sufficient to warm that in the bath, for washing those that are sickly. There should also be an *oven:* nothing so effectually destroys vermin in clothes and bedding, nor purifies them so thoroughly when tainted with infection, as being a few hours in an oven moderately heated.

In 1971, the court, taking judicial notice of conditions in the Dallas County (Texas) jail found: that no laundry facility had been made available to the inmates who, as a consequence, still had to wash their own clothes in the small lavatory sinks found in the cells; that no apparent steps had been taken toward improving the ventilation of the cells; that the detainees were still not being provided with adequate cleaning and bathing materials. . .[5]

Howard, in 1777, proposed:

In order to cleanliness; nothing is of more importance in the whole economy of a gaol: the ceiling and walls of every ward and room should be well scraped; and then washed with the best stone-lime, taken hot from the kiln and flaked in boiling water and size, and used during the strong effervescence, at least twice a year . . . Each ward and room should be swept, and washed every day, by the respective inhabitants, and sometimes with hot vinegar . . . Every prisoner who comes to gaol dirty should be washed in the cold or warm bath; and his clothes should be put into the oven in a sack on a pair of iron dogs . . . He should be provided with coarse washing clothes to wear while his own are thus purifying: clothes should be kept ready in the gaol for this purpose. (It would be better if criminals were to wear a kind of *prison-uniform* during the whole of their confinement, as I have seen practiced in many foreign prisons . . . Among other good effects, this would make them more liable to be discovered on escaping. On the other hand, they should be tried in *their own clothes,* for the obvious reasons that they may be more easily recognized by the witnesses.

Judge Eisele, in 1971, found:

The inmates of Pulaski County jail ordinarily wear the clothing which they have on their backs when they enter that institution for the entire period of their stay. There is no prison garb. There is no laundry.[6]

Regarding physical features and overcrowding of jails, Howard wrote:

> I wish to have so many *small rooms* or cabins that each criminal may sleep alone . . .

In 1972, U.S. District Judge Sarah T. Hughes of the Northern District of Texas, observed of the Dallas County (Dallas) jail:

> Most inmates are lodged in cells each with eight to twelve bunks which open into a "day room." The entire area is referred to as a "tank" . . . All tanks are overcrowded, having fifteen more inmates than the number of bunks. Those not assigned to bunks sleep on mattresses on the floor.[7]

Judge Eisele stated, of the Pulaski County jail:

> It should be remembered that there are no single or double occupancy cells in this facility. Ordinarily there are four or more inmates in each cell and, of course, in the large "bullpen" areas, thirty or more are housed together.[8]

Howard (1777):

> No fighting should be suffered in gaol: no quarrelling or abusive language; nor the frequent occasion of them, gaming. If anyone be injured, let him complain to the keeper, who must hear both parties face to face, decide the matter, and punish the aggressor by closer confinement. Faults that deserve more severe animadversion, should be reserved for the cognizane of the magistrates, or an inspector . . .

Judge Eisele (1971):

> During the course of these proceedings the court has heard the evidence of vicious assaults, homosexual attacks, torture, and inadequate and untimely medical aid in emergency conditions.[9]

Judge Hughes (1972):

> Infraction of rules was punished by a supervisor on complaint of a guard or of a corridor boss who is merely an inmate chosen by the supervisor. It was not required that the inmate be advised of the charge, and he could be placed in solitary, without a hearing, for an indefinite time. There was no provision for a review.[10]

In both the Dallas and Pulaski County cases the jail inmates alleged that jail rules and regulations were more or less discretionary with the jail supervisors and that no statement of jail regulations were enumerated for inmates. In 1777 Howard proposed, of regulations:

> *Regulations made known*
> Tables, exposed to public view; intelligibly drawn up . . .

In Dallas County the court observed:

> Previously there have been no written rules relating to conduct in the jail and inmates were not advised of any unwritten rules . . . The sheriff testified that new rules have been promulgated and will be posted in each tank and corridor. New prisoners will likewise be given a copy. As of the date of the trial the rules had not been posted and even the Chief Jailer was unaware of their existence.[11]

In Pulaski County the inmates complain that they are not informed or apprised of the standards of conduct expected of them or of the punishment or discipline which might follow from their departure from such standards.

The Court ordered that "the defendants would provide each incoming detainee with a printed copy of all rules and regulations regarding conduct and privileges."[12]

WHAT, THEN, HAS BEEN DONE?

The preceding pages graphically illustrate the dearth of progress in jail administration since the birth of this nation. America has done little to correct its "universities of crime," and the plight of the offender incarcerated in jail is overwhelmingly one of abandonment of all that is good and decent, of all that respects the dignity and worth of man.

The vast majority of prisoners found in American jails are as much neglected today as were those John Howard observed and studied 194 years ago.

Gary C. Stracensky recently wrote,

> Innumerable examples of the effects of horrid jail conditions can still be seen amidst the modern day efforts in "enlightened" corrections in America. Marked progress has been made over the past quarter-century in such areas as sentencing policies, probation, and parole practices, bail procedures, diagnostic center classification, community treatment programs, and legal aid for the indigent, to name only a few . . . These advances, however, have benefitted mostly the offender who is ultimately committed to our state and

federal prisons and penitentiaries. The benefits accruing to the individuals committed to our city and county jails, and other local institutions, have been negligible, if not completely disregarded in many cases.[13]

This situation is untenable in the era of enlightened corrections. The jail is the most important of all our institutions of imprisonment. The President's Commission on Law Enforcement and Administration of Justice reported 3,473 local jails in this country with a projected daily population of 178,000 by 1975. A high percentage of all convicted persons serve out their sentences in jails, and the jail is, with small exception, the universal detention center for persons awaiting trial. The part the jail serves in the correctional continuum cannot be overestimated, yet, this is the last institution to be seriously studied, analyzed and reformed. Whether for good or evil, nearly every criminal that is apprehended is subject to its influence.

The President's Commission on Law Enforcement and Administration of Justice, recognizing the need for change in local jails and detention centers, states:

> The deeper the offender has to be plunged into the correctional process and the longer he has to be held under punitive (though humane) restraints, the more difficult is the road back to the point of social restoration. It is logical, then, to conclude that the correctional process ought to concentrate its greatest efforts at those points in the criminal justice continuum where the largest numbers of offenders are involved and the hope of avoiding social segregation is the greatest.[14]

On the correctional continuum, jails are at the beginning of the institutional segment. The key to rehabilitative efforts lies at this juncture of the criminal process, yet, all too often, this becomes the point of departure for the first offender towards a career in crime. There is a critical need for programs and policies within the jails of America designed to forestall further crime and to initiate the rehabilitation process for the offender.

The President's Commission on Law Enforcement and Administration of Justice, *Task Force Report: Corrections,* made recommendations oriented toward the overall reform of the jail in America, and other investigative bodies, researchers, academicians and penologists have added their expertise and voices to the demand for adequate, humane and constitutionally operated jails and correctional facilities.

It would perhaps be wise to look backwards occasionally, to utilize the past in order to improve the future. A view of past reform efforts indicates that modern-day programs are often unconscious plagerism of past suggestions, yet still unimplemented.

Presented below are further selections from "Of Correct Principles," *State of Prisons*, 1777, presented in juxtaposition with proposals of the Special Committee on Correctional Standards, selected by the President's Commission on Law Enforcement and Administration of Justice in 1965. Their standards represent the best professional thought in the organization and function of a correctional system available today.

Commission Standards:
> A system of correctional institutions should have facilities for diversification of custody by age, sex, custodial requirements, type of inmates, and program needs.

Howard's "Correct Principles":
> The women-felons ward should be quite distinct from that of the men; and the young criminals from old and hardened offenders. Each of these three classes should also have their day-room or kitchen with a fireplace; and their court and offices all separate.

Commission Standards:
> Besides the appropriate educational qualifications for his position, each correctional employee should have good health, emotional maturity, integrity, interest in the welfare of human beings, ability to establish interpersonal relationships and to work with aggressive persons, belief in the capacity of people to change, recognition of the dignity and value of the individual, resourcefulness, patience, ability to use authority responsibly, and a continuing interest in professional development.

Howard's "Correct Principles":
> The first care must be to find a good man for a gaoler; one that is honest, active, and humane . . . This officer must be sober himself, that he may, by example, as well as authority, restrain drunkeness, and other vices in his prison. To remove a strong temptation to the contrary, it is highly requisite that no gaoler, turnkey, or other

servant be suffered to . . . have any connexion, concern, or interest whatever in the sale of liquors of any kind.

Gaolers should have salaries proportioned to the trust and trouble; since no office if faithfully and humanely administered better deserves an adequate encouragement: yet not so much as to raise them above attention to their duty, and the daily inspection of their jails . . .

Commission Standards:

Though parts of the correctional system may be operated by local jurisdictions, the State government should be responsible for the quality of all correctional systems and programs within the State. If local jurisdictions operate parts of the correctional program, the State should clearly designate a parent agency responsible for consultation, standard setting, research, training, and financing of or subsidy to local programs.

Howard's "Correct Principles":

Finally, the care of a prison is too important to be left wholly to a gaoler, paid indeed for his attendance, but often tempted by his passions, or interest, to fail in his duty. For every prison there should be an inspector appointed; either by his colleagues in the magistracy or by Parliament . . . The inspector should make his visit once a week, changing his days . . .

Commission Standards:

There should be one clinically trained chaplain for each major faith group in an institution having fifty or more communicants.

Howard's "Correct Principles":

I am fully persuaded, proceeded, in a great degree, from the constant attention that is paid to impress the prisoners with a sense of religion, by plain, serious discourse, catechizing and familiar instruction from the chaplains, together with the influence of a good example, both in them and in the keepers. These circumstances make a much greater impression upon the minds of criminals, when in prison, than they would have done before they came there. We have too much adopted the gothic mode of correction, *viz.* by rigorous severity, which often hardens the heart; while many foreigners pursue the more rational plan of softening the mind in order to its amendment.

Commission Standards:

All employable prisoners should have the opportunity to work. Their assignments should be closely related to their ability, interests, training needs, and custodial requirements. Prisoners should be paid for their work.

Howard's "Correct Principles":

Employment: Proportioned to strength; and to degree of criminality; hours of; kinds of; within doors and without doors; number working together; . . . working at their own trades; . . . proportion of profit to be allowed to prisoners . . .

SUMMARY

The jail in America today is not fifty years behind times as the President's Commission suggested but is, in many instances, foundering in a state of disorganization, chaos and *anomie* characteristic of the English and colonial American *gaols* of the late eighteenth century.

Standards of jail management and treatment of prisons promulgated by reformers 200 years ago are still awaiting implementation today. Presidential commissions, penologists and the court systems are striving to bring conditions in jails and community prisons, in 1973, up to standards suggested in 1777, often to no avail.

The present problems of the jail today reflect the relatively low priority given it in the overall correctional continuum, yet this institution affects the vast majority of all persons who enter the process.

The costs of change will be substantial, but the reality of the present and the promise of the future of the American jails if left unchanged, demands decisive action.

REFERENCES

1. President's Commission on Law Enforcement and the Administration of Justice: *Task Force Report: Corrections.* Washington, D.C., 1967, p. 178.
2. Ibid, p. 162.
3. Hamilton v. Love, 328 F. Supp. (E.D. Ark, 1971) at page 10.
4. Ibid, p. 10.
5. Ibid, p. 6.
6. Ibid, p. 13.
7. Taylor v. Sterrett, 344 F. Supp. 411 (N.D. Tex. 1972).
8. Hamilton v. Love, op. cit., p. 11.

9. Ibid, pp. 11-12.
10. Taylor v. Sterrett, op. cit., p. 7.
11. Ibid, p. 7.
12. Hamilton v. Love, op. cit., p. 5.
13. Stracensky, Gary C.: *Texas jails—Problems and reformation. Criminal Justice Monograph,* 3(4):2, 1971.
14. President's Commission on Law Enforcement and Administration of Justice: *Task Force Report: Corrections.* Washington, D.C., 1967.

CHAPTER 3

INCARCERATING THE INNOCENT:
Pretrial Detention in Our Nation's Jails

Mike Place and David A. Sands*

THE NATURE OF THE PROBLEM

WHILE THE TRAGIC EPITAPH INSCRIBED BY recent events at Attica has thrust the issue of prison reform into national prominence, our nation's jails simmer with similar explosive potential but are largely viewed with apathetic disregard. Eminent corrections officials have repeatedly urged that the overcrowded, unsanitary and dehumanizing conditions prevalent in jails must be relieved.[1] And occasionally, the detention facilities themselves erupt in violent warning of the exigency of this problem, as in the 1970 riot in New York City's Manhattan House of Detention for Men (commonly known as "The Tombs").[2] Nevertheless, the pace of reform is at best uninspired, causing a destructive threat to loom in Damoclean fashion over our entire system of criminal justice.

With national attention currently focused on correctional reform, it is significant to note that Norman A. Carlson, Director of the United States Justice Department's Bureau of Prisons, has recently declared that "[p]robably the most pressing problem in the correctional sphere is the tragic situation in our nation's jails."[3]

---
*Reprinted from *Buffalo Law Review*, Spring, 1972. (Copyright © 1972 by *Buffalo Law Review*.)

One commentator has described the extent of this "pressing problem" in the following manner:

> Conditions in short-term detention facilities are a national disgrace. Report after report of investigating commissions and grand juries disclose the existence of squalid, dehumanizing conditions in jails. The public should now be aware that jails are overcrowded; unsanitary; heavily populated with perpetrators of 'victimless' crimes — drunks, prostitutes, and vagrants — with older offenders mingled with young first-timers, and with convicted criminals mixed with those awaiting trial but unable to make bail; staffed by underpaid and untrained jailers who cannot prevent—or who even participate in assaults, homosexual attacks and other forms of brutality; lacking in facilities, money, and personnel to provide decent medical care, adequate nutrition, minimal recreational activities, or any educational or vocational program.[4]

Indeed, conditions in jails are consistently rated as being worse or harsher than those in penal institutions,[5] and one study has reported that prisoners preferred penal institutions to detention facilities in the ratio of twelve to one.[6]

Certainly one element contributing to the substandard and deteriorating state of our jails is the age of the physical plants. In a revealing study of jails in Illinois, it is reported that almost 30 percent of all jails in use in that state are more than seventy-five years old.[7] Moreover, more than half of all jails are more than fifty years old, and that figure swells to nearly 70 percent if only county jails, where inmates are confined for longer periods than in city jails, are considered.[8] On a national level, a recent survey by the United States Census Bureau for the Law Enforcement Assistance Administration observed that more than 25 percent of detention cells were housed in buildings more than fifty years old and 6 percent in buildings more than 100 years old.[9] The potential for deterioration is undoubtedly proportional to the age of the physical facility, but the age factor presents even more subtle ramifications. As the Illinois study pointed out:

> Generally speaking, the architecture of a jail reflects the ideas about human nature that were in the minds of the teachers and textbooks that taught the architects who designed them. Therefore, the fact that a jail is 25, 50, or 100 years old means that it embodies ideas about how human beings ought to be handled and treated that are 75, 100, and 150 years old.[10]

Of course age alone does not render a detention facility incapable of constructive service if it has been adequately maintained and/or modernized to meet current heating, lighting and ventilation standards. But largely due to limited municipal and county budgets and an unenlightened public interest, such maintenance programs have failed to materialize. The Illinois study reports that in that state "[o]ver 40 percent of the jails have not been touched since their dedication" nor are there plans for any physical improvements contemplated in over 85 percent of all jails.[11] As a result many jails exist in a high state of disrepair; lacking in proper lighting, ventilation or heating equipment; devoid of properly operative sanitary facilities; and often plainly insecure.[12] Many are quite literally fire traps; and, while some have been condemned, "it does not follow that they have been replaced."[13]

Compounding these factors and creating the most crucial stress on our aged and inadequate detention facilities is the problem of overcrowding. In 1966 it was estimated that 1,016,748 persons had been held in local jails, the average daily population being 141,303.[14] Plainly, facilities that were built to accommodate populations of twenty-five, fifty or more years ago cannot cope with such numbers of inmates. As the country's population has increased, the number of crimes committed has risen correspondingly. Utilization of modern and more efficient police methods is causing the apprehension and detention of more criminal offenders. The result is a serious crush on our nation's jails. A New York City study has estimated that detention facilities in that metropolis are filled to 161 percent of acceptable capacity.[15] and other figures indicate that this number occasionally reaches 200 percent.[16] Crowded conditions mean multiple inmate assignments to cells designed for single persons. The already inadequate sanitation facilities are so overtaxed that many jails offer toilets and washbasins at ratios that exceed one per every twelve inmates.[17] Strained jail budgets fail to provide for purchase of basic articles of personal hygiene such as soap, towels and toilet tissue, not to mention major items like clothing, mattresses and linens. Inmates are consequently compelled to exist in conditions of squalor and misery. The Illinois Jail study has concluded that "provision of personal hygiene articles is far less than what is required for simple human decency . . . ."[18]

Finally, it must be noted that since most jails are locally operated short-term detention facilities, construction programs generally anticipated only basic accommodations. Therefore, as the recent Census Bureau report points out, 86 percent of city and county jails across the nation have no recreational facilities, 50 percent have no medical facilities, and 25 percent are without prisoner visitation areas.[19]

At this point the reader should be acutely aware that these institutions of justice, once mockingly labeled "crucibles of crime,"[20] are indeed a "national disgrace."[21] Richard A. McGee, long-time corrections official, has conceded that "[w]hile I readily grant the necessity for places of temporary detention for most offenders . . . this initial step in the correctional process is more often destructive than corrective."[22] And in an impassioned article which decries the atrocities of our jails, Karl Menninger, author of *The Crime of Punishment,* has been moved to write:

> One-hundred and fifty thousand human beings, mostly young ones, are locked up in cages and dungeons in the name of 'justice' and mercy by agents of the very people who are being wronged. This expensive, futile, absurd, cruel business does not rehabilitate anyone; it does not reform anyone; it does not change anyone for the better. It only enrages and stupefies and crushes already unstable, misdirected and confused people. It ruins them for life in the shape of a light disciplinary slap on the wrist. After a jail sentence, the best of prisons cannot accomplish much.[23]

Thus, whether incarceration is viewed as an essential element of a deterrent criminal justice system or a primitive and regressive punishment not to be tolerated by a society enlightened by psychology and the social sciences, basic dysfunctions in the jail milieu must be acknowledged.

Such is the environment into which the jail inmate is cast. While the humanitarian may legitimately question the subjugation of any person to these environs, this comment is intended to focus upon only one segment of the total jail population—the pretrial detainee—whose confinement under such conditions is even more repugnant. These detainees are not incarcerated for punishment or rehabilitation, but solely because they are accused of committing a punishable offense and cannot "make" or are not allowed benefit of bail. Our system of criminal justice proclaims that the accused is to be presumed innocent until proven otherwise by judicial determination. Yet persons detained in local jails "who have not yet been convicted of a crime are subjected to the worst aspects of the American correctional system."[24]

While any investigation centered about restriction of personal freedoms will inevitably evoke consideration of constitutional protections, the instant discussion is not intended to concentrate on the constitutional questions.[25] Instead, the legitimate bounds of restrictions placed upon pretrial detainees will be explored with reference to the few recent cases that have dared venture into the realm of jail litigation. Such cases are important not only for the decisional principles established thereunder but also because they may herald a reversal of the traditional judicial disinclination to interfere in matters of institutional operation. The underlying thesis of this comment is that only a positive showing of legitimate state interest in assuring the presence of accused persons at trial can justify *any* restrictions upon the freedoms of such individuals. Even when pretrial detention is deemed imperative, the presumption of innocence must operate to insure that the detainee retains rights commensurate with those of his counterpart who is liberated by the bail system. Only those restrictions which are necessarily inherent in imprisonment can be tolerated.[26]

THE BURDENS OF CONFINEMENT

As a prelude to discussion of recent jail litigation, it is appropriate to briefly investigate the composition of jail populations and the consequences of detention, with special emphasis on the pretrial detainee. Such an investigation is essential for an understanding of the potential abuses of inmates' rights and for a determination of those areas most appropriate for judicial and administrative relief.

The Jail Population

Jails are operated primarily by county or municipal administrations as short-term detention facilities. These institutions house two basic classifications of persons—convicted misdemeanants sentenced to terms of confinement of one year or less, and accused persons awaiting trial. Inmates in the former category probably do not present a clear danger to society—being "annoying but . . . seldom vicious."[27] Thus a leading correctional official has recently written:

> As a practical matter . . . we find the local jail being occupied principally by drunks, addicts, and petty thieves. And as for the women, if the prostitutes were eliminated from the jail populations, most of the women's quarters would be virtually empty most of the time.[28]

However, the instant concern centers about those persons awaiting trial and, perhaps surprisingly, the United States Census Bureau has recently determined that this group constitutes more than half of all populations in our nation's jails.[29] Other studies have indicated that in some metropolitan jurisdictions as many as 60[30] or 70[31] percent of jail inmates are unconvicted.

The reasons usually suggested as justification for the confinement of these presumably innocent persons are twofold: to insure the appearance of the accused at trial and to protect such persons who may be called to appear as witnesses from harassment by the accused.[32] The former rationale is certainly the most widely espoused and has been described as basic to our system of criminal justice. Thus one commentator has written:

> [We] have realized that a deterrent system cannot function at all unless society can successfully prosecute lawbreakers. Hence we have traditionally detained individuals likely to flee or otherwise avoid prosecution. This limited form of pretrial detention is considered essential to the preservation of a system that seeks to control crime by threat of subsequent punishment . . . .[33]

However, it is not every accused that is subject to this "traditional" scheme of secured appearance. Since the passage of the Judiciary Act of 1789,[34] persons accused of noncapital offenses may obtain release before trial by giving adequate assurance that they will stand trial and submit to sentence if judged guilty.[35] Our society has determined that such "adequate assurance" shall be the deposit of money, or bail, held by the "court" and forfeited upon nonappearance. As a practical matter the bail system is administered by professional bail bondsmen who charge fees commonly fixed by statute.[36] This right to have bail set in noncapital cases is guaranteed to federal prisoners by Federal Rule of Criminal Procedure 46(a)(1). Most states have similar provisions guaranteed either by state constitution[37] or by statute;[38] however, a few permit discretionary denial of bail where a felony is charged.[39] This brief digression into the operation of the bail system indicates that most pretrial detainees are confined either because they are accused of a non-bailable offense or because individual poverty prohibits payment of the required sum when bail is granted. As this latter point suggests, the indigent defendant will more often be subjected to pretrial detention than will the accused who enjoys an economically superior status.[40]

Several additional means through which accused persons may be jailed before trial deserve mention. Persons who are accused of violating probation or parole are generally not eligible for bail. In addition, there is some current movement toward institution of a system of preventive detention. Under this practice, which has been advocated by President Nixon as part of his omnibus recommendations for crime control,[41] certain "hardcore recidivists" could be held in pretrial detention when accused of crimes and when their release would pose a danger to the community.[42] Implementation of this procedure has been widely attacked[43] and consequently not yet widely accepted. But a practice closely akin to the notions underlying preventive detention is exercised by many jurisdictions. This involves requiring a higher than normal bail amount for defendants having records of multiple arrests or facing serious criminal charges. The increased amount of bail frequently frustrates the accused's designs upon liberty and assures his membership in the jail population.

Given this sketch of the typical jail population with its heavy concentration of indigent inmates, and bearing in mind the inhumane conditions prevalent in our detention facilities, the layman may still be able to persuade himself that pretrial detention involves only minimal sacrifices of human rights. After all, are not detainees merely held for the brief period between arrest and trial? Unfortunately this conception that pretrial detention is limited to an abbreviated length of a few hours or days has become, for many, a utopian myth. In a study of Illinois jails released in 1970, researchers compiled detailed information concerning length of detention periods of unconvicted persons. The findings relative to average periods of confinement awaiting trial were presented in the following table:[44]

TABLE 3-I

Average Stay Awaiting Trial	Percent of Total Jails
Less than 8 hrs.	5.6
8-12 hrs.	12.5
13-24 hrs.	9.4
1- 2 days	12.5
3- 7 days	23.7
8-14 days	6.9
15-30 days	11.2
1- 2 months	8.8
More than 2 months	6.3
No response	3.1

An analysis of these figures reveals that almost one-third (33.2%) of all inmates are detained for periods of more than one week. Fifteen percent are confined for more than a month. It should be noted, however, that this study made no attempt to exclude cases in which payment of bail resulted in quick release from detention. A New York City study which eliminated such periods determined the average jail stay to be 140 days.[45] A more recent investigation conducted in New York City suggested that average periods of detention were increasing so that "it was not uncommon for men to be in detention for six to twelve months, with some prisoners detained more than a year."[46] Clearly, the average stay computed by the latter studies exceeds the median stay of three to seven days established in the Illinois report.

Several factors explain this discrepancy. As already indicated the Illinois report includes periods of confinement for all persons arrested during the study, whereas the New York City studies excluded cases in which quick release was obtained by payment of bail. Second, the Illinois report surveyed all jails throughout the state, both city and county, located in large cities and small towns. The New York City reports were confined to that metropolis. Undoubtedly, the length of pretrial detention in any jail bears some correlation to the level of activity of the courts responsible for adjudicating cases in those jails. The notorious overcrowding of court calendars in our metropolitan tribunals may cause lengthy delays in the trial process, and New York City courts are the rule rather than the exception. Courts serving smaller populations, on the other hand, are frequently more able to provide defendants with a speedy trial. These differences relating to the character of the samples used are reflected in the results of each study. Consequently, the studies limited to city jails have yielded a longer average detention period. Of course the regional fluctuation in crime rates and the generally difficult task of standardization affect attempts at generalization and are not to be discounted in assessing the differential. Thus, the 1967 Presidential Crime Commission Report irresolutely stated that the "average time served in detention ranged from six weeks to eight months in some jurisdictions."[47]

The central point, however, must not escape us. For persons not convicted of any offense, any period of detention is intolerable when five and six inmates are crowded into a cell designed for one; when homosexual attacks are frequent and unchecked; when toilets are cracked and leaking and showers and washbasins are unavailable; when the basic implements of personal hygiene are unsecurable, and the detainee's only clean clothes are those on his back when arrested.

The Consequences of Detention

The imprisonment of an accused prior to a determination of guilt is a rather awesome thing: it costs the taxpayers tremendous sums of money; it deprives the affected individual of his most precious freedom, liberty; it deprives him of the ability to support himself and his family; it quite possibly costs him his job; it restricts his ability to participate in his own defense; it subjects him to the dehumanization of prison; it separates him from his family; and without trial, it casts over him an aura of criminality and guilt.[48]

However essential to a "deterrent" system of criminal justice pretrial detention is thought to be,[49] the presumption of innocence dictates that such confinement itself is not supposed to deter or punish criminal acts.[50] Yet the preceding discussion of jail conditions and a reading of the passage quoted immediately above make it eminently clear that grave burdens are being placed upon pretrial detainees.[51] Whatever the strength of positions which claim that these burdens are inherent incidents of confinement, it cannot be rationally maintained that the detrimental consequences of detention should be allowed to fall upon one who is presumed innocent of any transgression. And yet we permit this fate to befall more than a million persons annually.

The burdens of confinement even spread to the innocent members of the detainee's family, as they are forced to work or otherwise provide for their own welfare. Imprisonment often frustrates the individual's efforts to prepare, or assist legal counsel in preparation of an adequate defense,[52] and may hamper the ability to secure witnesses.[53] And even though many pretrial detainees are subsequently discharged of all criminal liability and released,[54] the individual may discover that he has lost his employment and is tinged with the stigma of criminality.

Even more shocking, if one's sensibilities are not already numbed, is information which suggests that failure to secure pretrial release may affect the ultimate disposition of one's case and even the sentencing process.[55] One recent case study reports that "inhumane conditions in . . . jails frequently lead [detainees] to plead guilty in order to insure a quick transferral to a 'more humane' state prison."[56] When a case does go to trial, the unkempt appearance of an accused who has spent weeks or months in jail may influence the "demeanor" aspect of his testimony.[57] It has also been suggested that since the accused has already been confined to jail, presumptions of guilt may arise in the minds of jury members and even the judge.[58] A recent American Bar Association report noted that studies conducted in New York, Philadelphia, and the District of Columbia "all indicate that the conviction rate for jailed defendants materially exceeds that of bailed defendants."[59] Effects on sentencing may be similarly adverse. One investigation revealed that the likelihood of receiving a prison sentence increased proportionally with the period of detention before trial. Even persons who were jailed for only a portion of the period between arrest and trial were found to receive more favorable sentences than those continuously jailed, regardless of the brevity of this continuous detention.[60] Even more disturbing were the statistical effects of pretrial detention on first offenders.

> [J]ailed first offenders not only are twice as likely to be convicted and six times as likely to receive prison sentences as are bailed first offenders, but . . . jailed first offenders are half again as likely to receive prison sentences as bailed repeat offenders.[61]

The burdens associated with pretrial detention are by no means limited to the accused and his family but extend to the tax-paying public in an expensive and real fashion. The yearly cost of housing and feeding defendants detained pending trial in Philadelphia alone was recently estimated at nearly $5 million.[62] Even as early as 1962, New York City reportedly spent twice that amount in annual detention costs and "[o]ther cities report similar figures."[63] On the national level, a recent estimate of yearly operating expenditures for all jails was placed at $147,794,214.[64] And it should be noted that such figures do not express ancillary costs such as welfare payments made to detainees' families. The total supportive costs of pretrial confinement clearly constitute a substantial fiscal resource drain. But while monetary considerations are often accorded a preferred priority in our society, pretrial detention spawns additional, more subtle, social burdens, the effects of which are certainly more acute.

For many accused, pretrial detention represents the initial and sole contact with our correctional institutions. Thus, the part which the jail plays in our criminal justice system "cannot be overestimated."[65] Exposure to the kinds of physical conditions and individual burdens associated with our jails can only operate to demoralize the spirit and attitude of the accused. When release is effectuated, whether it be by acquittal or after service of sentence, the resentments and attitudinal prejudices gleaned from the jail experience remain. When the jail environment has been the first contact with our penal system, this first dose of American "justice" can prove particularly disillusioning. These acquired feelings of suspicion and distrust for the criminal justice system are internalized and carried with the detainee back into his particular social milieu, where they are communicated to family and friends. Each year hundreds of thousands of persons move through this process of demoralization, internalization and communication until vast segments of our population are affected. And since the poor[66] and minority groups[67] constitute a large percentage of the jail population, it is not surprising that the fears and suspicions enumerated are perhaps most prevalent in these segments of our society. The outward manifestations of these acquired prejudices are distrust and resentment toward the courts and police, this latter group being perceived as having caused the unpleasant ordeal at the outset by effecting the arrest. The resentment of police breeds friction; and friction contempt.

REFERENCES

1. Writing in 1959, elder statesman of corrections Richard A. McGee advocated comprehensive jail reform to alleviate the social and psychological damage wrought by these inadequate facilities that even at that time had "been so obvious to every student of this problem for the past fifty years." McGee, *The Administration of Justice: The Correctional Process,* 5 NPPA J. 225, 228 (1959). In a recent article this author persists in his campaign. McGee, *Our Sick Jails,* 35 Fed. Prob. 3 (Mar. 1971).
2. *New York Times,* Aug. 11, 1970, at 1, col. 1.
3. Carlson, *The Law and Corrections,* 6 U. San Francisco L. Rev. 77, 83 (1971).
4. Turner, *Establishing the Rule of Law in Prisons: A Manual for Prisoner's Rights Litigation,* 23 Stan. L. Rev. 473, 475 (1971) (footnotes omitted).
5. President's Commission on Law Enforcement and Administration of Justice, Task Force Report: Corrections 24 (1967) [hereinafter cited as President's Crime Commission Report]; Council of the City of New York Subcommittee on Penal and Judicial Reform, Report on Prison Reform 11 (1971) [hereinafter cited as Burden Report]; Note, *Pre-Trial Detention in the New York City Jails,* 7 Colum. J.L. & Soc. Prob. 350 (1971).
6. Foote, *The Coming Constitutional Crisis in Bail: II,* 113 U. Pa. L. Rev. 1125, 1144 n.235 (1965), *citing* A. Trebach, The Rationing of Justice: Constitutional Rights and the Criminal Process 83, 264 (1964).
7. H. Mattick and D. Sweet, Illinois Jails: Challenge and Opportunity for the 1970's 80 (Illinois Law Enforcement Commission 1970) [hereinafter cited as Illinois Jails].
8. *Id.* at 80-81.
9. U.S. Dept. of Justice, Law Enforcement Assistance Administration, 1970 National Jail Census 3-4 (Nat'l Criminal Justice Information and Statistics Serv., Series SC, No. 1, 1971) [hereinafter cited as 1970 National Jail Census].
10. Illinois Jails, op. cit. note 7, at 79.
11. *Id.* at 107.
12. The Mattick and Sweet study reveals that "[i]n one jail, inmates carried the door of their cell to the jailer—the hinges had rotted away." Illinois Jails, op. cit. note 7, at 81.

13. *Id.* at 80.
14. Burns, *The American Jail in Perspective,* 17 Crime & Delin. 446, 451 (1971).
15. Burden Report, op. cit. note 5, at 20.
16. *See* Note, op. cit. note 5, at 355.
17. *See e.g.,* Illinois Jails, op. cit. note 7, at 95-96.
18. *Id.* at 181. The report further suggests that the filthy conditions created when jails fail to make adequate provision for inmate hygiene has demoralizing effects on the inmates which contribute to security and handling problems. *Id. See also* Note, op. cit. note 5, at 357-59.
19. 1970 National Jail Census, op. cit. note 9.
20. This phrase is attributed to J. Fishman, Crucibles of Crime: A Shocking Story of American Jails (1923).
21. *See* Turner, op. cit. note 4 and accompanying text.
22. McGee, *The Administration of Justice: The Correctional Process,* op. cit. note 1, at 228.
23. Menninger, *Our Dreadful Jails,* 6 U. San Francisco L. Rev. 1 (1971). This article appears as a preface to a series of articles entitled *Symposium: The Purposes of Corrections—Directions for Improvement. Id.*
24. President's Crime Commission Report, op cit. note 5, at 24.
25. For an examination of constitutional considerations relating to pretrial confinement the reader is referred to Note, *Constitutional Limitations on the Conditions of Pretrial Detention,* 79 Yale L.J. 941 (1970).
26. At least one court has supported this assertion. The opinion in Butler v. Crumlish, 229 F. Supp. 565, 567 (E.D. Pa. 1964) proclaimed that:
    The constitutional authority for the State to distinguish between criminal defendants by freeing those who supply bail pending trial and confining those who do not, furnishes no justification for any additional inequality of treatment beyond that which is inherent in the confinement itself.
    See also Coffin v. Reichard, 143 F.2d 443, 445 (6th Cir. 1944).
27. Burns, op. cit. note 14, at 454.
28. McGee, *Our Sick Jails,* op. cit. note 1, at 4.
29. 1970 National Jail Census, op. cit. note 9, at 2.
30. McGee, *Our Sick Jails,* op. cit. note 1, at 4. The Mattick and Sweet study of Illinois detention facilities produced the following table concerning the status of inmates in all state jails:

Inmate Status	Percentage of Total Jail Population
Awaiting Trial	60.1
Under Jail Sentence	30.4
Awaiting Transfer	4.0
Held for Other Authorities	5.2

    Illinois Jails, op. cit. note 7, at 72 (headings supplied).

31. Burden Report, op. cit. note 5, at 7.
32. Note, op. cit. note 5, at 351-52 & n.14.
33. Tribe, *An Ounce of Detention: Preventive Justice in the World of John Mitchell,* 56 Va. L. Rev. 371, 376-77 (1970).
34. 1 Stat. 73 (1789).
35. *Id.* at 91, *See* Stack v. Boyle, 342 U.S. 1, 4 (1951). Pertinent sections of the Judiciary Act of 1789 are now embodied in Fed. R. Crim. P. 46(a)(1) which provides in part: "A person arrested for an offense not punishable by death shall be admitted to bail."
36. In fairness it must be mentioned that bondsmen do not exercise control over the fate of every accused. The Federal Bail Reform Act of 1966, applicable to those accused of federal offenses, provides for release without bail whenever possible. 18 U.S.C. § 3146 (1970). In addition a number of states have some form of bail release program which attempts to extend this same benefit. *See* Ares, Rankin & Sturz, *The Manhattan Bail Project,* 38 N.Y.U.L. Rev. 67 (1963); R. Molleur, Bail Reform in the Nation's Capital (1966).
37. *See, e.g.,* N.J. Const. art 1, ¶ 11.
38. *See, e.g.,* Ga. Code Ann. § 27:901 (1953).
39. *See, e.g.,* N.Y. Crim. Proc. Law § 530.20(2) (McKinney 1971).
40. *See* R. Clark, Crime in America (1970) wherein the author remarked: "For the want of a few hundred dollars millions of impoverished Americans have suffered in jail awaiting American justice." *Id.* at 299. *See also* Foote, op. cit. note 6.
41. N.Y. Times, Feb. 1, 1969, at 15, col. 4.
42. *See also* Mitchell, *Bail Reform and the Constitutionality of Pretrial Detention,* 55 Va. L. Rev. 1223 (1969) wherein the former Attorney General defends the necessity and propriety of this recommendation.
43. *See, e.g.,* R. Clark, op. cit. note 40; Tribe, op. cit. note 33; Note, *Preventive Detention Before Trial,* 79 Harv. L. Rev. 1489 (1970).
44. Illinois Jails, op. cit. note 7, at 74 table 20.
45. Note, op. cit. note 5, at 373, *citing* Vera Institute, A Report to the Mayor's Criminal Justice Coordinating Council: The Problems of Overcrowding in the Detention Institutions of New York City 59 (1969). The period expressed in this report roughly coincides with an estimated figure of more than four months reached by a more recent New York City survey. Burden Report, op. cit. note 5, at 20.
46. Note, op. cit. note 5, at 373, *citing* N.Y. State Senate Committee on Crime and Correction, Report on the Tombs Disturbances 48 (1970).
47. President's Crime Commission Report, op. cit. note 5, at 25.
48. Commonwealth *ex rel.* Hartage v. Hendrick, 439 Pa. 584, 601, 268 A.2d 451, 459 (1970) (Roberts, J., dissenting) (footnote omitted).
49. *See* op cit. note 33 and accompanying text.

50. Anderson v. Nosser, 438 F.2d 183, 190 (5th Cir. 1971). *See also* Note, op. cit. note 5, at 352.
51. *See generally* ABA Project on Minimum Standards for Criminal Justice: Standards Relating to Pretrial Release (Tent. Draft, Mar. 1968) [hereinafter cited as ABA Report].
52. Because of the recognized importance of the period between arrest and trial on preparation of a defendant's case the Supreme Court has described this time as "perhaps the most critical period in the judicial proceedings." Powell v. Alabama, 287 U.S. 45, 57 (1932).
53. *See* Note, *A Study of the Administration of Bail in New York City*, 106 U. Pa. L. Rev. 693, 725 (1958).
54. For statistical data supportive of this assertion, see ABA Report, op. cit. note 51, at 24.
55. *See* Rankin, *The Effect of Pretrial Detention,* 39 N.Y.U.L. Rev. 641 (1964).
56. Note, *Pre-Trial Detention in the New York City Jails,* 7 Column. J.L. & Soc. Prob. 350, 353 & n.20 (1971).
57. Wald, *Pretrial Detention and Ultimate Freedom: A Statistical Study,* 39 N.Y.U.L. Rev. 631, 632 (1964). This article appears as a prefatory summary to statistical investigation by Anne Rankin relating the effects of pretrial detention to judicial disposition of the detainee's case. *See* Rankin, op. cit. note 55.
58. Foote, *The Coming Constitutional Crisis in Bail: II, 113* U. Pa. L. Rev. 1125 (1965).
59. ABA Report, op. cit. note 51, at 3. Similar conclusions were reached in another study and published in the following table:

Disposition	Bail (%)	Jail (%)
Sentenced to Prison	17	64
Convicted without Prison	36	9
Not Convicted	47	27
Number of Defendants	374	358

Rankin, op. cit. note 55, table 1 at 642. This researcher determined that the correlation between detention and ultimate sentence existed independent of such common factors as prior criminal record, employment stability, familial influences and type of legal counsel.
60. Wald, op. cit. note 57, at 635.
61. *Id.,* citing Rankin, op. cit. note 55, table 3 at 647 (footnote omitted).
62. Commonwealth *ex rel.* Hartage v. Hendrick, 439 Pa. 584, 601 n.11, 268 A.2d 451, 459 n.11 (1970) (Roberts J., dissenting).
63. ABA Report, op. cit. note 51, at 3.
64. Burns, op. cit. note 14, at 451.
65. *Id.* at 449.
66. It is widely acknowledged that the bail system as presently administered in this country inevitably discriminates against the poor. In-

digents are therefore more frequently committed to detention than accused persons of economically superior status and consequently constitute a large percentage of the jail population. *See generally* R. Clark, op. cit. note 40, at 298-306; ABA Report, op. cit. note 51, at 1; Foote, op. cit. note 58.

67. In his recent book, former Attorney General Ramsey Clark presented figures which indicate that blacks were involved in certain crimes in a greater proportion than their numbers in the total population (warning, however, that this is a function of the "brutalization and dehumanization of racism, poverty, and injustice" and is not to be misconstrued as supportive of racist arguments). R. Clark, op. cit. note 40, at 50-51. Such crime rates are certainly one factor contributing to the large numbers of blacks being arrested and subjected to pretrial detention.

SECTION TWO

MANAGEMENT and ADMINISTRATION

CHAPTER 4

LOCAL ADULT INSTITUTIONS

NATIONAL ADVISORY COMMISSION ON CRIMINAL
JUSTICE STANDARDS AND GOALS*

REMOTE FROM PUBLIC VIEW and concern, the jail has evolved more by default than by plan. Perpetuated without major change from the days of Alfred the Great, it has been a disgrace to every generation.

Colonists brought to the new world the concept of the jail as an instrument of confinement, coercion and correction of those who broke the law or were merely nuisances. In the early nineteenth century, the American innovation of the State penitentiary made punitive confinement the principal response to criminal acts and removed the serious offender from the local jail. Gradually, with the building of insane asylums, orphanages and hospitals, the jail ceased to be the repository of some social casualties.[1] But it continued to house the town's minor offenders along with the poor and the vagrant, all crowded together without regard to sex, age and history, typically in squalor and misery.

Many European visitors came to examine and admire the new American penitentiaries. Two observers—Beaumont and Tocqueville—also saw, side by side with the new penitentiaries, jails in the old familiar form: ". . . nothing has been changed; disorder, con-

---
*Reprinted from Task Force: *Report on Corrections,* Wash., D.C., 1973.

fusion, mixture of different ages and moral characters, all the vices of the old system still exist." In an observation that should have served as a warning, they said:

> There is evidently a deficiency in a prison system which offers anomalies of this kind. These shocking contradictions proceed chiefly from the want of unison in the various parts of government in the United States.[2]

By and large, the deficiencies the two travellers found remain today, the intervening decades having brought only the deterioration of jail facilities from use and age. Changes have been limited to minor variations in the clientele. Jails became residual organizations into which were shunted the more vexing and unpalatable social problems of each locality. Thus, "the poor, the sick, the morally deviant, and the merely unaesthetic, in addition to the truly criminal—all end in jail."[2]

Although larger urban areas have built some facilities for special groups of offenders, in most parts of the country a single local institution today retains the dual purposes of custodial confinement and misdemeanant punishment. The most conspicuous additions to the jail's function have been the homeless and the drunks. Thus jails are the catchall for social and law enforcement problems.

Jails are the intake point for our entire criminal justice system. There are more jails than any other type of "correctional" institution. Indeed, the current trend toward the decreased use of confinement in major state institutions promises to increase the size and scope of the burden jails must bear. Perhaps this is a short-term expedient that will not become permanent. There are some faint stirrings of hope that it will not be so. For the first time since the colonial era, attention is being given to the place where social problems originate—the community—as the logical location for solving these problems.

MAJOR CHARACTERISTICS OF THE JAIL

A jail census conducted in 1970 by the U.S. Bureau of the Census under an agreement with the Law Enforcement Assistance Administration found 4,037 jails meeting the definition of "any facility operated by a unit of local government for the detention or correction of adults suspected or convicted of a crime and which has authority to detain longer than forty-eight hours[4] These institutions ranged from New York City's festering "Tombs" to the infrequently utilized small municipal lockup.

With more than 4,000 jails, implementing recommendations and standards delineated in this chapter will require localities to make precise specification of their needs and resources. The prescriptive content of this chapter will consist of elements that may be combined into a suitable solution for any given situation. There is no single answer to the problems of jails.

Local control, multiple functions, and a transient, heterogeneous population have shaped the major organizational characteristics of jails. Typically, they are under the jurisdiction of the county government. In most instances, the local area has neither the necessary tax base from which to finance a jail adequately nor sufficient size to justify even the most rudimentary correctional programs. Local control inevitably has meant involvement with local politics. Jails are left in a paradoxical situation: localities cling tenaciously to them but are unwilling or unable to meet even minimal standards. "The problem of American jails, put most concisely, is the problem of local control."[5]

Beyond their formally acknowledged tasks of correction and detention, jails have been adapted to perform a variety of "social welfare" tasks and provide easy answers to law enforcement problems. For example, Stuart Queen, a jail critic of fifty years ago, noted the "floater custom" in California counties by which transients were arrested, brought to the jail, and from there "ordered to disappear."[6] Similarly, Sutherland and Cressey observed the "Golden Rule disposition" of misdemeanant arrest in which the individual is held with no intention of bringing him to trial but only until his condition changes (as with drunkenness, disorderliness, etc.).[7] Such uses, as well as detention of suspects and witnesses, are understandable responses to difficulties encountered by law enforcement personnel. They are, however, short-term expedients that rarely solve anything.

Because of their multiple uses, jails house a population more diverse than any other correctional institution. The 1970 jail census found that, of 160,863 persons held on the census date, 27,460 had not been arraigned, 8,688 were awaiting some postconviction legal action, 69,096 were serving sentences (10,496 for more than a year), and 7,800 were juveniles.[8] Thus accused felons and misdemeanants and juveniles all are found in American jails, often unsegregated from each other.

However, jail populations do share common socioeconomic characteristics. Inmates are typically poor, undereducated and unemployed. Minority groups are greatly overrepresented. Fifty-two percent (83,079) of the inmates in the 1970 census were unconvicted, awaiting arraignment or trial.

It is crucial to note that the population of a jail bears no necessary or logical relationship to the size of the general population it serves. A study of Nebraska's county jails found that counties with the largest populations do not necessarily have the largest number of jail inmates.[9] The National Council on Crime and Delinquency recently advised that area population growth is not a suitable basis for projecting future jail population. "Jail populations are controlled more by statute and court practices than they are by population growth."[10] Variations in law enforcement practices, availability of alternatives (detoxification centers, state misdemeanant institutions, etc.), and attitudes of the local citizenry also affect jail admissions. It is doubtful that variations in crime rates cause the large disparities in jail population among localities. These facts require considerable flexibility in planning for the future.

For the most part, jails are not places of final deposition. In Illinois, an estimated 169,192 jail confinements occurred during 1967.[11] Extrapolating from these and other states' figures, an estimated 1.5 to 5.5 million jail commitments occur in this country annually.[12] The obvious result is a highly transient jail population. Yet the Illinois survey found that pretrial detention can stretch into years through legal maneuvering by both prosecution and defense. In general, the processing rate of any given jail depends on local practices and on availability of alternative placements for certain population groups.

In many of the jail riots in recent years, a trial has been a major, if not the only, demand by inmates. Nor is this demand surprising. The great number of men who spend months and even years in jail awaiting trial exacerbates miserable jail conditions.

In the District of Columbia Jail in the spring of 1971, 80 percent of the inmates were there awaiting trial. At the same time, the jail was housing 1,100 inmates in a facility designed to hold 550.[13]

JAIL CONDITIONS TODAY

In addition to the problem of local control, the principal problems facing the nation's jails today are condition of physical facilities, inadequate personnel, poor administration, and underutilization of alternative programs and dispositions.

A study of conditions in the District of Columbia Jail which was undertaken for the American Civil Liberties Union by volunteer lawyers and law students documents the results:

> The District of Columbia Jail is a filthy example of man's inhumanity to man. It is a case study in cruel and unusual punishment, in the denial of due process, in the failure of justice.
> The Jail is a century old and crumbling. It is overcrowded. It offers inferior medical attention to its inmates, when it offers any at all. It chains sick men to beds. It allows—forces—men to live in crowded cells with rodents and roaches, vomit and excreta. It is the scene of arbitrary and capricious punishment and discipline. While there is little evidence of racial discrimination (the Jail "serves" the male population of the District of Columbia and is, therefore, virtually an all-black institution), there are some categories of prisoners who receive better treatment than others.
> The eating and living conditions would not be tolerated anywhere else. The staff seems, at best, indifferent to the horror over which it presides. This, they say, is the job society wants them to do. The facilities and amounts of time available for recreation and exercise are limited, sometimes by a guard's whim. Except for a few privileged prisoners on various details, there is no means by which an inmate may combat idleness—certainly nothing that could be called education, counselling or self-help.[14]

The sad fact is that conditions in the D.C. Jail are by no means unique.

Physical Facilities

The most striking inadequacy of jails is their abominable physical condition. The National Jail Census found that 25 percent of the cells in use in 1970 were built before 1920.[15] And the chronological age of the facility is aggravated by the manner in which it is used. Jails that hold few persons tend to be neglected, and those that are overcrowded repeatedly push their equipment and fixtures beyond the breaking point. Given the fact that most jails are either overutilized, and hence overcrowded, or are using only a portion of their capacity, it is not surprising that most of the physical facilities are in crisis condition.

The National Jail Census found 5 percent of jails included in their survey overcrowded, with the propensity to be overcrowded increasing with design capacity.[16] On the other hand, on four census dates, a survey found 35 percent to 45 percent of Idaho's jails unoccupied.[17] Neither the situation of the overcrowded urban jail nor that of the underutilized rural facility will be ameliorated merely by constructing new buildings. The means of delivering detention and correctional services must be reexamined. Otherwise, the new will merely repeat and perpetuate mistakes of the old.

In nearly all jails, the available space is divided into inflexible cells or cage-like day rooms. Rows of cells compose self-contained cellblocks that face a large cage or "bullpen." The arrangement is designed "so that a relatively small number of staff can insure the secure confinement of a comparatively large number of inmates."[18] Items are passed into the bullpens through slotted doors, largely preventing contact between staff and inmates.

Many jail cells have neither toilets nor washbasins. The majority of inmates have access to shower facilities less than once a day. These inadequacies, combined with the short supply or complete lack of such items as soap, towels, toothbrushes, safety razors, clean bedding, and toilet paper, create a clear public health problem, not to mention the depressing psychological effects on inmates. Mattick declares that, "If cleanliness is next to godliness, most jails lie securely in the province of hell." He points out further disheartening physical conditions in jails:

> Considering that sanitary fixtures are a necessity, yet are often absent, it is not too surprising to find that other facilities for handling and treating prisoners, some of which are not as indispensable, are also lacking. Only the largest jails have such luxuries as classrooms, an adequate infirmary, a laundry, a separate dining area, recreation space, and a chapel.[19]

Lack of Adequate Staff

The neglect of local jails is as apparent in staff as in dismal physical facilities. Jail employees almost invariably are untrained, too few in number, and underpaid. They are second-level victims of the societal arrangements that perpetuate the jail.[20]

A 1970 jail survey in California found 25 percent of the deputies and 41 percent of the nonsworn personnel in fifty-eight county sheriff's offices engaged in custodial activities.[21] Although these are full-time employees, assignment to the jail frequently is only one of several roles they must perform. Moreover, "the law enforcement psychology of a policeman is to arrest offenders and see to it that they get *into* jail; the rehabilitative psychology of a correctional worker should be to prepare an inmate to get *out* of jail and take his place in the free community as a law-abiding citizen."[22] When law enforcement officers are not used, the solution has been to hire low-paid custodians who are even less qualified than those they replace.

While staff-inmate ratios often appear satisfactory, the need to operate three shifts and the erratic nature of many employees' duties must be considered in interpreting such figures. Nationally, there were 5.6 inmates per full-time equivalent employee in 1970. State ratios ranged from 1.3 to 11.4.[23] Interpreting these ratios on the basis of a twenty-four-hour, seven-day operation gives an average of 1-2/3 full-time workers per shift with an average of forty inmates.[24] Given the nature of jail architecture and the numerous duties the employees must perform both inside and outside the facility, these staffing levels are simply too low to permit regular supervision of inmates. In Nebraska, staff members were able to see all prisoners from their station in only five of the ninety county jails.[25] During the night, lack of supervision becomes more acute. In Idaho, for example, only 32 percent of the jails had a full-time staff member present at night.[26]

Professional workers, too often missing from jail staffs, are necessary for the initiation and operation of any reintegration or referral program and for training other staff members. A 1965 survey by the National Council on Crime and Delinquency ferreted out only 501 professional jail employees in the nation. These employees were primarily social workers and vocational and academic instructors, with a scattering of psychologists and psychiatrists.[27] All of these professionals were working in the larger urban jails.

This should not be construed as an argument for jails staffed by psychologists and social workers. The skills involved in relating to another human being are inexact, and professionals do not monopolize them, although training provided by the professional staff to fellow jail employees can be helpful. The need is to break the now-ancient pattern of uninterested and reluctant jail employees who lack the minimal training needed for the efficient performance of an extraordinarily difficult task.

Administration by "Custodial Convenience"

The fundamental principle underlying the relationship between jailers and inmates is that of "custodial convenience," in which "everyone who can, takes the easy way out and makes only the minimal effort."[28] Because of insufficient staffing and funding and the lack of effective screening for incoming inmates, the population is separated into several large groups and placed in specific cell blocks. Each division represents an attempt to replace continuous, or even frequent, staff supervision with a maximum security setting. With such an arrangement, jailers effectively abandon their control and concentrate solely on any untoward occurrences.

Thus the inmates are left to work out their own internal order. For this reason, "control over inmate behavior usually can be achieved by other inmates more immediately, directly, and completely in jails than in other types of confinement institutions, such as penitentiaries or state hospitals."[29] In past eras, kangaroo courts flourished in many jails and still do in some.

While most such "judicial" trappings have gone the way of many traditions, the basic features remain in force. Jail inmates face many uncertainties arising from a threatening environment and an ambiguous relationship to the machinery of the criminal justice system. Under these conditions, individuals experienced in crime and accustomed to life in state penitentiaries assume positions of leadership and control.

The "custodial convenience" philosophy is marked by an almost fanatic concern with security, but one practice totally contradictory to security is found in many jails. To operate and maintain the jail, selected inmates are granted the rank of trusty. They have free access throughout the jail and frequently to the outside as well. All too often, the result is a jail run by its inmates. In most instances, trusties, or at least their "barn boss" or foreman, are well-schooled in prison life, and jailers must offer them privileges in return for cooperation.

"Custodial convenience" also dictates a solution for the multitude of social and medical problems entering the jail. Here, too, inmates are left to solve their mutual problems, with the elderly, sick, intoxicated, suicide-prone, and addicted all thrown together. The assumption is that they somehow will arrange to take care of each other.

Jail inmates do not have the opportunity for even the momentary or limited privacy available to most prison inmates. Participation and conformity to the prevailing expectations of the jailhouse subculture are mandatory for all.[30] The daily routine generally is one of unrelieved idleness. Card playing, conversations, meditation, and, occasionally, television viewing are the only options available. In the nation as a whole, 86 percent of all jails counted in 1970 had no recreational facilities, and 89 percent had no educational facilities.[31]

Even acknowledging the resource limitations, such solutions produce reprehensible results. When the police department and the district attorney's office studied sexual assaults in the Philadelphia jail system during 1968, they found that such assaults were epidemic. "As Superintendent Hendrick and three of the wardens admitted, virtually every slightly built young man committed by the courts is sexually approached within a day or two after his admission to prison. Many of these young men are repeatedly raped by gangs of inmates."[32]

Daniel Glaser has captured the overall effect of current jail conditions as follows:

> The major costs to society from jail conditions probably stem not from the clear violations of moral norms that the inmates suffer there, but rather, from the prolonged idleness of the inmates in highly diverse groups cut off from much communication with out-

siders. In this inactivity and crowdedness day after day, those inmates most committed to crime "brainwash" the inexperienced to convert initial feelings of guilt or shame into smug rationalizations for crime. Also, jail prisoners become extremely habituated to "killing time," especially during pretrial confinement. Thus, deficiencies of ability to support themselves in legitimate employment, which may have contributed to their criminality, are enhanced at their release. While reformatories and prisons are often called "schools for crime," it is a far more fitting label for the typical urban jail.[33]

SHORTCOMINGS OF STATE SUPERVISION

In addressing the needs presented by current jail conditions, the trend toward seeking change through State-set standards and inspections of local jails is open to question. *The Passing of the County Jail,* published fifty years ago, was no isolated utopian exercise but the product of an era of jail reform, written by an experienced and tough-minded practitioner. The book assessed the growing State involvement in local correctional efforts that had occurred in the preceding two decades. State boards of charities and corrections had been established in several States and charged with inspection of jails. Results of inspection surveys were published in California and Illinois. In Alabama, a State prison inspector was granted broad powers by statute to oversee jail activities; including the right to set standards. By and large, however, these measures did not meet expectations.

In the fall of 1971, the National Clearinghouse for Criminal Justice Planning and Architecture attempted to assess the status of current State inspection efforts. Letters sent to the fifty state agencies responsible for corrections requested them to send a copy of any jail standards in use or to notify the clearinghouse if no standards existed. Twenty states replied that they had no responsibility for local jails and no statewide standards were in force. Three states provided standards governing planning and construction but not operation. Two states replied that, while minimal standards existed, they were old and, in one instance, were about to be replaced by pending legislation (See Figure 4-1).

Twenty-four states replied with copies of their current standards. One state answered that the need for standards had been eliminated through state operation of all county jails.

Standards now in use vary considerably—from minimal statutory requirements to detailed instructions, from mimeographed sheet to printed book. But such standards neglect the myriad connections jails have with other components of the criminal justice

FIGURE 4-1
EXISTING STATE JAIL STANDARDS*

	Operational Standards		Facility Planning and Construction	
	Yes	No	Yes	No
Alabama				
Alaska				
Arizona		X		X
Arkansas		X		X
California	X		X	
Colorado		X		X
Connecticut		X		
Delaware		X		X
Dist. of Columbia		X		X
Florida	X		X	
Georgia		X		X
Hawaii		X		X
Idaho	X			X
Illinois	X		X	
Indiana	X			X
Iowa	X		X	
Kansas		X		X
Kentucky				
Louisiana		X		X
Maine	X		X	
Maryland	X		X	
Massachusetts	X			X
Michigan	X		X	
Minnesota	X		X	
Mississippi				
Missouri	X			X
Montana		X		X
Nebraska		X		X
Nevada				
New Hampshire				
New Jersey				
New Mexico		X		X
New York	X		X	
North Carolina	X		X	
North Dakota	X			X
Ohio		X		X
Oklahoma	X			X
Oregon		X	X	
Pennsylvania	X		X	
Rhode Island				X
South Carolina	X		X	
South Dakota	X			X
Tennessee		X		X

	Operational Standards		Facility Planning and Construction	
	Yes	No	Yes	No
Texas	X		X	
Utah	X			X
Vermont	X		X	
Virginia	X		X	
Washington	X		X	
West Virginia				
Wisconsin	X		X	
Wyoming				X

*Survey conducted by National Clearinghouse for Criminal Justice Planning and Architecture, Fall 1971.

system. Many standards are vague and thus difficult to enforce. Several state agencies theoretically responsible for such enforcement complained of insufficient funds to carry out the inspection function. The all too frequent difficulty in identifying the specific department of state government responsible for supervision is probably indicative of the quality of the inspection services.[34]

Existing state standards and inspection procedures may have alleviated some of the most glaring physical defects in local jails. However, they do not constitute a program of action; they fail to cover the large complex of processes and agencies to which the jail is related. Furthermore, they inevitably involve political considerations. Standards and inspections aimed at institutional procedures are only two necessary components of the process by which jails may be dramatically reformed. Minimal standards that include only a small portion of the problem's components inevitably will perpetuate a haphazard approach to jail reform.

For individuals seeking reform of local adult corrections, precautions must be taken not to set off in the wrong direction. Hans Mattick has articulated well what must be avoided.

> At least two kinds of investment should be *postponed* in any statewide jail reform program based on a phased-stage implementation of state standards: the building of new jails and the hiring of more personnel. Investment in new jails, or the major refurbishing of old ones, would merely cement-in the old problems under somewhat more decent conditions. . . . Increasing the number of personnel in existing jails would only have the effect of giving more persons a vested interest in maintaining the status quo and contribute to greater resistance to future change. By and large, new buildings and more staff should come only after the potential effects of criminal law reform and diversion alternatives have been fully considered.

Such collateral reforms, combined with an increasing tendency toward regionalization of jails, would require fewer jails and fewer, but better qualified and trained jail personnel.[35]

This position may be difficult for some to accept because at first blush the answer to poor jails seems to be to build better ones; the response to inadequate personnel, to hire more. It must be remembered, however, that this is not the first generation to confront the plight of American jails. Concerned individuals have been speaking out for at least a hundred years. But, for the most part, the situation has not improved. New jails have been built, but they now present the same problems as those they were built to replace. History shows clearly that only a different attack on the problem holds real promise. The new approach must involve all components of the criminal justice system.

REFERENCES

1. For an account of this development, see David J. Rothman, *The Discovery of the Asylum: Social Order and Disorder in the New Republic* (Little, Brown, 1971).
2. de Beaumont, Gustave, and de Tocqueville, Alexis: *On the Penitentiary System of the United States and Its Application in France*, H. R. Lantz, Ed., Southern Illinois University Press, 1964, p. 49.
3. Mattick, Hans W., Aikman, Alexander: The cloacal region of American corrections. *Annals of the American Academy of Political and Social Science, 381*:114, 1969.
4. Law Enforcement Assistance Administration: *National Jail Census, 1970: A Report on the Nation's Local Jails and Types of Inmates.* Government Printing Office, 1970, pp. 6-7.
5. Mattick, Hans W.: Contemporary jails in the United States: An unknown and neglected area of justice, in Glaser, Daniel (Ed.): *Handbook of Corrections.* Rand McNally, forthcoming. Draft page 144.
6. Queen, Stuart A.: *The Passing of the County Jail.* Banta, 1920, p. 7.
7. Sutherland, Edwin, and Cressey, Donald: *Principles of Criminology,* 6th ed. Lippincott, 1960, p. 364.
8. *National Jail Census, 1970,* pp. 10-11.
9. Nebraska Commission on Law Enforcement and Criminal Justice: *For Better or for Worse? Nebraska's Misdemeanant Correctional System.* Lincoln, 1970, pp. 97-105.
10. National Council on Crime and Delinquency: *A Regional Approach to Jail Improvement in South Mississippi: A Plan—Maybe a Dream.* New York: NCCD, 1971, p. 40.

11. Mattick, Hans W., and Sweet, Ronald: *Illinois Jails: Challenge and Opportunity for the 1970's.* Washington, Law Enforcement Assistance Administration, 1970, p. 49.
12. Mattick, "Contemporary Jails," draft p. 47.
13. American Civil Liberties Union: *The Seeds of Anguish: An ACLU Study of the D.C. Jail.* Washington, ACLU, 1972, pp. 3, 5.
14. *The Seeds of Anguish,* p. 1 .
15. *National Jail Census, 1970,* p. 4.
16. *National Jail Census, 1970,* pp. 4-5.
17. Idaho Law Enforcement Planning Commission: *State of Idaho Jail Survey of City and County Law Enforcement Agencies.* Boise, 1969, pp. 12-13.
18. Glaser, Daniel: Some notes on urban jails. In Glaser, Daniel (Ed.): *Crime in the City,* Harper and Row, 1971, p. 238.
19. Mattick, "Contemporary Jails," draft page 67.
20. Mattick and Sweet, *Illinois Jails,* p. 368.
21. California Board of Corrections: *A Study of California County Jails.* California, Council on Criminal Justice, 1970, p. 102.
22. Mattick and Sweet, *Illinois Jails,* pp. 255-256.
23. *National Jail Census, 1970,* p. 9.
24. Mattick, "Contemporary Jails," draft page 74.
25. Nebraska Commission on Law Enforcement and Criminal Justice: *For Better or for Worse?.* p. 27.
26. Idaho Law Enforcement Planning Commission: *Idaho Jail Survey.* p. 9.
27. President's Commission on Law Enforcement and Administration of Justice: *Task Force Report: Corrections.* Washington, Government Printing Office, 1967, p. 164.
28. Mattick, "Contemporary Jails," draft page 88.
29. Glaser, "Some Notes on Urban Jails," p. 239.
30. Kimberly, John R., and Rottman, David B.: Patterns of Behavior in Isolating Organizations: An Examination of Three County Jails. University of Illinois Department of Sociology, 1972.
31. *National Jail Census, 1970,* p. 191.
32. Davis, Allan J.: Sexual assaults in the Philadelphia prison systems and sheriff's vans. *Trans-Action,* 6:9, 1968.
33. Glaser, "Some Notes on Urban Jails," p. 241.
34. National Clearinghouse for Criminal Justice Planning: "Spring 1972 Survey of State Jail Standards," unpublished source documents. Urbana, Ill., 1972.
35. Mattick, "Contemporary Jails," draft page 147.

CHAPTER 5

PRISONER MANAGEMENT AND CONTROL

MARK S. RICHMOND*

R ESPONSIBILITY FOR EFFECTIVE PRISONER MANAGEMENT and control is a burdensome problem for every correctional administrator. He lives with the ever-present potentials of prisoner disorder and its consequences. He knows that correctional objectives are not clearly understood and that they may even be in conflict with each other. He is also acutely aware that he is expected to achieve essential security without imposing adverse restrictions on prisoners' rights and expanding programs and services for prisoners. And he is constantly reminded that the levels of expectation are increasing before tradition-bound policies and procedures can be modified and before corrections and the criminal justice system can be examined from a common point of view.

Prisoner management and control is an area of correctional administration for which there are few generally accepted principles and standards of practice. Policies and procedures have been dictated by deep-seated traditions which have not kept pace with the times. In "landmark" decisions and otherwise, the courts have

---

*Reprinted from *Prisoner Management and Control,* a monograph published by the United States Bureau of Prisons (1969).

proscribed specific practices in selected situations. Legislative bodies have provided general guideline in others. Under the harassment of pressure from all sides, some correctional officials have tried to "second-guess" the courts and special-interest groups by introducing new procedures or by summarily adopting policies that seem to "work" in some other jurisdiction. While changes brought about in these ways may eventually produce universal standards of practice, the process will be long and predictably painful at times.

The pages that follow are intended to assist a more rational approach to the problem. It analyzes a number of major factors in prisoner unrest. It discusses preventive measures with special attention to personnel management, policies and operating procedures and improvement of correctional programs. Finally, attention is directed to the handling of emergencies, in which emphasis is given the development of plans for escapes, riots and disturbances. This is guideline material with which the administrator can assess conditions as they are, set goals, and formulate policies that are both coherent and consistent with long-range objectives.

FACTORS IN PRISONER UNREST

". . . and him safely keep," whether directly expressed or not, is the universal mandate that accompanies every order of commitment to a lock-up, jail, prison or other correctional facility. Ultimate responsibility for this rests upon the administrator of the facility, together with responsibility for the training, use and performance of personnel. He also bears stewardship responsibilities for the proper care and use of government property and the wise expenditure of public funds. For these reasons, if no other, the institution administrator is very much concerned over the ever-present potentials of prisoner disorder.

The possible consequences of prisoner unrest, whether in misconduct, escape or riot, can be serious. At the least, disorder of any significant magnitude can interfere with the efficient operation of the institution. For example, staff time and energies that are devoted to handling an excessive number of misconduct reports detracts from more productive pursuits of the personnel involved. Escapes not only can be disruptive of normal operations but require the deployment of personnel who have other primary duties to perform. In extreme degree, a major riot which results in extensive property damage can cripple an institution for months. Beyond this, disorder can produce negative reactions in officials and the general public by undermining confidence in the management of the institution and by reinforcing existing rejective attitudes toward offenders and employees as classes of people.

It is generally true that the potentials for disorder within an institution are in inverse ratio to the effectiveness of institutional management and control. But this explains nothing, and any attempt either to apply preventive measures or to cope successfully with incidents as they occur can fall short unless there is, first, some understanding of the many factors which figure prominently in prisoner unrest. In the discussion that follows, an arbitrary distinction is made between "external" and "internal" factors. This distinction may not appear in real life. Likewise, the discussion deals with a number of separate items when, in reality, all may be interrelated.

External Factors

Indifference

It is entirely possible that what appears as indifference is actually a perfectly "natural" reaction of people who look upon irrational, irresponsible and, at times, unpredictable and threatening behavior with a mixture of fear, frustration and frank bewilderment. Rather than indifference, the reaction may be outright rejection. The term "offender," alone, expresses an attitude of rejection. Certainly imprisonment is a form of rejection or banishment, however brief.

Whatever the reasons for it, the most visible evidence of indifference is withholding support. The expenditure of public funds for the operation of prisons and jails is politically unpopular under ordinary circumstances. Hospitals, schools, highways, aid to needy children, and other competing demands on the public treasury have far more appeal than the correctional needs of offenders. Hand-to-mouth budget practices and deficit financing can account heavily for the inadequacies of personnel, facilities and programs.

Politics

Typically, jail management is the responsibility of elected local officials. Unlike schools, hospitals and mental health programs where the need for competent, trained and full-time leadership has long been recognized, the administration of local correctional facilities is more often than not one of the many responsibilities of the sheriff. He, in turn, must rely on subordinates who ordinarily have had no preparation for their jobs.

In any institution there can be less visible but more insidious kinds of politically-motivated activity which sap the vitality and undermine the integrity of operations. Some of these involve pressures to extend improper favors to certain prisoners, efforts to obtain early releases, favoritism in the assignment of personnel, and misuse of institutional property and supplies.

Unwise Commitment and Release Procedures

Prisoners, like other people, tend to excuse and rationalize their own behavior. Unfortunately, many of the excuses are easily found in the machinery of criminal justice where there are all-too-obvious inequities and injustices. Problems in this area are numerous.

The system which permits accused persons with money to be free awaiting trial while those without resources have to stay in jail is both a blot on our notions of equal justice and the cause of many people's being in jail needlessly. The mystique of a "taste of jail" is still popular in the minds of police, prosecutors and judges with the resultant confinement of many people who otherwise might have been released on bond or their own recognizance, placed on probation or assessed a fine.

Disparity in sentencing practices is a prime source of prisoner discontent. All judges do not think alike about how the law should be administered. Legislatures may impose unwise limits on judicial discretion, as when laws are enacted that require long minimum sentences or which establish ineligibility for probation or parole. In addition, decisions to release from jail are often viewed by prisoners as having been based on prejudice, caprice, or the "right connections."

Overcrowding

Emotional tensions are developed by the irritations of people upon each other. The more congested the conditions under which they must live, the greater the risks of frustration, anger and open conflict. All too frequently institutions have to operate over capacity. Examples abound of two beds being placed in cells built for one, mattresses spread on corridor floors, overtaxed facilities, overworked personnel and failure generally to meet the most elementary requirements of differentiating among prisoners and maintaining acceptable standards of decency.

Emotional Tone of the Community

Prisoners are not nearly so isolated from the free community as may be supposed. They are aware of the attitudes of employees and visitors who live in the outside world. They have access to newspapers, radio, television and other means of communication with the outside. It is widely believed by institution people that the emotional tone of the free community is reflected inside the walls as truly as upon other groups. In fact, there are many who believe that the tone is magnified because prisoners are held in confinement under duress and they tend to seek support for their own reactions to real or fancied wrongs.

Internal Factors

Seeds of discontent abound in the very nature of life in a prison, jail or other correctional facility. An institution is a community of people set apart. It has its society of inmates, its society of personnel, and its own peculiar culture of many conflicts.

The Society of Prisoners

Of the hundreds of thousands of offenders who pass through correctional institutions in the course of a year, some are committed irrevocably to criminal careers while others subscribe to quite conventional values or are aimless and uncommitted to goals of any kind. Some are alcoholics, some narcotic addicts, some sexual deviates and so on through the catalog of human frailties and personal problems. Behind the visible few who are conspicuous by their offenses are nameless numbers of nondescript human beings, more characterized by imprudence and inability to cope with the demands of a complex society than by any pattern of malicious willfulness.

Many offenders are members of minority groups whose values and objectives may be quite different from the middle-class standards to which members of the staff subscribe and upon which correctional goals are based. Poverty may be a common denominator among them. They may have a language barrier. A sense of low status may lie at the root of the frustration and hostility that often mark minority attitudes toward the dominant society. Almost all minority groups will have had some bad experiences with authority.

Confinement is a stressful experience under the best of circumstances. Under the worst it can become intolerable. There are many sources of stress for the prisoner. The closing of the front gate behind him is a denial of his freedom, a frustration of his accustomed ways of life, a humiliation, and a label of being an undesirable member of society. Isolation, inflexible routine and monotony are characteristic of most correctional institutions. Its most visible feature is enforced idleness which imposes a heavy burden on all concerned and may produce deterioration in onceable people who leave with neither the ability nor the will to earn an honest living.

The Society of Personnel

Not all institutional problems of management and control are generated by the society of prisoners. A second set of problems can be created by the staff.

Without question, the greatest single resource for correctional management and control is personnel. Prisons and jails are run by people. The quality of the operation depends directly upon the skills, experience, performance standards, and morale of the staff. Well-qualified and promising recruits can be attracted to correctional work only as they are offered appropriate salaries and conditions of service which encourage lifetime, rather than casual, periods of employment. Lack of a sufficient number of employees to provide adequate supervision for safety, to say nothing of correctional programs, is too often the rule rather than the exception.

In many jurisdictions, the number of positions allowed is usually far below an acceptable level of efficient service and safe coverage.

Employees who are expected to promote the aims of the institution in keeping with philosophies and procedures laid down for them, and who are the first to bear the brunt of inmate pressures, are human beings too. To a great extent, their effectiveness is determined by what they and the administration perceive their roles to be.

There are many factors which may result in a curious combination of laxity, harshness and even brutality. One is insensitivity to the legitimate needs and rights of prisoners. Another is inattention to bona fide complaints and grievances. Laxity may result from the necessity of using prisoners to perform work which should be done by personnel. Compensation for these services may be in the form of unwarranted trust or special and unusual privileges. Laxity can be found where personnel are unqualified for the jobs they perform.

Staff failure to recognize the existence of cultural differences among offenders or to understand why people who are shaped by them fail to respond "like everybody else" can interfere seriously with working relationships between inmates and staff. When intolerance and lack of understanding foster beliefs among members of the staff that prisoners are possessed of traits that are unacceptable, inferior or repugnant, effective working relationships are impossible. Personnel are subject to emotional stress, too, and when this happens they are inclined to be less tolerant of beliefs which they consider to be different from their own. This may result in their unwillingness to accept policies and programs established by the administration, as well as the philosophies upon which they are based. They may become intolerant of anything that disturbs their own perceptions, their sense of knowing where they stand. They tend to resent challenges to the familiar signposts of values upon which they have counted.

Social Caste in Institutions

Life in a correctional institution is actually a caste system in which prisoners and personnel are divided into two distinctly separate groups. The prisoner caste is at the bottom of the ladder and even though some inmates may share some of the same values and ways of behaving as staff members, they cannot enjoy the same status and rewards. As a result, communication and collaboration between inmates and staff are hindered. The pressures upon inmates to adapt themselves to social relationships within their own caste may be greater than pressures for them to identify with the upper caste.

Traditional prisons and other correctional institutions are highly authoritarian communities. Mass handling, countless ways of making inmates subservient to rules and orders, and special forms of "etiquette" have the effect of creating and maintaining social distance between keepers and prisoners. Frisking of inmates and regimented movement about the institution tend to depersonalize prisoners and make their stance toward authority increasingly obdurate. The admonition "do your own time" is a slogan which endorses alienation and indifference to the interests of both staff and other inmates.

PREVENTIVE MEASURES

Many of the factors in prisoner unrest—forces that influence the environment in which prisoner management and control takes place—cannot be changed immediately or directly. The institution manager by himself can do little about public indifference, overcrowding, political meddling, or unwise commitments and releases. These are matters for which responsibility must be shared with others outside the institution. There are, however, many things that can be done to improve the climate within the institution.

Borrowing from military experience, it is too easy to think of the problems of prisoner management and control as being represented by good morale or poor morale among inmates and personnel. Not only is this a dangerous oversimplification of the problems involved but, like the military formula of command—organize, deputize, supervise—it is not particularly instructive. A shortsighted resolve to improve morale, alone, can result in misspent effort and a further complication of the underlying problems that contributed to poor morale in the first place. For example, an unwise institution manager may be tempted to accede to demands (real or anticipated) for more privileges. Unless the privileges sought will contribute directly to operational and program objectives, to grant them would risk strengthening the manager's own position at the expense of the total responsibilities he holds. Moreover, by pursuing such a course of action long enough he might discover one day that he had no more privileges to offer. The basic error in such an approach, however, is that the symptoms, rather than the causes, become the object of attention. It is not unlike taking aspirin for the temporary relief of a headache which may have serious unrelieved causes.

Obviously, the immediate purposes of prisoner management and control are security and the protection of persons and property. But there are additional concerns that are consistent with the broad objectives of imprisonment and that contain the clues to the *manner* in which management and control is achieved. These involve (a) reducing the damaging effects of confinement, (b) minimizing the offender's alienation from the rest of society, (c) maintaining human dignity and self-respect and (d) developing a sense of constructive purpose.

These concerns do not stem from maudlin sympathy toward offenders at all. They are based on facts. One fact is that there is nothing in the language or intent of existing statutes that says prisoners should be subjected to degradation, humiliation, privation or that confinement should be a debilitating, handicapping experience. On the contrary, there is a growing body of court decisions which state that, while prison and jail administrators must be accorded wide latitude in their actions, this shall not be disproportionate to the latitude accorded officials at every other point along the process of criminal justice. The thrust of these decisions is that prisoners *do* have rights, including rights to humane and equitable treatment, and that it is incumbent upon institution administrators to achieve essential security without imposing adverse restrictions.*

The other basic fact is that with few exceptions every person committed to a jail or prison is released sooner or later. A large percentage of awaiting trial prisoners are released on bail within

---

*For a more complete discussion of the rights of prisoners in confinement, see *The Prison Journal*, Vol. XLVIII, No. 1, 1968, published by the Pennsylvania Prison Society, Philadelphia, Pennsylvania.

days and many others do not return from court because they were acquitted or have been fined or their sentences were suspended. Most of the sentenced prisoners committed to jail are released in a matter of days, weeks or months. If released prisoners are bitter, hostile or further incapacitated by the experience of confinement, the institution has done nothing to contribute to the control of crime—to say the least.

The manner in which prisoner management and control is achieved is largely in the hands of the administrator and his staff. For the administrator this becomes a matter of applying philosophies and techniques to personnel management, the formulation of policies and operating procedures, and the improvement of correctional programs.

Personnel Administration

There are several personnel problems which plague penal institutions. According to a recent survey conducted for the Joint Commission on Correctional Manpower and Training, correctional workers feel that their programs must be improved. Their concern over existing program results causes frustration and can lead to apathy or cynicism. Competent personnel faced with system shortcomings they cannot overcome will resign rather than continue their association with an organization which appears to them to be prone to failure. While dissatisfaction with the ineffectiveness of programs is general among correctional personnel, the higher the educational achievement of employees, the greater is their dissatisfaction. The field of corrections, which has always found it difficult to recruit highly trained personnel, can ill afford to suffer steady loss of those it succeeds in hiring. Moreover, when a sizable group of workers in an institution or agency holds views opposed to those of the administration, disruptions in correctional operations can be expected.

Development of Correctional Careers

It is an established fact that careers in correctional work are not well defined. The manner and conditions of entry into this work differ widely from one jurisdiction to another and between correctional agencies. The circumstances also differ considerably from entry into education, social welfare and other government programs of private industry. Job dissatisfaction soon arises from an awareness that promotions are slow in coming and may bear little apparent relationship to experience and ability.

The need to provide real career opportunities in correctional work is obvious. Correctional managers must begin the development of such careers by taking the initiative in aggressive recruitment of qualified people, as industry, education, and other public services have done for a long time. Correctional agencies must begin to compete seriously for qualified or trainable people if they are not to continue to be second and third career choices for applicants years after graduation from school and probably on the heels of dissatisfactions in other jobs.

But even the most aggressive recruitment will fail unless program managers are given more freedom in offering jobs. Age and residence requirements, which are now imposed formally or informally, should be eliminated. Some requirements of previous experience should be reconsidered if young people are to be attracted to available jobs.

Education and training must be recognized in the corrections career ladder. Management trainee posts should be established. Young people today are attracted to jobs which offer challenge and some potential for personal success. Once a person starts in correctional work, he should be able to look upon his choice as a career matching others in prestige, salary and opportunity for advancement.

Support of Staff Development Programs

In today's world, knowledge increases so rapidly that the need for continuing education and training for most occupations is generally acknowledged. There is no reason to dispute this need in corrections. While few correctional systems now offer well-developed training programs, many have the capability for this, either by utilizing their own resources or in collaboration with nearby industries and institutions of higher learning. These programs should include training in principles of management and supervision, as well as in the dynamics of human behavior, community relations, law and correctional methods.

If staff development is to be improved in both quality and quantity, correctional leaders will need to provide the necessary funds and other forms of support required. Legislators and government officials must be impressed with the urgency of the need for staff development. This is a broader need than training alone. It includes exchange of personnel, tuition support for employees who wish to take academic courses, opportunities to conduct research, visits to other agencies, and involvement in professional organizations.

Removal of Job Dissatisfactions

Since administrators are responsible for the establishment of policy, they must be continually alert to employees' dissatisfactions with this work. Aggressive efforts should be made to obtain higher salaries and to provide opportunities for upward mobility. Other sources of dissatisfaction are no less important. Understaffing is more than a matter of overwork for the employees on duty. The necessity of dealing with excessive numbers of offenders may result in less than adequate supervision and control, gross inefficiency, and inability to help any of them. There is need to re-examine traditional utilization of personnel in the light of techniques which will improve program effectiveness. Even the nature of the services themselves should be studied carefully.

Much more than this needs to be said about personnel. But personnel administration is not the only area which can contribute to reduction of management and control problems.

Policies and Operating Procedures

There is an old prison saying to the effect that an institution is but the lengthened shadow of the warden. In a literal sense, this is only a partial truth since the shadow is actually a composite of many. However, it is meant to imply that institutional programs and policies and the operating procedures which dictate the ways in which things are done reflect an underlying administrative philosophy of correctional treatment and control. There is also the accurate inference that this philosophy pervades all activities throughout the entire institution, as well as the relationships which exist between the institution and other agencies, organizations, and the public. Broadly, the physical appearance of the institution and every regulation, activity and personal contact has a bearing on prisoner management and control. Four representative situations have been singled out for attention here.

Prisoner Rights and Attention to Complaints

It has long been established that lawful imprisonment necessarily causes the withdrawal or limitation of many rights to which the average citizen is fully entitled. This does not mean that the institution manager can do as he wishes without fear of criticism, censure or judicial intervention. Neither does it mean that a prisoner is without rights. One of the great problems for the administrator is determination of what restrictions and conditions may appropriately be imposed upon prisoners when the guidelines seem to be ever-changing. Yesterday's preposterous expectations can well be today's privileges and tomorrow's rights. It is nearly impossible to predict which administrative decisions will become the subject of judicial disapproval or new legislation, but there are many indications to be found. The earlier reference to a particular issue of *The Prison Journal* is only one of many sources of information. The trick is to utilize these indications to insure that reasonable rules are established which will insure fair treatment of prisoners and, at the same time, allow the administrator to do his job without undue hindrance. Prisoner rights comprise only one point of view from which the new administrator should carefully study the rules and policy decisions which he inherits. This is only one reason why all regulations and procedures should be re-examined frequently.

Food service is an example of the importance of other reasons. It is assumed that every prisoner has the legal right to be adequately nourished throughout his confinement. Presumably, this means that his food intake for an average day will be in ample quantity and nutritive value to sustain him. From a nutritional point of view this amounts simply to meeting needs based on such factors as age, weight, size, sex, physical activity and conditions of health. But in jails and prisons, as elsewhere, adequate food service depends upon budgetary allowance, procurement, storage, preparation, the manner in which meals are served, sanitation, appearance and many other considerations. Not the least of them is menu planning. Menus can be effective substitutes for calendars in determining the day of the week, or they can provide variety and reflect the particular tastes of the people being fed.

Numerous similar examples can be found in the day-to-day operation of any institution. Take clothing. A prisoner's right to human dignity demands that his nakedness be covered. His right to humane treatment requires that this covering be appropriate to the climate and circumstances in which he finds himself. Health standards dictate that clothing shall be free from vermin and reasonably clean. But these are not the only considerations. If an institution is to furnish clothing, it should also be reasonably well-fitting and in an acceptable state of repair.

Beyond the issue of rights, the problems underlying the examples given are less a matter of what policies and rules may require than of how they are carried out. Thus, the administrator should be concerned both with the substance or content of programs, policies and rules and with ways of implementing them. In part, this becomes a matter of sensitizing personnel to the fact that they deal with fellow human beings, even though they be prisoners. To illustrate further: every correctional institution conducts a "count" several times a day. This can be done promptly, accurately, and with a minimum of confusion, or it can be a recurring aggravation and an unnecessarily harassing inconvenience to the inmates. A strip search for contraband can be conducted efficiently, privately and with as much dignity as circumstances permit, or it can be a disgusting, humiliating spectacle. A cell "shake-down" can accomplish its purpose and leave authorized personal belongings in good order, or it can make a shambles of the cell with ruthless destruction of "junk" items which the prisoner happens to value highly.

The kinds of sensitivity and good judgment that apply to operating procedures and daily activities are equally applicable to the attention given prisoner complaints. Inattention to prisoner complaints can lead from uncertainty and dismay to distrust and rebellion that may produce an incident to attract attention. This is particularly likely to happen if the prisoner believes that his problem would be solved if it reached the proper officials. Areas in which complaints and grievances are most often expressed are: food, handling of mail and visits, disciplinary procedures and punishments, and work or quarters assignments which are thought to be inappropriate for some reason.

It goes without saying that legitimate complaints should be heard and the condition corrected as soon as possible. Not all situations can be corrected. In this event, the matter should be discussed with the complaining prisoner and dealt with openly. A number of jurisdictions have adopted a technique having at least psychological value. A special mailbox is installed in a prominent place within the institution. Any prisoner, at any time, may deposit a letter for prompt mailing without inspection or censorship to listed government officials whose office has some responsibility for the handling of prisoners' cases or for the operation of the institution.

Communications

It is probable that maintaining effective communications in a prison or jail is more of a problem than in other organizations. In addition to communications between management and staff, there must be communication between prisoners, staff and management.

There are many ways in which communication occurs. The choice of method may well depend upon circumstances, but it should also be considered in terms of why communication is necessary. Obviously one purpose is to instruct personnel. This can be accomplished by staff training, whether formal or informal, the issuance of policies and rules, written post orders which contain a detailed listing of duties, staff meetings, roll-call announcements, and conversations with supervisors. Another purpose is to keep management informed of what is going on. There is no good substitute for day-to-day personal observations of management personnel, but these can be augmented by personal interviews, whether scheduled or casual, staff meetings, reports, and reviews of records. Communication is an inevitable part of effective planning. Various techniques of utilizing subordinate personnel in planning assignments claim the advantages of employing staff knowledge and skills and, at the same time, insuring a sense of involvement on the part of staff in the solution of problems, program development, or other planning purpose.

Adaptations of these methods are equally applicable to communications between prisoners and staff. It is just as important that prisoners know from official sources, rather than from rumors, what is expected of them and what management is doing or planning that affects their welfare. Similarly, management needs to know what the prisoners are thinking and how they feel about things in general. Beyond this, is only by increasing communications between staff and inmates that correctional programs, such as counseling, can be introduced or improved. Additional benefits are that loosening of inmate-to-staff and inmate-to-inmate communication tends to reduce the inmate politicians' power and to minimize the traditional stigma and physical danger of cooperating with the staff.

Correspondence Regulations

Correspondence with members of the family and with close friends and associates is essential to the morale of all confined persons and may form the basis for both present and future good adjustment.

Traditionally, inmate correspondence has been surrounded by restrictions designed to limit the number of letters which could be posted or received, including elaborate record-keeping systems to assure that quotas were not violated. Close scrutiny of both outgoing and incoming mail was considered essential to the security of the institution and for the maintenance of prisoner discipline and control. Censorship was thought to be necessary to prevent the introduction of contraband, to minimize involvement in criminal activities and to prevent correspondence's becoming a tool for planning escapes or plots of violence. Experience in a number of jurisdictions has demonstrated that some of these restrictions can be eliminated with safety in certain institutions and substantially revised in others, without loss of essential control and with important savings in time, expense and inconvenience.

The size and complexity of each institution, the status and degree of sophistication of the inmates confined, along with other variables, will determine the extent of regulations required. Generally, they should include the following:

Ordinarily there should be no question about the propriety of correspondence with members of the immediate family. Friends, former business associates, and others may be considered whenever it appears that the proposed correspondence will not be detrimental to the inmate or the correspondent. Inmates should be permitted correspondence with attorneys of record or attorneys under contract without limitation. Such correspondence should be regarded as privileged in that it should be subjected to inspection only to prevent the introduction of contraband or other threat to the good order and security of the institution.

A number of institutions have demonstrated that it may not be necessary to limit the number of persons on the approved correspondence list.

Similarly, to the extent that administrative considerations permit, no limit need be placed on the number of outgoing letters authorized for mailing. (Experience has shown that the volume of correspondence remains fairly constant whether or not limitations are imposed.) Recognizing the importance of maintaining family and community contacts, the institution should expect to pay postage on a "reasonable" number of letters if the inmate is substantially lacking funds.

At time of commitment, each prisoner should be expected to sign an authorization for the head of the institution or his representative to open, read and inspect all mail. Failure to sign this authorization may result in withholding of all correspondence privileges.

While all mail of a particular inmate may need to be subjected to close scrutiny, more flexible procedures for reading, scanning or otherwise spot-checking incoming and outgoing mail will suffice for most prisoners. This should be done frequently enough to maintain security, to learn about any particular problem confronting the inmate or to alert other members of the staff to any matter that may help in evaluating the inmate. "Censorship" of mail for any purpose is indefensible. That which violates postal regulations can be referred for possible prosecution. The institution cannot assume responsibility for the content of incoming or outgoing letters.

Prisoners should be informed of the reasons for which incoming and outgoing mail will be rejected, and they should understand that they and their correspondents are responsible for the contents of their letters.

Petitions, motions, appeals, and other legal papers related to a prisoner's commitment or sentence or touching upon some legal question affecting his status in the institution, should be forwarded promptly to the appropriate court.

Visiting Regulations

The formulation and administration of visiting regulations should encourage as much visiting as personnel and facilities will permit. The setting in which visits take place should also be as informal and attractive as facilities will permit with due regard for necessary controls. Visits should be conducted and supervised in such manner that an atmosphere of friendliness and lack of tension is achieved.

The following general principles underly the reasons for granting visits:

Like correspondence, visits are a means of maintaining family ties and wholesome personal relationships with relatives and friends.

These ties and relationships are important factors in prisoner morale and future adjustment.

Visits by family and friends provide an opportunity for closer relationships with staff members for the purpose of more effective program planning.

Properly handled, visits can contribute to good public relations and a better understanding of the institution's objectives.

The practical considerations which impose limits on visits include the size of visiting facilities, the time and expense of supervision, and the need for maintaining other important institutional activities without unnecessary or extended interference.

Generally, persons who can be approved as correspondents are suitable as visitors. While it is reasonable to expect that most of the essential legal work which a recognized attorney performs for an inmate will be handled on the basis of correspondence between the attorney and his client, personal visits will be necessary when pending legal problems require, especially with persons awaiting trial and sentence. Such visits should be supervised by observation only for the purpose of contraband control and good order. The attorney and his client should be permitted to converse privately.

As with correspondence, both the prisoners and their visitors should clearly understand what the visiting regulations are.

Prisoner Discipline

There probably is no aspect of correctional institution management more filled with emotion and less open to calm appraisal than that of discipline. Yet, there is no activity more in need of objective study and complete overhauling than the traditional ways of handling prisoners who misbehave and violate institution rules. Not only does tradition exact a double standard of behavior but frequently it may ignore guarantees of civil rights and due process.

The objectives of prisoner discipline and control should be fully consistent with the correctional objectives of the institution, the focus being on (a) individual adjustment to the programs, behavior standards and limitations imposed by the administration and (b) the general welfare of the institution community. Disciplinary policy and methods should reflect this statement of purpose and recognize that disciplinary sanction is but one factor in correctional treatment and control. As applied to a prisoner who has misbehaved, this means that the sole objective is his future voluntary acceptance of certain limitations which are being imposed upon him.

Following are essential principles in acceptable and effective disciplinary policy and procedures.

1. Disciplinary action shall be taken only at such times and in such measures and degree as is necessary to regulate a prisoner's behavior within acceptable limits.

2. Prisoner behavior must be controlled in a completely impersonal, impartial and consistent manner.

3. Disciplinary action shall not be capricious nor in the nature of retaliation or revenge.

4. Program assignments and changes are made to achieve treatment goals, not as punishment or reward.

5. Corporal punishment of any kind is strictly prohibited.

6. The intiation of disciplinary measures against any prisoner is the responsibility only of staff members (preferably a committee) to whom this authority has been defined and delegated.

7. Disciplinary action should be taken as soon after the occurrence of misconduct as circumstances permit.

8. Case records should include misconduct reports, their dispositions, and should also include evaluative staff statements regarding them.

Delegation of disciplinary authority: Basic authority for the administration of prisoner discipline should be delegated by the chief executive officer of the institution. Where circumstances permit, this delegation should be to a committee of at least three staff members who are competent and who broadly represent the primary areas of correctional treatment. Such delegation should be accompanied by a specific charge which outlines duties and responsibilities.

In addition to receiving reports of misconduct, conducting hearings, making findings and imposing disciplinary actions, the adjustment committee should make referrals for diagnosis and special handling, make program changes indicated and otherwise have authoritative concern over institutional policies and operating procedures which affect discipline. The committee should also be concerned with evaluating the effectiveness of its decisions and other factors which have a bearing upon prisoner discipline and morale.

The adjustment committee should be given a broad range of dispositional alternatives. Its choice of alternatives in the disposition of each case should be consistent with the objectives of disciplinary policy. Committee action should be a composite group judgment which takes cognizance of the reasons for the adverse behavior, the setting and circumstances in which it occurred, the involved prisoner's accountability, and the correctional program goals set for him. The choice of disposition goes far beyond mere compliance with regulations. To be fully effective, the prisoner must understand and accept the reasonableness of the limitations being imposed upon him. A system should be devised to provide follow-up of at least the more serious and persistent behavior problems dealt with.

Use of segregation: In most institutions there is a separate housing for prisoners who, at times, need to be segregated from the regular population. In keeping with the statement of disciplinary policy above, this unit should be operated in accordance with the following basic requirements of control and supervision.

1. *Segregation conditions.* The quarters used for segregation should be well-ventilated, adequately lighted, appropriately heated, and maintained in a sanitary condition at all times.

2. *Cell occupancy.* Except in emergencies, the number of prisoners confined to each cell or room should not exceed the number for which the space was designed. Whenever an emergency arises which indicates that excess occupancy may be needed temporarily, an immediate report should be made to the head of the institution and his approval obtained.

3. *Clothing and bedding.* All prisoners should be admitted to segregation (after thorough search for contraband), dressed in normal institution clothing, and should be furnished a mattress and bedding. In no circumstance should a prisoner be segregated without clothing except when prescribed by the institution physician for medical or psychiatric reasons. If a prisoner is so seriously disturbed that he is likely to destroy his clothing or bedding, the institution physician should be notified immediately and a regimen of treatment and control instituted with his concurrence.

4. *Food.* Segregated prisoners should be fed three times a day on the standard ration and menu of the day for the institution.

5. *Personal hygiene.* Segregated prisoners should have the same opportunities to maintain the level of personal hygiene available to all other prisoners. This should include the availability of toilet tissue, washbasin, drinking water, comb, eye glasses, dentures, and opportunities for shaving and brushing teeth.

6. *Duration of segregation.* Consistent with the need for segregation, no prisoner should be held in this status longer than necessary. Special care should be taken that segregation does not become a haven for those who persistently fail to face their problems. The adjustment committee should be responsible

for the program needs of prisoners who require or demand long-term segregation. The committee should conduct a formal review of such cases at least once each month and make recommendations to the head of the institution.

7. *Supervision.* In addition to the direct supervision afforded by the unit officer, each segregated prisoner should be seen daily by the institution physician or medical technician and one or more other responsible officers designated by the head of the institution.

8. *Correspondence and visits.* In the absence of direct and compelling reasons to the contrary, prisoners in segregation should not be required to forfeit correspondence and visiting privileges.

9. *Records.* A permanent log should be maintained in the segregation unit. All admissions should be recorded indicating date, reason for admission, and the authorizing official. All releases from the unit should be similarly recorded. Officials required to visit the unit should sign the log indicating time, date and purpose of visit. Unusual activity or behavior of individual prisoners should be recorded in the log with a follow-up memorandum to the head of the institution.

Improvement of Correctional Programs

The third general area in which the administrator can effect improvements in prisoner management and control is program. While this is not the place to attempt a blueprint of program design, it is appropriate to examine the philosophy of correctional treatment and certain program premises.

To a great extent, many of the problems of correctional institution management are based on philosophical conflicts and controversies. Foremost among them, of course, is the argument of punishment versus treatment. Most administrators today tend to believe that correctional institutions serve to protect the public by keeping offenders locked up, as ordered by the courts, and by making an effort to at least reduce the future threat of offenders through correctional treatment. This is not a universal point of view. Thus, some of the problems of management relate to false ideas that punishment and treatment are inconsistent objectives.

This may help account for the fact that, despite the belief of administrators, the vast majority of correctional institutions still operate in traditional ways, in which the motive force is punishment, vengeful in character and expression.

Thoughtful observation has produced another point of view. While the philosophy of individualism has done much to advance correctional treatment, it has also produced a number of distortions. For example, both the law and operation of the criminal justice system tend to focus responsibility for crime and guilt on the individual offender. Thus the courts and correctional agencies become preoccupied with reforming the individual offender as an isolated problem. By channeling resources exclusively on the reformation of the offender, attention is diverted from correcting conditions in the community which encourage development of criminal behavior. Moreover, the treatment preoccupation with individual offenders has tended to obscure the fact that they do not function as unrelated individuals. As prisoners they are members of a social system, as they were in the community, and they are subject to the heavy impact of the total confinement experience.

The framework within which program planning and development are beginning to occur consists of a number of assumptions because the state of the art of correctional treatment is still not very far advanced. Other than the theories that have been advanced, very little is known about the direct causes of criminal behavior. More discriminating selection factors with which to classify offenders are needed. Much more must be learned about the character types which can make the most and least effective use of correctional programs and services. There is a basic need for knowledge with which to train staff and prisoners in the specific behaviors which are required to master the specific tasks for successful adjustment in the community. In the meantime, primary program assumptions are:

 1. The focus of corrections is intervention in delinquent and criminal careers, through management and control of crises and programs and services designed to overcome handicapping deficiencies.

 2. The deeper an offender has to be plunged into correctional processes and the longer he has to be locked up, however hu-

manely, the greater the cost and the more difficult the road back to the point of socialization that will permit successful reentry in the community.

3. A person's needs for control or for help are not necessarily related to his legal status.

These assumptions have lead to a number of alternatives to confinement that are being tried in a number of jurisdictions, and they suggest new functions and new program directions which open the possibility of more efficient and constructive uses of correctional institutions. As realistic programs are developed, the majority of prisoners will be eager to participate in them, both because of the opportunities they afford and because their mere existence is evidence that somebody cares.

HANDLING EMERGENCIES

The factors contributing to prisoner unrest, whether any singly or in combination can be identified as causing a particular problem or incident, is another matter. Similarly, inattention to the control of locks and keys, arms and ammunition, tools, items of contraband, and security inspections may well contribute to problems of management and control or, in a particular situation, become the cause of a particular emergency. Not all problems and incidents can be prevented and not all of them occur as emergencies. Being prepared is both a form of prevention, among others, and a means of minimizing the magnitude of disorder when it occurs.

The kinds of emergencies with which correctional institutions are most likely to deal are escapes and riots or disturbances. This chapter will be devoted mainly to the handling of these problems. But in these days of mass social protest and challenge of authority, local jails and correctional institutions, especially, are likely to be involved in the control of civil disorder in the community. For this reason, attention will be given the problem of emergency detention occasioned by mass arrests. Fire and civil disaster are emergency situations which will be mentioned.

Escape Plans

Although escapes or attempted escapes are comparatively rare in well-managed institutions, the entire staff must be constantly alert to prevent them. It is possible to reduce successful escapes to a minimum only through cooperative and coordinated planning. While the methods and circumstances of an escape will vary, certain basic policies and procedures are applicable to all of them. Every correctional institution should maintain a carefully developed and detailed plan for the prevention and apprehension of escapes. It is important that the plan be reviewed frequently and kept up to date. A copy should be furnished each employee with the requirement that all become thoroughly familiar with its contents.

In developing a comprehensive plan, an escape should be viewed as an incident which must be assessed in phases or series of action steps.

    1. The alert—a period of time in which it may be possible to prevent the incident or to prepare for it.

    2. Sounding the alarm—a brief interval for decision that an incident has occurred and for notifying others.

    3. Mobilizing resources—final preparation for command and action.

    4. Establishing control—thwarting the attempt or apprehending the escapee and assuring security of the institution.

    5. Returning to normal operations—including investigations, reports and necessary repairs.

The elements of a comprehensive escape plan will establish policy, define responsibility, and outline procedures to be followed in each of these phases. The plan itself should be developed around the following action steps.

Prevention

The plan statement should indicate the most common and immediate ways of preventing escapes. This should include reference to such items as: alertness to detect and report signs of unrest or tension; observation of anything unusual about participation in programs and activities; expression of complaints and requests for change; prompt and decisive action when the occasion demands; thorough security inspections and counts; and effective methods of selecting prisoners for work and quarters assignments.

Sounding the Alarm

The plan should provide that any unauthorized absence from a work detail, living quarters or other location will be reported immediately to the supervisor in charge. When it is determined from the information at hand that an escape has occurred, prearranged signals should be sounded to notify all employees. The plan should distinguish the kinds of signals and the circumstances of their use as the sound of a general alarm can create unnecessary tension and excitement.

Mobilization of Resources

A list of all employees with addresses and telephone numbers should be maintained and arranged so that a maximum number of employees may be contacted with a minimum number of calls. As soon as an escape occurs, an employee should be designated to contact the off-duty employees required and have them report for duty immediately.

The security posts and maintenance operations essential to continued functioning of the institution during an escape emergency should be identified. All other posts should be vacated and nonessential activities shut down so that all available personnel can report promptly to a central place for special duty assignments. Personnel in charge of nonessential activities should place all tools in a convenient, safe place, secure the area and check their prisoners in. The officer assigned to the armory, with whatever additional help may be needed, should prepare immediately to issue arms, ammunition and other equipment that may be requisitioned. The record clerk should be prepared to issue escape notices, including identification pictures, for prompt distribution and mailing.

Concurrent with the initial assignment of personnel to escape posts and duties, one employee should be designated to notify all law enforcement agencies in the surrounding area by telephone or radio. Addresses and telephone numbers of the agencies to be notified should be part of the escape and apprehension plan. (In the development of the plan it will be helpful to determine with local law enforcement officials exactly what involvement each agency will have. A confidential copy of the plan might well be furnished each law enforcement agency for reference.) The possibility of asking nearby radio and television stations to assist by spot announcements of escape essentials should not be overlooked.

Establishing Control

A complete list of all posts to be covered during a search should be maintained. These may be divided into various categories. The posts to be manned will depend on the information available as to the time the escape occurred, means of departure, direction of travel, and other factors that will help insure that the search effort can be pinpointed as closely as possible. An instruction kit should be prepared for each post and handed to the officer at the time he is assigned. For posts located beyond the immediate vicinity of the institution, the instruction kit should include a map of the area, directions for transportation, the duties to be performed, and other information, such as location of the nearest telephone and the anticipated relief schedule, that will be helpful to the officer assigned to the post.

The establishment of a special communications center, apart from the command post, can be most useful in conducting an orderly, efficient search. The person in charge of this center is usually authorized to issue press releases, answer numerous inquiries, receive and place telephone or radio calls, and otherwise process and record messages and information incidental to the search.

While task forces are being deployed, the plan should establish procedures for starting the investigation. This may include the assignment of an employee to search the personal locker and effects of the escapee for evidence that may provide clues for the hunt. At this time, too, the preliminary investigation should be organized, starting with interviews with both staff members and prisoners who were in a position to know the escapee well and who might be able to shed some light on the escape.

It should be clearly established in policy that if a hostage is taken in an attempt to escape, all personnel should have clear instructions that orders given by any person under duress, including executive officers, are not valid and under no circumstances should the prisoner be permitted to escape from the institution.

The plan should make clear what authority is granted for the use of firearms and in what circumstances these should be used.

Generally, firearms should be used as a last resort to prevent escape, prevent injury or loss of life to personnel or prisoners not involved, and to protect property. Orders to halt or desist should be given first and, if ignored, a warning shot should be fired. Should this be ignored, subsequent shots should be aimed to disable rather than kill.

Also, the plan should include instructions to all personnel on all posts regarding the importance of tact and good judgment in contacts with other people, the authority granted for stop and search, and the tasks that are to be performed in collaboration with representatives of other law enforcement agencies.

Returning to Normal

As soon as the decision is made to discontinue the initial search effort, all law enforcement agencies, news media, and other persons who were notified of the escape should be informed.

When an escape involves cutting of bars, window sash, or other property damage, a careful record, both photographic and written should be made and arrangements made for repairs. Attention should be given the gathering and safekeeping of other evidence that may be important to prosecution. Particular care must be taken in interviewing the apprehended escapee and other suspects. It is best that this be done only with the advice of the prosecuting attorney.

One of the important concluding steps in handling an escape incident is assessment and report of the experience. The adoption of a general reporting format will facilitate the process involved and provide clues to the lessons that can be learned from the incident.

Plans for Riots and Disturbances

Prisoner disturbances are of two basic types: (1) a disturbance of a riotous nature between two or more prisoner factions which is related to animosities between prisoner groups and may not be well-organized; and (2) a more general disturbance directed against the institution because of some real or fancied grievance or other objective, such as mass escape. Whenever prisoners or personnel are under great stress, "spontaneous" disturbances can erupt for any reason. Once a disturbance starts, the measures taken to regain control may be the same, regardless of its type or precipitating causes. Yet, it is important that distinctions be made among them because of the few moments of decision as to how to proceed and because of the critical importance of keeping the disorder as isolated and as small as possible.

While it is impossible to detail the procedures that should be followed for the effective handling of all kinds of disturbances in all institutions, experience has shown that the following guidelines are generally applicable.

That each correctional institution should maintain a carefully developed plan for handling group disturbances of all kinds, that the plan be kept up to date, and that all employees be familiar with its contents is evident enough. The steps involved in handling a riot or disturbance, as with an escape, must be thought through. These are: the interval of alert, sounding the alarm, mobilizing resources, establishing control, and returning to normal. The same basic policies and principles expressed in the preceding discussion of an escape plan are applicable to plans for riots and disturbances.

As with escapes, there usually are signs of tensions among prisoners which portend a group disturbance. It is known that precipitating factors may be unresolved racial problems, complaints over food, dissatisfaction with the performance or attitudes of personnel, complaints over recreation, visiting or formation. With this knowledge, promptness in detecting and reporting unusual activity or bad "climate" may enable getting at the root of the trouble and possibly forestalling incidents that could result in a riot.

An action plan should be developed from the primary responsibilities of institution management and in this order: public safety; safety and welfare of hostages; prevention of loss of life or injury to other personnel; prisoner welfare; protection of property.

When, despite all efforts to prevent them, riots or disturbances do occur, they begin with startling suddenness, spread rapidly, and can cause major damage. Prompt activation of the riot plan, in which the following elements are incorporated, is absolutely necessary.

Containment

Immediate steps to close any possible avenues of escape are

mandatory. The trouble should be localized and access to other areas cut off to prevent the disorder from spreading. Careful appraisal of the situation should be made before rushing in or committing personnel to a situation that might result in their being taken hostage. The immediate objective should be determined, the necessary reinforcements called, and equipment required assembled. The safety of employees and prisoners must be considered if it becomes apparent that force and the use of defensive equipment will be necessary. Force and the use of defensive equipment should be used only when ordered by the head of the institution or his representative. Any person held hostage has no authority while under duress, regardless of rank.

It is noteworthy that even in the worst prison riots only a relatively small percentage of the total prisoner population has been actively involved. It is important that prisoners not wishing to participate be given an opportunity to withdraw from the area of disturbance. They should be provided safe conduct to secure quarters.

Employees should be instructed to observe the activity closely to identify ringleaders and subsequently report their participation. Recurring efforts should be made to determine the cause of the disturbance and participants should be urged to select one or more spokesmen to confer with the head of the institution or his representative. No promises should be made to demands other than assurance of fair hearing.

Use of Force and Defensive Equipment

When the decision has been made to use force or defensive equipment, the kind and amount will be dictated by the situation but only for the purposes of control and protection.

RIOT SQUADS. As part of a basic riot control plan, it is assumed that a number of personnel will have been selected, organized and trained both in the proper use of special equipment and in the tactics to be used in various situations. When it is necessary to use riot squads, their members should be properly equipped. Injury should not be risked unnecessarily. Each squad should be instructed in the specific tasks it is to perform. Squads should enter the area of disturbance simultaneously from as many entrances as are available.

WATER. A riot can often be brought under control by the effective use of water. The riot control plan should identify the location of hydrants and other water outlets, the availability of hose and other fire fighting equipment. Further, the plan should afford protection of hydrants, valves and exposed water pipes during a disturbance. Water may be used to disperse participants, to bring sporadic fires under control, and to create dampness necessary to the most effective concentrations of gas should its use be required.

GAS. Gas of various types may be useful in situations where it would otherwise be hazardous to break up a rioting group. Sufficient gas should be used in the first attempt. (Minimum and maximum amounts that can be used safely under various circumstances should be computed in advance and this information should be incorporated in the riot plan.) Provisions must be made for follow-up. Gas will break resistance, but participating prisoners may have to be removed forcibly. A squad equipped with gas masks should be assigned this task. The gas should be permitted to develop fully, but not to dissipate, before the squad enters the area. Sometimes a single gas shell or grenade will break up a large group so that smaller groups can be split off. When this tactic is used, the group will quickly re-form unless the follow-up is properly timed. Whenever gas is to be used in an enclosed area, it should be determined in advance that dispersed participants can exit easily.

FIREARMS. As with escapes, firearms should be used only as a last resort to prevent escapes, injury or loss of life of personnel or prisoners held hostage, and to protect property. Orders to halt or desist should be given first, and, if these are ignored, a warning shot should be fired. Subsequent shots should be aimed to disable rather than kill.

Post-riot Procedures

Steps should be taken as soon as the disturbance is under control to insure that nobody has escaped and that the institution is physically secure. Initially, all participants in the disturbance should be confined and supervision augmented to insure that the disturbance will not break out anew. Extra help should also be assigned to all living quarters and other areas where it is necessary for groups of prisoners to congregate until it is certain that the disorder has completely subsided. If necessary, all nonessential activities can be suspended and feeding schedules rearranged to provide supervision over smaller groups and to meet supervision needs elsewhere.

The remaining steps are similar to those identified for escapes in the preceding section: photographic and written reports of damage, repair of damage, collection and preservation of evidence, notification of persons and agencies that had been informed of the disturbance, and, finally, assessment and report of the experience.

Plans for Civil Disorder

The local jail or correctional institution is very likely to be involved in community efforts to control group protests and demstrations. When mass arrests are made, temporary detention facilities will be needed for large numbers of people, including women and juveniles. Obviously, correctional officials should participate in advance law enforcement planning for such emergency, and the plans should include definitions of what specific services temporary detention facilities will be expected to provide for what numbers and kinds of arrested persons. It is possible that these services can be provided by existing jail and detention facilities under emergency conditions. In this event, operating problems will center around vast overcrowding, the processing of large numbers of people in and out of the institution, and such accommodations as housing, feeding, telephone calls, visits and interviews with investigating officials and attorneys.

When it is known that existing facilities lack the capabilities required to meet anticipated needs, a much greater planning problem will involve the staffing and operation of an emergency detention center in some other setting such as an armory, stadium or warehouse. Based on two such experiences of its own, the Bureau of Prisons has published an Emergency Detention Manual, copies of which are available upon request.

It is possible that situations may arise in which trained personnel of the local jail or correctional institution will be called upon to assist law enforcement agencies in controlling civil disturbances in the community. The riot squads referred to in the preceding section would be appropriate for this purpose under emergency conditions. Service of this kind should be based on important high-level policy decisions and careful planning.

Plans for Civil Disaster

The local institution may be a valuable resource for emergency services to the community in the face of disaster brought about by flood, fire, earthquake or other major happenings involving extensive property damage, personal injury, or large-scale displacement of people. The precise needs in such dire circumstances and the capabilities of local institutions to provide services vary so greatly that generalizations about them would be of little value. The institution manager should confer with local police, fire and civil defense officials about such matters. While it may not be possible to formulate definite plans in advance, at least general agreement can be reached as to the kinds of services the local institution might offer under given conditions.

Fire Plans

That the institution manager bears responsibility for the protection of lives and property goes without saying. It is equally evident that this responsibility cannot be borne without planning for fire prevention and fire fighting. Fire marshals and other officials can assist greatly in the development of such plans, in training personnel and prisoners in fire fighting techniques, and in making periodic inspections and investigations.

CONCLUSION

Disorder, including violent and destructive behavior of prisoners, is not unknown to jails, prisons and other correctional institutions. Mass demonstrations, organized social protest and natural disasters not only can cause institutions to operate under emergency conditions, but they can contribute directly to emotional stress in prisoner populations.

The potential dangers inherent in these situations are sobering, indeed, especially when it is realized that so many of the basic causes, and even the triggering incidents, are beyond the immediate control of institution managers and personnel. Yet, there need be no feeling of alarm. On the contrary, institution managers and personnel can draw much self-assurance from the knowledge that they can acquire the capability of handling disorder and are prepared for it.

The preceding discussions have emphasized the importance of planning for emergency conditions. This is a difficult, time-consuming and continuing task. Yet, only in this way can the unnecessary handicaps of surprise, confusion and costly indecision be avoided.

CHAPTER 6

CUSTODY and SECURITY

Manual of Correctional Standards*

The fundamental responsibility of prison management is the secure custody and control of prisoners. This is universally prescribed by law, custom and public opinion. Although at times such a concept may seem at variance with attempts to introduce rehabilitative services, it is doubtful that any correctional program which ignores this reality will long endure. Actually services and facilities for rehabilitative treatment can operate effectively only in a climate where control is constant. Conversely, good control cannot be consistently maintained without energizing it with positive correctional and training resources.

Wise prison management recognizes this "frame of reference" within which the correctional program must operate. The many chapters in this *Manual* indicate the broad aspects of current correctional practice. A well-rounded correctional program, including medical, food, educational, industrial, and other rehabilitative services must be correlated with and into a system of sound custody, security and control of inmates.

ESSENTIALS FOR CUSTODY AND SECURITY

The following are among the most important provisions in establishing sound custody, security and control:

---

*Reprinted with the permission of the American Correctional Association.

95

1. *An Adequate System of Classification of Prisoners.* Careful study, diagnosis and recommendations for treatment documented into case histories give prison workers the knowledge they need to handle inmates.
2. *Inspection of Security Facilities.* Regular, formalized inspections reinforced by constant observation of the physical plant, help assure its best use.
3. *An Adequate System of Counting Inmates.* An adequate system of counting inmates to make certain "all are present and accounted for" at prescribed periods day and night.
4. *Control of Firearms.* A plan for firearms control specifying its purpose, use, safety precautions, proper inventory, storage and standardization; all should be included in the plan for all institutions.
5. *Gas Control.* A plan for gas control specifies its purpose, use, safety precautions, proper inventory, storage and standardization.
6. *Control of Contraband.* A plan for the control of contraband defines such items and provides for their regulation.
7. *Key Control.* A plan for control of keys assures that all are accounted for and under control of free personnel.
8. *Tools and Equipment.* A plan for control of those tools and equipment items that pose a threat to persons or to the physical security of the plant must be developed.
9. *Job Analysis.* A comprehensive and up-to-date job analysis for all posts aids employees in understanding their tasks.
10. *Locking Devices.* Proper locking devices must be kept in good operating condition.
11. *Proper Cell Equipment.* Proper cell equipment should be designed to minimize the necessity of permitting custodial risks to leave their cells after lock-in.
12. *Emergency Doors.* Emergency doors must be provided into housing and to the areas where prisoners are congregated.
13. *Special Emergencies.* Plans should be developed and be available to place into effect for operation during special emergencies: (a) riots, (b) escape, (c) fire fighting, (d) emergency lighting and stand-by power, and (e) civil defense.

Perhaps, in the final analysis, the soundest and safest security measure of all *is the existence of a positive program of inmate activities*. Such a program includes all the things such as work, recreation and education that are discussed in other chapters of this *Manual*. Such multi-faceted programs are sometimes referred to as "calculated risks" against security. Actually, these positive programs have become important security factors in well-managed institutions of all types and have become primary security features in many institutions such as prison camps, and minimum custody type institutions in California and the Federal Prison System.

Prisoners who are receiving decent food and humane treatment and who are busily engaged in useful work programs, carefully organized and purposeful leisure time activities, and self-improvement, seldom resort to disturbances or escape attempts. No matter how modern the buildings, how secure the facilities, how efficient the operating procedures may be, or how well the personnel may be trained, it should be emphasized that security cannot be assured if it is predicated entirely in procedures which are operated wholly against the will of the prisoners. If the prisoners are committed to inactivity, moral degradation, humiliation, and mental stultification, then the desire within them to escape or to throw off the shackles of these unnatural restraints will become so strong that security facilities and procedures will be breached sooner or later.

The fundamental custodial procedures outlined in this chapter have been tested in the strains of day-to-day prison operations. If adopted as a part of the total program of administration advocated by the American Correctional Association in this *Manual*, they can assure a high degree of security in any prison. The greatest effectiveness will most certainly be attained where sound security procedures, combined with enlightened humane treatment of prisoners, gain their willingness to cooperate in the difficult prison situation.

DISCUSSION OF STANDARDS

An Adequate System of Classification of Prisoners

Careful study, diagnosis, and recommendations for treatment documented into case histories give prison workers the knowledge they need to handle inmates.

Ideally, a state correctional system should include several types of institutions to provide different degrees of custody; however, in a state with a small prison population this is impractical and uneconomical. Whether it is provided in several institutions in a system or in a single prison, an administration should provide for these varying degrees of security. Since the total inmate treatment and training program is conditioned largely by custody requirements, its success is almost wholly dependent on flexibility of custody classification and handling of prisoners. Elsewhere in this manual there is a brief discussion of custody as it relates to different types of institutions. This section will attempt to define briefly the degrees of custody within the institutions in a correctional system.

Under most operating conditions an institution should provide for three or four different degrees of custody. The basic three are *Close, Medium,* and *Minimum.* In most cases the fourth, or maximum custody classification, is used only for the known "escape risk" inmates or those considered incorrigible. In practice, *Close Custody* inmates are housed in the institution's most secure housing units, are assigned to work within the institution enclosure, and are under constant supervision. *Close* custody classification is intended not only to reduce the escape hazards but to provide close supervision for sex deviates, abnormal, or unusually difficult types of prisoners. *Medium Custody* classification should normally provide that inmates be available for work on the inside without constant or direct supervision and on the outside of the regular enclosure under supervision. This group is considered eligible for housing in the less expensive units such as dormitories and outside cell blocks. *Minimum Custody* inmates are considered eligible for outside assignments such as farms, camps, logging operations, etc., and usually under general or intermittent supervision only.

It is important that the classification program in any state correctional system provide for at least an automatic annual review of the custody of each prisoner. The degree of custody under which an individual is held is frequently an important factor in his adjustment. Many times the expression of confidence shown by a reduction in custody has a tremendous favorable impact on an individual prisoner's adjustment. It can be an important morale factor in an institution, since it is specific evidence that custody-classification is vital, alive and continuous.

Inspection of Security Facilities

Regular, formalized inspections reinforced by constant observation of physical plant for security, safety, sanitation and appearance help assure its best use.

Security measures inside a prison are the day-to-day control and supervision procedures designed to expedite the movements of prisoners, to assure control of their whereabouts at all times, to guard against flagrant violation of rules, and to promote discipline and good order while institution routines are carried out.

At least once a week, or more often if considered necessary, all bars, locks, windows, doors, and other security facilities should be checked carefully for evidence that they are in good condition and have not been tampered with. The results of these inspections should be submitted in writing to the head of the institution or the officer specifically in charge of security. Inspections of this sort often reveal attempts at escape and are discouraging to prisoners who may feel that the net value of such an attempt is not worth the effort.

In addition to formal inspections already described, all employees should be trained to observe any unusual conditions, as they apply to the security facilities, during their regular rounds of the prisoner's quarters. All defective security equipment should be replaced or repaired immediately. Failure to do so is false economy that can but end in serious consequences for the prison administration.

An Adequate System of Counting Inmates

Two things are accepted as axiomatic in the operation of any prison in any state or federal system—meals must be served and counts must be made. No matter what type of institution is involved, or what types of programs are in operation, no one has yet come up with a plan to eliminate the counting of prisoners. It is the one method of knowing that the ever-present and all-compelling responsibility imposed for detention of prisoners is being carried out.

The count system in any type of institution should provide for at least four official counts in a twenty-four hour period. These counts may be spaced to facilitate the work program and to interfere as little as possible with the inmate education and leisure time activity programs. It is usually found expedient to schedule at least two official counts at or near the time of officer shift changes so that plenty of help will be available to make efficient counts and to have a large number of officers on hand if discrepancies in the count are found.

In addition to the complete official counts made on schedule, each detail officer and housing unit officer should be required to make irregular, but periodic, "census" checks of inmates under his supervision. If an official count is not scheduled between the morning and evening counts, then a comprehensive census by details should be made at the noon hour.

The master count in an institution is usually maintained in the control room or operations center. It is imperative that the officer responsible for maintaining this master count be provided with up-to-the-minute information regarding all inmate housing moves and work assignment changes, admissions to the prison hospital, etc. He also must be so situated that he can apply himself to this important task without harassing interruptions.

Certain fundamentals in making counts are listed here as aids to individual officers.

1. *Concentrate ONLY on the count as the round is made.* Do not speak to prisoners or other personnel or allow distraction in any way.

2. *When the count in one part of the unit is complete, list it on a temporary count sheet.* When counting the next part, such as one side of a cell block gallery, one floor of a dormitory, or one section of a shop, make that count separate and again list it on the temporary count sheet.

3. *See flesh or movement or hear the prisoner speak before recording him as counted.* Many escapes have been perpetrated by the skillful substitution of dummies. The greatest success with dummies has been attained by "building up" the officer to accept certain practices. For instance, in one successful escape an inmate who was supposed to be standing near his cell door for the count, by degrees and over a period of time began to recline on the bed, at or near count time. The officer did not enforce the count regula-

tions and after about three weeks of "build up" the prisoner was able to fashion a dummy, sitting upright on the foot of his bed, which deceived the officer throughout an entire shift. The ruse was discovered when his relief officer, who observed the rules, discovered the dummy. The prisoner had been gone since he left the dining room, some six hours before.

4. *Counts in dormitory or open type units should never be made by one officer.* It is a simple matter for prisoners to move from one side to the other to be counted twice to cover up for an escapee. One officer should make the count while a second officer stands in a position to observe any movement.

5. *Up-to-the-minute count records should be maintained in the control room or operation office.* This not only is a matter of good administration, but is essential in case of sudden escapes, accidents or violence.

REMEMBER — THE WELL-TRAINED, ALERT OFFICER KNOWS HOW MANY PRISONERS HE HAS AT ALL TIMES AND WHERE THEY ARE.

Control of Firearms

It is obviously necessary that firearms equipment be included in the plan for security of an institution. The system for control of these weapons must be carefully established and must be adhered to by all employees at all times. Defects in the system or carelessness on the part of an employee in observing the established security controls can result in violent deaths of employees, prisoners and others. This has happened many times in the past.

Certain rules that apply to basic control procedures in all institutions may be listed as:

1. The weapons arsenal should be located *outside* the inmate housing and activities area. Under most conditions, an armory tower is the most secure arsenal location for all weapons and ammunition not in use. It should be borne in mind that weapons are not needed *inside,* so that the proper place for storage is outside if possible. Firearms are used only as a last resort to prevent escape or in extreme cases of violence. Therefore, they are usually needed only when escaping prisoners are gaining egress from the institution

perimeter. When prisoners have reached the outside, weapons stored inside the institution in a vault or an inside armory are practically useless.

2. *All employees* must be trained to safely handle and shoot all weapons they may be called upon to use. Many law enforcement officers, who do not have the opportunity or desire to attend training courses in the use of firearms, feel that the very fact that they are carrying a weapon is sufficient to protect them and to enforce their authority. This may be true for months or years, but sooner or later the time comes when the weapon must be used quickly and expertly to save lives, perhaps that of the law enforcement officer himself. Prison officers should be required to qualify on regulation shooting courses as a requisite for their position initially, and should later be required to qualify at least once each year.

3. When it is necessary for firearms to be checked out of the arsenal or when they are being transported in areas adjacent to prisoners, there should be two or more officers available. In most cases where it is necessary for weapons to be transported from the arsenal to towers that are manned only for certain shifts, it is advisable for one officer to transport the weapons, and after he has posted himself in the tower, to receive the ammunition from another officer. This procedure may be varied depending on location of tower lines, etc.

4. Precautions should always be taken to assure that shipments of weapons or ammunition coming into institutions are plainly labeled and that instructions on the outside of the cases direct that the institution will be notified prior to delivery.

It should be emphasized to all new prison trainees that there is no more flagrant example of false security than an ostentatious show of weapons and the habitual use of such weapons in close proximity to prisoners. It is an open challenge, and the histories of many bloody riots show without question that it almost inevitably leads to death or terrible violence or both, sooner or later. The untrained or blustery prison officer who swaggers among prisoners with a gun on his person is usually trying to compensate for fear or lack of knowledge in how to handle prisoners. Any prison system that permits such use of weapons is inviting disaster.

A Plan for Gas Control

All penal institutions should be equipped with a sufficient quantity of gas for use in quelling violent disturbances. Ordinarily, institutions of from 500 to 1000 inmates should have a minimum stock of approximately 50 CN gas grenades, several 1.5 inch gas projection guns with at least ten rounds of tear gas projectiles for each gun, and these should be divided about equally between short-blast and long-range projectiles, and at least twenty-five billies. Other types of gas dispensers are available and most are satisfactory.

Prison administrators should ascertain where additional supply of gas equipment can be readily obtained in the event of a major disturbance. Because gas munitions deteriorate rapidly, it is not economically sound to keep large quantities on hand in the institution.

The use of gas in prisons has been a controversial question for years. Those who oppose its use in quelling disturbances probably do so because of unfortunate experiences in critical situations. However, the use of gas has undeniably prevented bloodshed in many cases of violence. The degree of success in the use of gas depends almost entirely on the skill, judgment and planning of those who use it. *Gas should never be used by personnel who are not trained in its use.*

Advantages

The use of tear gas in suppressing disturbances is more humane than bullets, since it causes no serious or lasting damage. Unless there has been prolonged exposure to intense concentrations, tear gas has a physiological effect only for a short period of time varying from a few minutes to a few hours. It provides a means, if properly used, of overpowering and subduing a man or a group of men without wounding or mutilating them. The psychological effect of using tear gas is also helpful. Actually, the threat and availability of gas at the scene of a disturbance has probably halted more incipient disorders than its actual use.

Disadvantages

The proper use of gas is not understood by the public generally and may lead to unfavorable reactions. The physical effects of tear gas tend to make a man oblivious of everything except his desire to get out of the gas. This may prove to be a disadvantage. If the gas is used unwisely, it might precipitate a disturbance worse than the one which exists at the time, and it might cause temporarily blinded prisoners to injure themselves by rushing into an unseen hazard.

Conditions must be favorable for the use of gas, so that when released, it will reach the intended objective; an adverse wind could cause the gas to be disadvantageous. There are also limitations to its use inside a building because of dangers of starting fires from burning grenades, getting a concentration which is too dense, or gassing adjoining areas not affected by a disturbance.

Use of DM or Nauseating Gas

The use of DM is recommended only under the most extreme conditions. If extreme violence prevails and extensive property damage may result, then, as a last resort before use of firearms, DM gas may serve to subdue desperate rioters.

The effects of nauseating or DM gas are sneezing, coughing, nausea and vomiting in varying degrees of severity, depending upon the concentration inhaled. The victims of the gas become depressed, physically weak, and generally debilitated after a few minutes and can offer little resistance. The gas does not take effect as quickly on some persons as on others. Action has been known to be delayed about thirty minutes in rare cases. The effects are more lingering than those of tear gas and usually light concentrations only are necessary. It should be remembered that DM may readily contaminate water and cause poison if such water is used for drinking or cooking. An effective concentration may be produced with .002 of an ounce of Adamsite®, in 1,000 cubic feet of air at three-minute exposure.

For DM gas or a mixture of CN-DM the treatment usually recommended is rest, fresh air, and removal of the contaminated clothing. The nose and throat should be washed with salt water or a solution of bicarbonate of soda. Relief for the burning of the nose and throat is afforded by inhaling the following mixture:

> Alcohol 40%, chloroform 40%, ether 20%, and ammonia five to ten drops. Glycerin and menthol troches help to relieve the burning of the throat. Breathing chlorine given off from a bottle of chloride of lime is beneficial. Keep patient warm, but not near heat.

A Plan for Control of Contraband

Contraband items are a continual source of harassment in any prison. A somewhat succinct statement of how to control it might be given in one word: Supervision. Regulations are necessary to control narcotics and stimulating drugs. All types of medicine and stimulants should be under lock and key and should be absolutely inaccessible to prisoners. Any types of poison represent distinct hazards in an institution. Not only is there danger of accidental misuse, but dangerous or mentally deranged prisoners may cause great harm or death to themselves or others if they come into possession of poisons. Some of the most common causes of death, blindness or other permanent disabilities have been prisoner possession of lye, insecticides, anti-freeze and denatured alcohol. These items should never be in the possession of prisoners, even the most carefully selected prisoners, unless they are under constant supervision of qualified employee specialists. It is imperative that regulations assure the closest possible control of such substances at all times.

For consistent control of contraband items, whether they be dangerous articles such as guns, knives, or other weapons or poisonous or hazardous substances, can best be assured by these few basic procedures being faithfully carried out:

1. Periodic but irregular search of cells, inmates, and inmate work areas.

2. Frequent search and careful supervision of so-called "trusties."

3. Discreet supervision of visitors to inmates.

4. Regular inspection of inmates' mail.

5. Inspection of all vehicular traffic and supplies coming into the institution.

6. Use of metal detector devices at gates of compound and entrances into cell blocks.

Key Control

Key control is an extremely important factor in the matter of security and cannot be left to sporadic checks by supervisors or occasional system overhauls. At any hour of the day or night the system of control should indicate where each ring of keys is and in

whose possession. Certain procedures are fundamental and should be adopted in any key control system.
 1. All keys should be issued from a central location such as the institution control room.
 2. The key control center should have a log book in which all keys are listed, showing the number of each key, trade name of lock and where located, and the number of keys available for each lock. It is usually most practicable to number keys in series, such as series "100" for administration building, "200" for the next building, and so on for all other buildings listed on the same plan.
 3. The control center should have panel boards with sufficient hooks for all bunches of keys.
 4. The key control center should have at all times at least one duplicate set for each bunch of keys.

Proper control of keys can be maintained only if an inviolable rule is enforced to assure that all officers who withdraw keys from the control center give a receipt for the keys. A simple and speedy method is to provide all officers with metal tags on which their names are stamped and require that a tag be turned into the control center for each bunch of keys withdrawn. This tag is placed on the hook in lieu of the keys issued and is returned to the officer when he checks in the keys. This system must be enforced rigidly since any exception to receipting for keys soon breaks down the system.

It is sometimes discouraging to enter a unit and find the officer practically staggering under a huge bunch of keys dangling from a laundry pin, a piece of string, or rawhide attached to his belt. All too frequently it develops that many of the keys have been out of use for years but still remain on the ring because "they have always been there" or "no one has ever ordered them taken off." Periodic surveys should be made to assure that obsolete keys are discarded, that key records are up to date, and to see that no locks have been changed without notice to the key control center.

Key rings of good quality should be provided. Wherever it is feasible to use them, protecting covers of leather or other material should be provided to prevent inmate's studying the size and shape of keys and avoiding wear on officers' clothing.

Under no circumstances should prisoners be permitted to handle keys. The officer who passes keys to a "trusty" or any other inmate is shirking his own responsibility and endangering the security of the institution. Even if it is not possible for the prisoner entrusted with the keys to use them advantageously during the time they are in his possession, it is a simple matter for him to make prints of keys in soap, chewing gum, or other substances so that he may manufacture a key later.

The most frequent violation of the fundamentals of key control is that of officers entering cell blocks or other units where prisoners are confined with keys to outside doors in their possession. Keys which actually permit egress from the housing unit proper should be locked up securely or under direct supervision of a paid employee at all times. There simply should be no opportunity for prisoners to come into possession of keys to the outside doors.

Tools and Equipment

If any one thing can be compared to keys and guns as potential escape aids, it is tools. Untrained prison officers all too frequently are prone to take tools for granted whenever they are found in the institution. Lack of attention to these highly dangerous means of escape has brought many an officer to grief—some have died as a result.

Most institution bars can be twisted or pried loose with a six-inch crescent wrench. Consider then the hazards involved in the huge wrenches and other types of tools so frequently found unattended in prisons. Locks may be removed with screwdrivers. Bars may be sawed with a two-inch coping saw blade. The institution which does not have a system of checking tools in and out, for supervision and control of tools at all times is flirting with disaster. Some of the bloodiest and most violent escapes have been made possible by prisoners being able to gain possession of *one* seemingly harmless tool or piece of pipe from which a bar spreader could be fashioned.

Several fundamental principles of tool control might be listed as follows.
1. Have a shadow board with outlines drawn to indicate what type tool belongs in that certain place.
2. Check tools to see that they are where they belong. This should be done as regularly as counts are made.

3. Check tools out to employees only and get a receipt.
4. If tools are allocated to various departments, have the tools for each department marked so that responsibility for them may be placed properly.
5. Never allow prisoners to use or possess tools inside buldings within the enclosure except under supervision.
6. To insure against loss or misuse, kitchen knives and other items in and around a kitchen should be checked as carefully as tools.

Good tool control is not only essential to security—it is evidence of good administration and efficient operation.

Job Analysis

Every custodial post in any correctional institution should be provided with a set of general procedural orders and a specific job analysis of every post should be made and kept available in the institution. Every officer who is assigned to a post regularly, or as a relief, should be required to read the post orders and to know the responsibilities and requirements of the post. This provides specific information for the officer, assures that procedures will be uniform on a post regardless of changes in personnel and, of utmost importance, states in writing what is expected of the officer. This serves as a protection for competent officers and enables the administration to protect itself against incompetent or disloyal employees.

Locking Devices

Proper locking devices must be kept in good operating condition. Obviously, many of the older institutions in operation today are poorly designed and make the control and security of prisoners a hazardous task. However, in many cases, maximum utilization of existing facilities is not made. It is essential that locking devices always be kept in good operating condition and that plumbing facilities be kept in good order. It is not uncommon for locking devices to be neglected until they become corroded and rusty to the point of being inoperative. This is a most dangerous "economy."

Some institutions are forced to discontinue the use of multiple locking devices entirely and resort to the use of individual door locks when routine repairs and maintenance have been so long neglected that the cost of overhaul becomes prohibitive.

The staff of every major institution should include a competent locksmith. In small institutions the locksmith may be assigned other duties, but it is essential that such an employee be on the staff.

Proper Cell Equipment

Proper cell equipment should be designed to minimize the necessity of permitting custodial risks to leave their cells after lock-in. Single cells are obviously most desirable for housing prisoners, but whether single or multiple cells are used, they should be equipped with necessary plumbing to assure that cells need not be opened at night. Escape records of small institutions having only communal plumbing facilities show a high incidence of escapes, assaults, and attempted escapes during night hours when prisoners are let out of their cells. The importance of modern plumbing equipment and its proper maintenance cannot be stressed too strongly from the standpoint of security alone.

Emergency Doors

Emergency doors must be provided into housing and to the areas where prisoners are congregated. All housing units should have an emergency entrance door with a lock opening on the outside only and the door made to swing outward only. This provides an entrance into units that may be otherwise barricaded at main doors. An additional security feature that is invaluable during a riot or disturbance is a grille cage, or sallyport, just inside this emergency entrance. Such a cage should be at least six feet square and should have a second grille door opening into the housing unit area. This security facility makes it possible for officers to enter a strife-torn unit without being exposed to assault when opening the doors. Another powerful justification for this emergency opening is its availability for exit during any emergency such as fire or bombing.

Special Emergencies

Riots

No matter how well-trained the institution personnel may be, or how efficient the operating procedures, it is inevitable that there will be some escape attempts, an occasional riot or disturbance that requires immediate emergency action. While it is not possible to foresee the exact nature of a disturbance, nor the time it may occur, there should be predetermined and well-defined plans of action for coping with such emergencies. Basic procedures for dealing with riots in the dining room, recreation yard, auditorium, communal shower rooms, or any place where large groups of inmates congregate, should be developed and available to be used for training of personnel and in order that supervisors may be familiar with recommended emergency procedures. Such written plans should include such information as instructions for separating and temporarily housing ringleaders, what law enforcement agencies to notify of the emergency, what temporary measures should be taken by the supervisor in charge pending arrival of the warden or other responsible officials, and any other instructions peculiar to particular institutions such as manning special security posts, locking specific doors, or placing emergency security guards on the powerhouse and utility facilities, and what stand-by sources of power exist.

Obviously, it is desirable to prevent riots or disturbances, and every effort should be pointed toward such prevention; but just as there are fires in a community in spite of every modern preventive measure, it is still necessary to have trained fire departments and to carry fire insurance on property, so it must be acknowledged that in the abnormal, always potentially inflammable prison situation, it must be accepted that emergencies may occur. The more thorough the established plans to deal with such emergencies, the greater the likelihood of bringing them to a quick and decisive end.

All inmate rule books should cover things most likely to be expected in case of riots and insurrections and state clearly that there will be no bargaining by authorities while disorder exists.

Experience indicates that bargaining with and publicizing actions of rioting psychopaths establishes ready-made alibis for the next hostile group. Publicly admitting baseless charges to be true simply as a means to end a disturbance sets the stage for similar incidents elsewhere. If law enforcement officers outside the prison refused to apprehend and prosecute the bank robber who tied up and terrorized a bank staff but sat supinely by and refused to act because the bank robber said the world "hadn't treated him right," or that society's "systems" were all wrong, then we would have chaos indeed. Just as surely any prison administration that condones terroristic actions is an administration with fear in its heart and is inviting chaos.

A well-developed emergency plan for dealing with riots or violent disturbances should include the following:
   a) *Prevention:*
      1) Alertness to detect and report any signs of unrest or tension.
      2) Consideration of legitimate complaints or needs.
      3) Provision of an adequate overall institutional program.
      4) Unbiased thinking on the part of the personnel.
      5) Early recognition and control of agitators.
      6) Use of organization as a sounding board.
   b) *Control:*
      1) Adoption and proper use of Master Riot Plan.
      2) Selection and training of personnel for squad.
      3) General knowledge of plan among all personnel.
      4) Prompt and decisive action.
      5) Adequate alarm system.
      6) Ready availability and proper use of equipment.
      7) Proper application of special controls by Mechanical Service personnel.
   c) *Post-Riot Procedures:*
      1) Have institution count made.
      2) Segregate ringleaders and agitators.
      3) Check security of institution.
      4) Conduct a thorough investigation of incident.
      5) Administer first aid to injured.
      6) Repair damage.
      7) Adopt effective measures to prevent repetition.

In putting into effect the Emergency Plan, there are a few things of vital importance to remember:
   a) When an emergency alarm is sounded, be sure that all available officers DO NOT rush to the scene. A rear guard or reserve force should remain away from the scene to take action after the situation has been evaluated. The histories of many unfortunate riots have shown that officers who rushed unguarded and unwarned into actual or staged group disorders have been taken as hostages, overpowered, or killed.
   b) Officers who are untrained with firearms should never be

given assignments calling for the use of arms to quell a disturbance. If gas or weapons are needed, use them methodically and only after detailed plans of operation have been prescribed.

c) Above all, have a plan and proceed calmly and quickly.

Procedures for Escapes

Since escapes usually occur without warning, it is essential that an institution have well developed plans for procedures that may be placed into effect quickly. Time is of the essence in blocking off the movements of escape and effecting recapture. While methods of escape will vary, certain basic procedures are applicable to all searches and these should be developed in writing, and all members of the institution staff should be familiar with the general plans. It is recommended that mimeographed copies of the Procedures for Escapes be available to personnel for study and that each employee be required to become familiar with the plan. The geographical location of an institution, its structural characteristics, the topography of contiguous terrain, and even the types of prisoners are all important factors in the development of Procedures for Escapes, but the following suggestions are considered essential to any plan:

1. The institution, usually in the office of the Custodial Supervisor, should maintain an up-to-date list of all employees, with addresses and telephone numbers so arranged that a minimum number of calls will contact a majority of officers.
2. The Procedures for Escapes should provide that when an unauthorized absence of any inmate from a work crew or living quarters is discovered, it will be reported at once to the supervisor responsible. When it is determined that an escape has probably occurred, the Procedures for Escapes should be placed into effect without loss of time, and prearranged signals should be sounded to notify all employees living in the area of the prison.
3. Procedures for Escapes should include a complete list of posts to be covered by officers while the search is in progress. These may be divided into schedule A, B, C, etc., depending on the information available as to how inmates escaped, time and means of departure. The posts covered may be only those

included in certain areas. For example: if inmates have departed by car and are known to be some distance from the institution, posts normally covered near the scene of the escape would not be manned. The Procedures for Escapes should provide that officers on assigned posts may be moved only by the person in charge of the search operation.

4. The Custodial Supervisor should have available a "kit of instructions" to be handed each officer on a post. For example: if post number sixteen provides for the covering of a particular crossroads, this kit marked "Post No. 16" would contain a map of the nearby area, information as to residents living in that area, location of the nearest telephone, location of the nearest law enforcement officers or agency, and any other information that will assist the officer when he arrives on the post.

5. Concurrent with initial assignments of officers on post, one employee should be designated to notify by telephone or radio all law enforcement agencies in the county or state. The telephone and communication lines should be covered as long as the search is in progress. Any well-developed Procedures for Escapes provide that law enforcement officers will have been contacted in advance and would be prepared to go into action when the prison gives notification that an escape has been made.

6. Plans should provide that in case of a general escape alarm, all personnel, custodial and noncustodial, not on duty will report immediately to the officers' assembly room or previously designated place.

7. Officers in charge of crews at work should place their tools and equipment in one place and proceed with their crews to the checking-in point. They should then make themselves available for emergency duty.

8. Officers assigned to essential maintenance posts such as powerhouse, kitchen, hospital, fire station, who have under their supervision inmates who must remain on duty, should take a count at the sound of the emergency alarm and report this count to the control center. The Procedures for Escapes should provide for specific instructions for officers on posts such as

the powerhouse, fire station and any other post that may exercise control over vital utilities.

9. At the sound of the escape alarm, officers assigned to armory towers or arsenal units should make immediate preparations to issue arms, ammunition, and such other equipment as may be needed.

10. The records clerk should stand by his office and be ready to prepare escape circulars for distribution and mailing. These circulars should be dispatched to the Chiefs of Police in all immediate cities and mailed to all law enforcement departments in each county in the state in which the escape occurs and to sheriffs, chiefs of police, and state patrol departments in neighboring states. Circulars and information also should be disseminated to railroad police, immigration agencies, and any other law enforcement agencies available. Under no circumstances should untrained officers be sent out with a gun. Also, under normal circumstances, correctional employees should not establish roadblocks, nor stop cars, unless accompanied by duly appointed law enforcement officers. Serious incidents have occurred when untrained, armed officers have fired into cars and injured innocent persons. Such organizations as state police, sheriffs, and county and city police are generally well trained in techniques of roadblocks and are well equipped to carry out operations if necessary.

11. The Procedures for Escapes should provide for use of nearby radio and television stations. If plans have been made previously, it is nearly always possible to secure the cooperation of these public service facilities.

Experience has indicated that most escapees prefer to remain under cover during daytime and move at night. When information is available that escapees are in a certain area, it is well to maintain groups in that area to apply continuous pressure in order to force the escapees into movement. Even when the majority of employees have been taken off the search, about the third or fourth day, it is well to continue some patrol of areas previously covered in order that investigations of all reports may be made. Above all, rely on the sincerity and integrity of community citizens who are extremely helpful in any escape hunt.

One thing not to be overlooked is that all law enforcement agencies and communities previously informed of the escape be *notified immediately* when the prisoners have been recaptured. This is good public relations and assures that the same agencies and groups of citizens will respond to later emergencies.

Fire Prevention and Control

Any institution that does not have a well-conceived basic plan for fire fighting is inviting disaster. Not only can fire inside a prison cause tremendous financial losses, but hundreds of lives are threatened when any fire of consequence breaks out in a housing unit or work area. It is essential that competent, well-trained inmate firemen under employees' supervision be available at all times. There should be up-to-date, efficient fire-fighting equipment available at all hours of the day or night.

Any basic plan for control of fires should include as a minimum:
1. A full-time crew of inmate firemen. These inmates should be suitable as to custody, intelligence, interest and training to cope with any types of fires in the main institution and in buildings outside the main security perimeter.
2. The fire crew should be housed in close proximity to the fire truck and other equipment. It is highly desirable that this crew be housed separate from other inmates in order that they may be checked and identified quickly if it becomes necessary to go outside the main compound.
3. Equipment should include as a minimum a modern fire truck, complete with pressure pumps and tanks. Modern portable extinguishers should be a part of this equipment. Fire extinguishers should be placed in close proximity to all housing units and should be located in strategic spots in all building areas. The types of extinguishers to be used should be those recommended by the local fire department since fire hazards differ according to types of structures and types of operations. It is important to use care in selecting the types of mixtures for use in fire extinguishers since inmates sometimes resort to emptying the instrument in order to drink the fluid or inhale the fumes. In some cases this can be dangerous to the inmate and, of course, it destroys the value of the extinguisher.
4. The institution should have specific plans for evacuation of

inmates in case of emergency, such as fire, earthquake, bombing and so forth. In the case of fire, it is well to remember that smoke, under normal conditions, rises upwards, and a plan for evacuating cell house tiers would include evacuating the upper tiers when a fire begins to get out of control in the housing unit. As a rule, it is not difficult to extinguish fires that occur in cells, but it must be borne in mind that a fire allowed to get out of control endangers the lives of all occupants who are locked in a cell house, since the danger of suffocation is greater than that of actually being burned.
5. Keys to all emergency exits and to stationary fire-fighting equipment that may be locked in storage places should be immediately available. Such keys should be marked distinctly to avoid confusion during the emergency. It is a good idea to paint the metal tags on these keys in a distinguishing color, such as red, in order that they may be located and issued with no delay.
6. Portable floodlight equipment should be readily available in the control room and fire station, since these are usually necessary in combatting fires at night. This type of equipment is especially necessary when approach to the fire must be gained across rooftops. These lights may be used as additional security protection also, along fence lines when many inmates are out in the compound at night engaged in fighting the fire.

The location of an institution, the types of buildings and the industry operations are all factors that must be taken into consideration in the development of any plan for dealing with fires. Two things, however, are of the utmost importance in developing any plans for the control of fires. First, prevention is axiomatically the most important. Inmates should be kept aware of the hazards involved in careless handling of cigarettes, improper control of inflammable fuels, welding equipment and so forth, and they should be given such training as property owners in communities are given. Many films dealing with fire hazards are available in universities and from public sources, and all modern city fire departments are ready and willing to cooperate in giving lectures and demonstrations of the proper measures for dealing with various types of fires. Perhaps the second most important thing is to have the plan so developed that inmates on the fire crew can get to the scene of any fire on a reservation in the shortest possible time. If inmates belonging to the first department are housed in various places around the institution, and in various degrees of custody clearance, then this becomes impossible. Members of this crew must be housed together, trained together, and they must have instilled in them a sense of responsibility and loyalty to their job.

Emergency Lighting and Stand-By Power

In considering to what extent emergency power and lighting should be supplied to an institution, many factors must be evaluated. Emergency power, by its very name, does not denote complete replacement of everyday public power. Therefore, an evaluation must determine what in an emergency must operate to best preserve life and property under recognized adverse conditions.

A correctional institution is in the business of providing custody, treatment, and the necessities of life for its inmates. One of the primary needs of good custody is the ability to see. This requires artificial lighting during the night hours involving electric power. Treatment covers education, various types of psychotherapy, recreation, craft work, etc. Lighting for these activities and power for tools is needed in the classrooms, shops, libraries, and assembly rooms of the institution.

Increasing attention to self-improvement, study, and counseling finds the institution making more and more use of night hours to carry on treatment programs. This increases the danger potential in the event of power failure, and subsequent loss of light where many large groups are gathered. The necessities of life also require electric power to ventilate, operate refrigeration, cooking equipment, hospital operating suites, etc.

No light can spell disaster to the control custody must maintain over the group. Therefore, some light must be maintained at all times in areas of inmate congregation or activity during occupancy. This does not mean that this light must be maintained after the area has been vacated and the inmates moved into housing units. Such areas can be isolated from the activity sphere of the institution during the emergency and the emergency light conserved for future use in other areas if the emergency is prolonged.

The normal treatment programs, other than those using electric power, could be carried on under restricted conditions during daylight hours in those areas with good, natural light. Other programs could and should be curtailed, and should present no undue danger to the security of the institution.

The necessities of life, such as food, water, heat and sanitation, must be provided. Ventilation could be compensated for by maximum use of natural sources or vacating certain areas. Food can be prepared, although menus will have to be revised. Refrigeration will not be affected for many hours. All institutions should have at least two days' supply of water and, with conservation practiced, more.

The recommended standards to meet emergencies created by power failures are the following.

1. Emergency power units, either battery or motor driven, for institution telephone system.
2. Emergency power units, either battery or motor driven, in all hospital operating suites.
3. Emergency power units, motor driven, in all boiler rooms ample to provide light and power for controls.
4. Emergency power units, motor driven, to adequately light the institution's perimeter fence.
5. Emergency power units, motor driven, to operate milking equipment and provide minimum lighting in institution dairies.
6. Emergency power units, motor driven, to operate the sewage plant.
7. A listing of available emergency generating equipment in the community and procedure for acquisition in case of need.
8. An established plan and procedure for isolating and vacating areas and collecting and moving all inmates into housing areas.
9. Adequate coverage of all interiors of buildings where inmates may be congregated, especially those areas used after dark, by wet battery trickle charged lights or comparable dry cell type. The same coverage may be provided by paralleling or using existing circuits activated by emergency power units, motor driven.

Civil Defense

A manual published for the guidance of correctional administrators, supervisors, and personnel has been prepared to assist in developing adequate plans for organized effective institutional action in the event of extreme emergency or disaster. It outlines information and procedures essential to institutional plans, programs and participation in emergency relief in the event of disaster to the community.

Defense against wartime hazards is, to a large extent, preparedness against natural hazards, and the same basic operational procedures are employed in both cases. Inmates confined in many correctional institutions represent a large manpower potential which can be used to assist during emergency or disaster conditions.

The Civil Defense authorities in the immediate area of the prison or institution will assist in setting up the procedures, develop mutual aid agreements regarding fire protection and the use of auxiliary equipment, and prepare the facility to meet the requirements of either a natural or war-caused disaster, or be of assistance if disaster strikes a nearby community.

Confronted with the need to prepare for disaster, each administrator should plan an effective course of action relative to his institution in response to the following questions.

1. What is the institution doing to train the inmates and staff for personal survival in case of disaster?
2. What can be done to educate and train personnel for positions of leadership to meet disaster conditions?
3. What is the institution prepared to do for itself in the event of enemy attack?
4. Is there a plan for early resumption of routine in the event of disaster?
5. What help can the institution offer to the community should disaster strike?

SUMMARY

It must be recognized that even in the best managed prison the desire to escape and attempts to escape will be found upon occasion. The deprivation of liberty, which is treasured by every individual, is a basic function of the prison which must be carried out against the wills of the prisoners. The safety of the prison depends upon how well the security procedures are developed and the degree of proficiency and alertness with which they are carried out.

As stated at the beginning of this chapter, the security and control procedures must be carried on without continuous flagrant authoritarian display of force, but in a manner best inclined to gain the cooperation of the majority of the inmates. To do this, there must be those positive and qualitative forces for good morale which mean so much to security—an adequate work program, a prisoner counseling service, a classification service, and a broad program of education and training. Only when these things exist in the prison can the suggested security and control procedures be expected to produce maximum results.

BIBLIOGRAPHY

American Prison Association—Committee on Classification and Casework: *Handbook on Classification in Correctional Institutions.* Preface by Lewis Drucker, vii, 88pp. 1947, The Association.

American Prison Association Committee on Education: *Prison Administration: An Educational Process; Second Yearbook.* Ed. by Walter M. Wallack. 281 pp., 1940, The Association.

American Prison Association—Committee on the Model State Plan: *Manual of Suggested Standards for a State Correctional System.* Sam A. Lewisohn, Chairman, 94 p. 1946, The Association.

American Prison Association—Committee on Personnel Standards and Training: *In-Service Training for Prison Custodial Officers.* Preface by Richard A. McGee, Chairman, vii, 64 p. illus. 1951, The Association.

American Prison Association—Committee on Riots: Statement concerning causes, preventive measures, and methods of controlling prison riots and disturbances; Richard A. McGee, chairman. 32 p., May, 1953, The Association.

Ragen, Joseph, and Finston, Charles: *Inside the World's Toughest Prison.* Charles C Thomas, Springfield, Illinois.

CHAPTER 7

DISCIPLINE

THE MANUAL OF CORRECTIONAL STANDARDS*

Definitions of discipline vary widely according to the setting in which they are applied. For example, disciplinary procedures in military services, in schools and colleges, and in industrial organizations, differ in varying degrees from those which are arbitrary and inflexible to those which are flexible and permissive. Discipline is the outcome of a process of training intended to produce order and controls and equal opportunities for achievement and is the essence of social behavior which permits community living.

Discipline as defined by Webster's New World Dictionary, Collegiate Edition (1962) is ". . . training that develops self-control, character, orderliness and efficiency: the result of such training; self-control; orderly conduct; . . . treatment that corrects or punishes."

> . . . discipline is directed toward the development of patterns of behavior which will be of help to the prisoner in his future adjustments in the free community. In this sense, discipline is a central objective in the aims of the administrator and his rehabilitative staff. The custodial staff may be more immediately concerned with discipline in its narrow sense: the prevention of misconduct and disturbances. The long-term objectives of discipline cannot be clearly

---

*Reprinted with the permission of the American Correctional Association.

separated from the immediate concerns of the custodial staff, and thus discipline becomes a function of the administrator and his entire personnel.[1]

Several of the old and existing principles of the American Correctional Association indicated endorsement of what has recently become known as the therapeutic community approach.[2] This newer term refers to the institutional phase of correctional practice and in which the total institutional environment by its very nature, so to speak, can contribute to the rehabilitation of those inmates held in it. This concept of the therapeutic community envisages an institutional climate wherein every staff employee, for example, is treatment-minded. It envisages that the interrelation between and among the staff and inmates is on such a level that high standards of human conduct including pride, honesty and other-regarding attitudes develop in such a way as to bring modification of anti-social attitudes. The concept of milieu therapy or the therapeutic community approach also operates around a sound program of varied educational offerings and the many other techniques of retraining to the end that the total climate of institutional life is geared to reform.

The position is taken that correctional administrators should develop those programs and train and indoctrinate personnel in such a way that both program and the staffs which operate it can make of the institutional environment a situation where the therapeutic community approach can function.[3]

From such definitions and positions, discipline is seen as "treatment . . . oriented toward enabling the (inmate) to clarify his self-concept and toward enabling him to practice new methods of adjustment in a protected setting."[4] It is recognized that "people need security in the group before they can afford to look at the underlying basis for their actions."[5]

"Everyone connected with prisons, including inmates, agrees that there must be 'discipline' among the inmates and among staff members."[6] Even the "incorrigibles," the recurrent maximum security section inmates, are . . . "especially concerned that there be known limits established and maintained," expressing a . . . "strong desire for certainty," believing that . . . "punishment is neccessary in order to maintain conformity," and wanting to know . . . "what the limits were in their relationship to authority."[7]

Even more important than imposed discipline and rules, however, is the necessary development of self-discipline and self-controls within the inmate: not merely the ability to conform to institutional rules and regulations, but the ability and the *desire* to conform to accepted standards for individual and community life in free society.

ESSENTIAL ELEMENTS OF CORRECTIONAL DISCIPLINE

1. *Good morale.* The only sound basis for good discipline is good morale. Conversely, proper discipline builds morale.

2. *Custody and control.* Custodial care is the supervision of inmates designed to prevent escapes or incidents. It does not mean that it is necessary that all prisoners be under close supervision at all times.

3. *Contributing disciplines.* The staff and all phases of the institutional program in their special ways contribute to the general discipline and morale of the institution.

4. *Individualized discipline.* Not only should discipline be consistent, reasonable, objective, firm and prompt, but it must be appropriately varied in terms of an understanding of the personalities of the inmates.

5. *Preventive discipline.* It is desirable to forestall punitive disciplinary practices with a workable program of preventive discipline.

6. *Good communication.* A good system of communication will replace mutual suspicion and other disturbed feelings between inmates and staff by greater mutual acceptance. It is particularly imperative to have good communication when instituting any change of program which affects masses of the inmate body.

7. *Program and procedures for maintaining proper standards of institutional control.* Since discipline in its broadest sense is one of the most important factors in institutional life, primary responsibility must rest with the senior officials who will develop good disciplinary practices and prevent undesirable practices which are now considered archaic.

Discipline, with the immediate aim of good order and good conduct, looks beyond the limits of the inmate's term of confinement. It must seek to insure carry-over value by inculcating standards which the inmate will maintain after release. It must always be objective and must develop in the inmate personal responsibility to that social community to which he will return.

DISCUSSION OF ESSENTIAL ELEMENTS OF CORRECTIONAL DISCIPLINE

Good Morale

The only sound basis for good discipline is good morale. Conversely, proper discipline builds morale. The two are almost synonymous. Good morale is a prevailing mood and spirit conducive to willing and dependable performance, steady self-control and steadfast conduct, based upon faith in group goals and its leaders and a conviction of being in the right and motivated for success through cooperation in common efforts.

A high level of morale within an institution is the most valuable aid to a custodial program. Good personnel and a good treatment program make for good inmate morale and self-discipline which aid immeasurably in the maintaining of proper custody and climate. Good will has a definite, practical and material value in prison operation and is of greater importance to morale and easy handling of men in confinement than all of the artificial restraints ever devised. While occasional disturbances may occur in the best managed institutions even when discipline and morale are high, these usually result from the actions of agitators, recalcitrants, or troubled people. In such instances, the existing high level of morale negates the chain reaction which could culminate in a major disturbance.

Good morale is not obtained by arbitrary rules or hard work alone. It comes with the development of activities which provide for the inmate's mental and physical needs, fair treatment, and reasonable opportunity to use his time constructively. It requires leadership and a balanced program in which work, training, recreation and other activities are carried on with a common objective—the welfare and reformation of the individual.

Custody and Control

Security and custody quite obviously are of vital import. In a general sense, custodial care is the supervision of inmates designed to prevent escapes or incidents and to make for smooth running of the institution. Strictly defined, custody is guarding or penal safekeeping. Through a system of in-service training and effective supervision, the custodial staff is trained in proper custodial and security measures, in locking and counting routines, in defensive tactics, procedures for searching cells and prisoners, elimination of contraband, and similar responsibilities.[8]

While custody, discipline and security have always been recognized as the first duties of correctional personnel and take precedence over all other functions, it is equally recognized that the correctional worker who is in contact with the inmate at work, in quarters, at school, on the recreation field, and so forth, is the individual who has the greatest influence upon the inmate during his institutional life. In some institutions, members of the custodial staff are taught the techniques of interviewing with the use of the central file and report writing and participate in the interviewing of inmates and their relatives. They make a report which is routed through channels to the central file. Further departure from the traditional duties and work of a member of the custodial force are the programs where custody and treatment personnel functions are merged.

Control involves supervision of prisoners to insure punctual and orderly movement to and from living quarters, work area, classrooms, vocational shops, the chapel, recreational facilities, clinics and sick lines in accordance with the daily schedule. Control does not mean that it is necessary that all prisoners be under close supervision at all times. Full use should be made of such devices as passes and strategically located checking points. Obviously, custody and control are closely interrelated.

It is vitally important that the system and control procedures be as simple as possible, practical, and well understood by inmates and personnel. Particular care should be used to avoid unnecessary requirements and complicated or conflicting procedures. Routines involving group movements and custodial controls which are unpleasant or expose inmates to inclement weather, such as waiting in line in open places for counts or mess call, should be kept to the absolute minimum.

Contributing Disciplines

Discipline—self-motivated or directed orderly acceptable conduct—is not accomplished by the disciplinary officer or disciplinary committee alone, or by any one part of the program. It is accomplished by the staff and all phases of the institutional program, all of which in their special ways are contributing to the general discipline and morale of the institution, as well as to the self-discipline of the inmate.

The conduct of a modern prison embraces such contributing disciplines as that exemplified by the correctional worker who confronts the inmate with his responsibilities to his family and to his community and shows him how to fulfill them; the psychiatric approach which looks beyond the name of the crime which a man committed and into the motivations which led him to do it; and the approach of group and individual psychotherapy sessions. Department supervisors and personnel—educational, vocational, maintenance, and industrial, for example—by encouraging and assisting the inmates to attain new goals through purposeful work activities and employment responsibilities, also make an important contribution to security and discipline. Through directed religious and recreational programs, library services, and the above captioned growth activities, staff members with special training can be of greater assistance through their technical skills to give the inmate better insight into his attitudes and actions to help him to improve them.

Individual Discipline

Factors which contribute to the making of delinquents and criminals are varied and complex. Hence, the techniques and services required in correctional treatment must be appropriately varied and, in terms of understanding the inmate as a person, discipline must be considered on an individualized basis. In taking the individualized approach in the handling of disciplinary problems, we need to understand the personalities of the inmates and accept them as individuals. In so doing, we need to examine social, psychological and psychiatric data; prior criminal history; and institutional program and disciplinary history. This does not mean that when a man is charged with a disciplinary infraction one should read his social history and let him off with a warning because he had a drunken father and a miserable childhood. We must examine carefully all available data to see what sort of man we are dealing with, what we can reasonably expect from him, and what treatment methods will be most effective. We need to know everything possible about every individual we hope to help. Individual, as distinct from group conduct, calls for individual treatment on the basis of all pertinent data on the man concerned. "No two men are alike, and that which will turn one man's thoughts toward changing his way of life may irretrievably antagonize another."[9]

Preventive Discipline

Present-day industrial management recognizes the importance of preventive maintenance in avoiding more costly repairs at a later time or, perhaps, complete breakdown or catastrophe in a plant. This same theory and practice applies as well in present-day prison management.

Despite the most sincere, intelligent and painstaking efforts by capable officials to maintain good discipline based on sound morale, disciplinary problems will arise in any prison. If they are group problems such as racial conflicts, strikes, near-riots, they must be dealt with firmly and without hesitation or vacillation. The capable and experienced official stops most outbreaks of this sort before they get started by constant correction of conditions that cause bitterness and unrest, by spotting and segregating ringleaders and agitators who are fomenting trouble.

> ..., we are also cognizant of the elementary truth that punishment assessed after an offense does not prevent the offense and is, therefore, a negative form of discipline that can be justified only to the extent that it creates fear of further punishment.[10]

Insofar as practicable, it would seem desirable to forestall punitive disciplinary practices with a workable program of preventive discipline.[11] In such a program, the correction of minor deviations before they become serious violation is essential.

> If every act of the inmate which violated regulations or was prejudicial to good order was reported for "Court" adjudication little else could be accomplished in a prison. The most significant control of behavior in a prison is that of mutual expectation, just as it is in any social group or community. Most prisoners plan to govern their behavior so that they will not come into conflict with the officials, and by far the greater proportion of all behavior is conformative. Minor infractions of rules where the behavior of the prisoner is not indicative of intentional violation should be handled

by the observing officer with a reprimand and no other punishment. The officer's leadership is an essential requirement in the correctional process. It cannot be expected that his leadership will be developed if some other agency is expanded to limit rigidly most of the inmate's behavior.[12]

In most situations, good control may be maintained by the principle of certainty—that is, certainty that misbehavior will not go unnoticed but that appropriate steps will be taken to correct it. This is an application of the concept that it is the certainty rather than the severity of correction that affords the greatest deterrent.

It is equally important that recognition of an improvement in self-discipline be promptly and consistently recognized and/or rewarded, through such programs as Meritorious Pay, Meritorious Good Time, etc.

> Rewards for conformance to the highest values in our culture should be given precedence over fear of punishment in guiding the development of human character in correctional systems as well as in society at large. Enlightened self-interest must be emphasized and made operative at all times.[13]

Correction is really a re-orientation or re-instruction of the individual with a view to preventing a repetition of the deviation without the necessity of taking punitive action. It may be used when the deviation or violation is trivial, is due to ignorance or lack of understanding, or is the result of careless or faulty habits. A word of caution or instruction, or even a significant glance or gesture, is often sufficient. A genuinely interested employee may in a fair and friendly way show the man how to avoid future errors. Conversely, in a like situation, an employee, lacking an interested and understanding approach, may, by his unprofessional, unfriendly, and even hostile attitudes and bearing, aggravate an inmate to the point where it is mandatory to take disciplinary action for misbehavior.

Good Communication

It is important that the management at all times knows what the prisoners are thinking and how they are reacting to the institutional program. It is also important that the prisoners not only know what is expected of them but also know what opportunities are available to them in the institutional program; that they have the opportunity of receiving facts relevant in daily living in contrast to dependence upon rumor and grapevine communications. It is also important that they know from official sources, and not from rumor, what the management is doing or planning which affects their welfare.

Inmates normally desire to live in an orderly, constructive atmosphere and, if avenues are available, will contribute by way of suggestion and participation in the maintaining and possible refining of existing practices.

A good system of communication helps relieve the inmate's feelings of insecurity about his situation. Through improved communication, mutual suspicion and other disturbed feelings between inmates and staff will be replaced by greater mutual acceptance.

It is particularly imperative to have good communication when instituting any change of program which affects the masses of the inmate body. Communication and explanation prior to the change will tend to obviate possible disturbances. If inmates are informed and given reasonable explanations so that they understand the reasons for daily routines as well as any pending changes, they are much more likely to accept and support the program.

Through proper orientation, the inmate may understand his own situation more clearly and the conditions under which he must live and work and study in prison. Such orientation will do much to relieve his uncertainty about his situation; will inform him of what is expected of him and, in this way, give him a feeling of security which is essential to good adjustment and progress.

During the reception period, newly admitted inmates should be given systematic instruction in the program and procedures of the institution; in their opportunities, privileges and responsibilities; and in the detailed rules and regulations with which they need to be familiar. The first portion of the orientation program would be devoted to acquainting inmates with those functions of the prison administration which concern them most directly. This would be accomplished through instruction and discussion classes regarding rules and regulations and operating procedures which apply to their day-to-day life in the institution. The necessity for institutional rules would be discussed with some of the more important ones analyzed with the civil and criminal laws which govern a free citizenry. It is important that inmates understand the reason for certain rules and routines of the institution. Explanation of requirements usually results in a greater degree of willing compliance and cooperation in any group situation. Prisoners are no exception.

Through talks by representatives of the various departments within the institution and through an orientation brochure, the inmate receives an introduction to the various treatment programs—educational and vocational schools; religious services; recreational program; correspondence school privileges; library facilities; as well as opportunities in development-group activities. The brochure could also include information with regard to commissary privileges, an interpretation of mail and visiting privileges, honor camp opportunities, and parole provisions. It is often combined with the manual of rules and regulations into a comprehensive Inmate Handbook.

Programs and Procedures for Maintaining Proper Standards of Institutional Control

Disciplinary and punitive action is ordinarily the responsibility of the deputy or associate warden or assistant superintendent in larger institutions; in smaller ones the warden or superintendent often exercises that function. When anyone other than the two senior officials is in charge of disciplinary matters, it is usually a person on the next lower administrative level (assistant deputy warden, for example), and the responsibility is only partially delegated, along with the authority. Since discipline in its broadest sense is one of the most important factors in institutional life, primary responsibility for maintaining it should not be delegated any further down the administrative scale than is absolutely necessary, taking into account the many demands on the senior official's time.

It is a common, although too limited, concept, of discipline that it consists of holding hearings on the cases of inmates reported for infractions of the rules, and prescribing punishment for them. This is only a part of discipline, sometimes the least important part. Nevertheless, infractions occur and must be dealt with promptly and justly.

Reports

Correctional employees, as a part of their function in a treatment process, must recognize that the writing of reports need not always be concerned with misconduct. Many institutions use behavior reports, incident reports, or monthly work and conduct reports as separate from misconduct reports. These are designed to call attention to inmate acts and attitudes which might otherwise be erroneously classified as misconduct. Such compulsive behavior as suspiciousness, withdrawal symptoms, incessant talkativeness, indifference to surroundings, persistent failure to understand simple commands and to follow orders, lack of self-control, etc., should be called to the attention of staff members who are responsible for classification and treatment. To label all such acts, especially where unintentional, as misbehavior, underemphasizes the officer's role in discipline. The officer who must make a decision as to which kind of report is best suited in the handling of minor infractions of rules has the opportunity to express his judgment, and he is more likely to recognize the importance of reports in the treatment of offenders.

Behavior reports, incident reports, and monthly work and conduct reports are also used to indicate exceptionally good work habits and attitudes which might not be recorded in the usual routine progress reports. This positive function can help every employee to recognize the importance of his role in correction.

Every infraction of discipline should be reported and the inmate given a hearing before any punishment is administered. The report should be in writing on a form prescribed for that purpose and should include the name of the inmate and other identifying data, the offense charged, a brief description of the circumstances, the names of the complainant and of witnesses, if any, and the signature of the staff member making the report. It should then be forwarded for review concerning its completeness and accuracy or for additional action before it is filed with the Disciplinary Committee.

Hearings

A hearing should take place as soon as practicable after the offense is reported, but it is customary to schedule routine hearings at an hour that interferes as little as possible with work, sickline, etc. If the offense needs immediate investigation, it should be initiated at once and the hearing on the offense may be postponed as long as necessary to complete the investigation. If the offense is serious enough to warrant it or there is a danger that the offender will try to influence witnesses, he may be placed in segregation pending investigation and hearing, but should not be in a punishment status. In some cases inmates should be brought at once to the officials in charge of discipline for questioning.

It is desirable that the more serious or repetitious types of misconduct and offenses be thoroughly investigated. This procedure reduces the incidence of violations through the discovery and correction of bad practices or unreasonable conditions or rules which contributed to the misconduct or offense and reassures the inmate that any hearings will be impartially and fairly conducted.

At the hearing the inmate reported should be given a full opportunity to state his case and, if the offense is a serious one and he claims that witnesses could establish his innocence or bring out important mitigating factors, such claims should be carefully investigated. It is usually not wise or practical to have staff members or inmates appear as witnesses at hearings. The administrative problems involved in having staff members and inmates at the hearing and the possibility of feelings of hate and resentment by the inmate against those testifying makes this practice undesirable in most cases. The soundest practice is to have a staff member investigate and report his findings to the disciplinary officer, including statements of witnesses, where applicable, for use at the time of hearings. In short, the hearing should be an orderly attempt to arrive at the truth and is not a formal court proceeding. As much of the inmate's case history and record of adjustment as is pertinent should be taken into account and not merely his criminal history and previous infractions.

Offenders shall be provided and advised of a regular channel of appeal from the finding made or the penalty assessed at any disciplinary hearing. For example, where a subordinate officer handles routine matters, disposition may be appealed to the Disciplinary Committee. Provision should be made for the inmate to send sealed uncensored letters to the Governor, the Director or Commissioner, or his deputy, and members of the paroling authority.

Records

A written record should be made of every infraction reported and how it is disposed of, even when it is dismissed or disposed of by mild reprimand. An entry should be made on the inmate's disciplinary card, in the classification committee's progress report files, and wherever else individual data are entered. In many institutions entries are also made on a bound disciplinary record book kept in chronological form, so that an inspecting official can see for any particular day what offenses were reported, what ones disposed of and how, what punishments were imposed, the inmate's physical condition, etc. These records can also be used for statistical purposes including frequency and type of incidents, budgetary justifications, program planning, research, etc. It is a practice in some institutions to place in the employee's file a copy of the citation when he makes a report to the Disciplinary Committee. The number of such citations in the file could be considered a factor in analyzing his effectiveness on an assignment.

Disciplinary Committee

It is better to have a three-person Disciplinary Committee conduct hearings rather than a single official and that this should be a regular and established practice. The Federal Prison System, the Army Correctional System, and many states have such committees in operation. They have proven to be practicable and desirable, especially in the cases of repeated petty offenders, those charged with serious misconduct, and chronic troublemakers of the agitator type.

The composition of a Disciplinary Committee will differ according to the size of the institution and personnel available. The person in charge of disciplinary matters (associate warden, assistant superintendent, etc.) should preside. A psychiatrist or psychologist may be used as a resource consultant in the handling of the complicated or aggravated cases. In selecting members of the Disciplinary Committee, weight should be given to personality, judgment, training and experience, as well as to the position occupied. The Committee must be fair and just in its decisions and recognized by the inmates as being so.

The manner in which disciplinary hearings are conducted is all-important. The Disciplinary Officer or Committee can further or destroy the treatment process, since discipline is a vital element of treatment. By calm, dispassionate hearings which seek to find and correct the causes of misconduct and which avoid a punitive, legalistic or courtroom type atmosphere, the disciplinary proceedings can be effectively utilized for correction.

ACCEPTED DISCIPLINARY PRACTICES

Good disciplinary practices are dependent upon a wholesome treatment program. In any institution where inmates are only serving time, persistent efforts of the administration and the upper management staff will be required to prevent and hold in check the spread of bad disciplinary practices. In those institutions which have a constructive correctional program, good or positive disciplinary practices can be created. It is not enough to have discipline consistent, reasonable, objective, firm and prompt. From a historical point of view, it is significant that the mitigation of severe punishments has accompanied the increase of reformative influences within the prison community.

The exercise of disciplinary authority is so vital to administration of institutions, both from the standpoint of public relations and treatment of inmates, that the types of disciplinary measures authorized should be established and strictly controlled by the central office or governing board of the state correctional system.

The routine use of severe disciplinary measures usually serves to embitter inmates rather than deter them. Except for serious offenses or chronic violators, more moderate controls can serve as effective deterrents.

Types of disciplinary measures which may be used constructively in the control of prisoners' behavior are as follows:

Counsel and Reprimand

A written report of misconduct which is filed in an inmate's case record may serve as an adequate warning for his future behavior. Inmates who recognize that a clean institutional record may help influence their earlier release from prison usually conform to rules. When such an inmate commits an occasional infraction, counsel and reprimand may be sufficient to discourage future misconduct.

Loss of Privileges

One of the most effective controls of prisoners' behavior is the possibility of losing valued privileges through misconduct. Recreation time, canteen purchases, package privileges, movies and other organized leisure time activities are privileges which may be taken away for the violation of institutional rules. It is not advisable to restrict inmates' letter writing or visiting privileges unless the offense is in violation of the regulations relating to these practices.

Loss of Good Time

In some jurisdictions, legislation provides for inmates to accrue "good time" or receive a partial remission of sentence as a reward for good conduct and industry. In such cases, it has become a practice to assess unruly prisoners a portion or all of their good time for institutional misconduct. It is good disciplinary practice to be cautious in the imposition of penalties which remove the possible incentive for future good behavior. It is desirable to have, at some future date, a review of "lost time" penalties in order to insure against overseverity and to provide for restoration of time lost when subsequent good conduct of the inmate merits such restoration.

Suspended Sentence

While a variety of penalties may be imposed upon an inmate such imposition of penalty may be suspended contingent upon his future good conduct, the suspension usually being for a specified probationary period. The suspension of a stronger penalty may serve to reinforce a reprimand or temporary loss of privileges and discourage future misconduct. To be most effective, this type of penalty must be followed by reward or appropriate recognition of the ensuing conduct of the inmate involved during or at the conclusion of the stipulated period of suspension. The basic and essential element of good disciplinary practice is the development of a good system of incentives for inmates.

Close Confinement

It is necessary to segregate some inmates from the main population and provide close confinement for varied periods of time for the purposes of punishment, for the protection of themselves or others, or because of their inability to get along in the general population.[14] But to use this as a standard disciplinary action for almost the entire range of offenses is hardly a sensible solution to disciplinary problems.

When inmates are restricted to close confinement it is necessary that they be closely supervised by experienced, competent personnel and that they be closely and regularly observed by the official exercising disciplinary responsibility and other key staff members. Procedures and requirements governing the equipment of close confinement quarters, and the care, treatment and supervision of inmates in close confinement should be carefully prescribed in detail by the warden or superintendent and every precaution taken against abuses of laxity. Segregation is sometimes subject to serious abuse, but if proper safeguards are provided and are carefully enforced, it can be safely used by a competent Committee.

Segregation when used as a type of punishment has been variously called isolation, segregation, punitive segregation, solitary confinement, etc. For this discussion the terms punitive segregation (punishment) and administrative segregation (restriction) will replace those formerly employed.

The deterrent values of punitive segregation lie not only in the amount of time served, which may be relatively short in duration, but also in the influence upon the actions of the paroling authorities. In some penal systems, such a disposition of disciplinary charges may affect an inmate's calendar status or may result in revoking of a parole hearing date.

Punitive and administrative segregation are not synonymous. If space permits, the quarters for punitive segregation should be detached from the administrative segregation area. Those sent to punitive segregation go there as punitive action, usually for a definite period of time. An administrative segregation unit for men with serious problems of maladjustment, such as homosexuality, should be used as a place for confinement and treatment of those who are unable to adjust to the ordinary routine of the institutional program until evidence of adjustment warrants return to the general population.

Punitive segregation is ordinarily used as punishment when reprimands, loss of privileges, suspended sentences, and similar measures have been tried without satisfactory results and when the infractions are not serious enough to warrant bringing the inmate to trial in a criminal court. In some cases it accompanies one or more of those other forms of punishment. It is a major disciplinary measure, which can have damaging effect upon some inmates, and should be used judiciously when other forms of action prove inadequate or where the safety of others or the serious nature of the offense makes it necessary. Perhaps we have been too dependent on isolation or solitary confinement as the principle methods of handling the violators of institutional rules. Isolation may bring short-term conformity for some, but brings increased disturbances and deeper grained hostility to more.[15]

We need continually to analyze our institutional programs, regulations and practices to determine whether we are not causing rather than preventing the development of severely recalcitrant inmates. It is essential that we abandon the purely punitive approach in the handling of such inmates and work towards solving the fundamental problems which make them "severely recalcitrant." If punitive segregation is indicated, it should be of as short duration as possible and there should be intensive therapeutic follow-up to the basic problems.

When an inmate is tried in an outside court and receives an additional sentence, it is not considered double punishment to segregate him on normal diet while awaiting action, or after conviction, as a precautionary safeguard. The distinction between administrative segregation and punitive segregation is occasionally confused when an inmate is segregated for a comparatively short period of punishment (for an assault with a knife on another inmate, for example) and is then placed in administrative segregation for an indefinite period for the general good of the institution. It may be said of the latter type that protection of the inmate and the institution is for mutual convenience rather than punishment of the individual. It is essential that inmates transferred to administrative segregation fully understand their new status and the purpose behind it.

Segregation may take any one of the following forms:

a) *Restriction to cell room.* This may be with full equipment of furniture, regular diet, reading and mail privileges, etc., or on restricted diet, with one's furniture removed during the working hours, and with no privileges. Restriction to quarters is used for short periods for infractions that call for loss of yard, movies and other privileges, but do not require transfer to a punishment section. This type of restriction may also be used for sexual deviates who do not need to be completely segregated, inmates who cannot control their tempers and are perpetually in trouble but are well-meaning and do not need to be confined in a separate section or building, and inmates who are not insane but are so defective that they cannot get along, or are easily taken advantage of, in the general inmate population.

b) *Segregation in a section of ordinary cells or rooms.* These are sometimes separated from the rest of the tier or corridor to prevent introduction of contraband. The restriction of diet, deprivation of privileges, etc., vary as above. A section of this type in an institution with cell blocks is often referred to as a segregation section and is properly located on a tier where few inmates or visitors are allowed access. In any location it is customary to extend wire screening from the edge of the gallery in front of the cells to the gallery above and to install a partition and door on the gallery. In an institution with rooms instead of cells the corridor is similarly cut off by wire screening or a solid partition.

Only one inmate should occupy each cell while confined in segregation.

There is ordinarily a small special yard where prisoners in this type of segregation are permitted to exercise under supervision. They should either be fed in their cells, seated at special tables separated from the other prisoners in the mess hall, or have a separate mess hall.

c) *Punitive segregation in a special punishment section or building.* This section is usually not a part of the regular living quarters. Inmates confined in this area usually receive a restricted diet and a loss of privileges. They should be in a punishment status and kept there for comparatively brief periods. Ordinarily no inmate should be retained in punitive segregation on restrictive diet more than fifteen days, and normally a shorter period is sufficient. Those who fail to make an adjustment under such conditions can often be treated more effectively in special administrative segregation facilities. The punitive segregation section should not be utilized for indefinite or permanent segregation. The not uncommon practice of confining insane inmates there is indefensible; *all* insane inmates should be transferred to a mental hospital or medical-psychiatric treatment facility.[16]

The punitive segregation section and all the cells in it should be evenly heated and adequately lighted and ventilated. Artificial ventilation is usually necessary. High sanitary standards should be maintained; bathing facilities should be provided in the section and inmates permitted to bathe frequently. Most of the cells should contain a washbowl and toilet. It is necessary to omit this equipment from a few cells and assign them to inmates who persist in misusing the plumbing facilities. A few cells may have toilets that can be flushed only by the officer from outside the cell; these are either ordinary seat toilets or "Oriental type" toilets, which are opening level with the floor. Toilets which the occupant of the cell cannot flush need constant supervision by the officer. Wholly dark cells should not be used, and if there is a solid door on the cell, it should be so designed that it does not exclude all light. Natural or artificial lighting should be provided during normal hours of the day or evening in keeping with standards for regular living quarters.

Punitive segregation cells should be so constructed that all parts are visible to the patrolling officer from the corridor. Such cells or at least some of them should be soundproofed for obvious reasons. Doors may be hollow with insulation in the hollow spaces. All efforts possible should be made to prevent the transmission of sound to the outside through ventilating shafts, ducts, etc.

Normally, inmates are not confined in cells with solid doors or placed on restricted diet unless they have created a disturbance while confined in standard cells in the segregation section. Occasionally they are put in cells of this type to prevent communication with other prisoners or to minimize noise from disturbances. Some institutions have solid fronts on all punishment cells, using wire glass or glass brick to admit some natural light and provide ample mechanical ventilation. The use of double doors with open grille gates supplemented by solid front doors makes it possible to maintain better observation by leaving solid doors open except when necessary to control the noise of a disturbed or unruly inmate for temporary periods. View ports or windows of tempered glass should be provided in such cells to permit good supervision and to prevent mutilation or suicide.

d) *Adjustment Center.* "An important index of the true humanitarian character and rehabilitative purpose of a prison system is its policies and procedures regarding the treatment of severely recalcitrant inmates."[17]

An Adjustment Center is an area of the institution designed solely for the intensive treatment of problem inmates. It represents a progressive development of the ordinary administrative segregation. In addition to drawing upon existing treatment facilities in an institution, such as education, library, and chaplains' services, etc., this Center is designed to provide for occupational therapy, recreational therapy, and individual and group counseling and psychotherapy. An appropriate staff is necessary.

Since most of the inmates confined in the Adjustment Center may be potentially dangerous, adequate provision must be made in both structural design and equipment to enable the staff to maintain control without exposure to unnecessary hazards. The limitations of physical facilities and the differing characteristics of their inmate residents, as would be expected, have considerable bearing upon the operation of Adjustment Centers. However, staff morale and competency to deal effectively with the expected problems as they arise are of greater importance.

Transfer

In any penal system embracing several institutions, transfer from one to another is often an effective disciplinary procedure as well as an administrative necessity. When all possible treatment and disciplinary resources of any one institution have been exhausted on a problem inmate without success in terms of his effecting a satisfactory adjustment, or if he constitutes a major threat to the welfare or security of that institution, transfer to an institution which affords greater custodial control or specialized treatment may be indicated. A chronic offender in one institution often adjusts surprisingly well when transferred to another institution where he is no longer compelled to keep up the "tough guy-big shot" pretense and can start anew in a changed environment. Special problem cases or chronic recalcitrants may need to be moved to an institution having an available administrative segregation unit or adjustment center when general population housing in institutions not equipped with such facilities ceases to be practical or safe.

UNDESIRABLE DISCIPLINARY PRACTICES

Most capable and experienced officials in the correctional field condemn certain forms of punishment and discipline as inhumane and because experience has shown them to be less effective than more progressive methods. They are frequently destructive to the good discipline they are designed to establish and maintain.

Overseverity

Restrictions, imposed chiefly to remind inmates that they are doing time, defeat work and training programs, put a premium on scheming and are the poorest sort of preparation for release. Rules and regulations that cover every minute detail of a prisoner's daily activities, specifically prohibiting everything that any inmate in the whole history of the institution has ever thought of doing, are certain to produce infractions, followed by punishments and more infractions in a vicious circle.

Punishments out of all proportion to the offense, employing inhumane and archaic methods dictated by brutality coupled with ignorance, incompetence, fear and weakness, are demoralizing to both inmates and staff. Such punishments substantially increase the chances that the inmates will continue to be disciplinary problems in the institution and will return to crime after release.

Physical Punishment

Corporal punishment should never be used under any circumstances. This includes such practices as flogging, strapping, beating with fists or clubs, spraying with a stream of water, stringing up by the wrists, exposure to extremes of heat or cold or to electric shock, confinement in the stocks or in cramped sweatboxes, handcuffing to cell doors or posts, shackling so as to enforce cramped position or to cut off circulation, standing for excessive periods "on the line" or barrel-heads, painted circles, etc., deprivation of sufficient light, ventilation, food or exercise to maintain physical and mental health, forcing a prisoner to remain awake until he is mentally exhausted, etc.

Use of Force

"Moral forces, organized persuasion and scientific treatment should be relied upon in the control and management of offenders, with as little dependence upon physical force as possible."[18] *The regulations of well-run prisons usually provide, in effect, that force may be used only when necessary to protect one's self or others from injury, or to prevent escape, or serious injury to property.* Only as much force is authorized as is necessary to control the person against whom it is directed. The use of force is never justified as punishment. If a certain amount of unjustified force is permitted or condoned it is not long before it gets out of hand and rises to dangerous proportions.

Officers should not be permitted to carry clubs, partly for the practical reason that inmates almost always seize them in case of serious trouble, and partly because experience has shown that clubs cause more trouble than they prevent. The threat of public scandal must also be considered, for it is demoralizing to the entire system to have a good record of constructive effort destroyed by one incident of the use of unwarranted force.

Laxity

Laxity in discipline, permitting unearned privileges, and other mistaken practices are indefensible. Most prisoners of normal mentality do not like an overly permissive institution.

> The prisoner who wants to do his time and get it over with has little liking for a prison where he can find no sense of direction in a maze of favoritism, prison politics, variable rules, indefinite procedures in discipline, and the hypocrisies that underlie weak administration.[19]

This is particularly true in new institutions or in those under new management. If one must err in a new institution, it would be better in the direction of too great strictness for awhile. It is easier to relax discipline that is too strict after an institution has been operating for awhile than to tighten up discipline after the prisoners have become conditioned to laxity.

Use of Rock Piles

Useless made-work for purposes of punishment or humiliation has no place in present-day practices. Even though the work is often less arduous than that being performed by many prisoners in good status, it is degrading and viewed by all prisoners as having punishment as its primary object. However, the production of gravel for roads, using proper equipment, does not fall in this category.

To assign some prisoners to especially hard work or disagreeable work with definite production value such as digging ditches that are actually needed, building dikes or levees to prevent the flooding of farm land, or clearing a piece of land of stumps and roots is an accepted practice. Usually enough useful work may be found to make the rock pile unnecessary.

AUTHORITY AND RESPONSIBILITY FOR DISCIPLINARY MATTERS

Definite precautions must be taken in the use of administrative segregation or punitive segregation.

Authority

Authority to segregate prisoners should be delegated by the warden or superintendent only to authorized committees such as the Disciplinary Committe or the Adjustment Center Committee. Subordinate personnel should only have authority to lock up an inmate when it is necessary to restrain him. They should be required to make an immediate report of their action to their superior officer. The latter should make an immediate investigation and report to the associate warden (associate superintendent) or to the senior official designated to deal with disciplinary matters.

Time Limits

Segregation for punishment should be for the shortest period that will accomplish the desired result of a favorable adjustment, and in any event not over thirty days. With most inmates and for most infractions a period of a few days proves sufficient. In other cases, a few days in punitive segregation followed by thirty to ninety days in administrative segregation, or in some other status that involves continued control or loss of privileges, is sufficient.

Excessively long periods of punishment defeat treatment goals by embittering and demoralizing the inmate. If he needs to be segregated for a long period, it should be in administrative segregation rather than punitive segregation.

The associate warden (assistant superintendent), or whoever is in charge of discipline, should visit inmates in punitive segregation daily, and more often if possible. He may make recommendations to the Disciplinary Committee for release of inmates from punitive segregation whenever he feels the desired results have been accomplished. The cases of those placed in indefinite segregation should be brought before the Classification Committee or Disciplinary Committee at regular intervals or should be considered periodically by the official in charge of discipline if no such committee or board has been established.

Supervision

In addition to the visits of the official in charge of discipline, the captain and watch commanders should visit segregation sections frequently and at varying times of the day and night. The officers in charge of the segregation sections should observe every prisoner carefully at least every thirty minutes and give particular attention to prisoners in solitary confinement. A card should be on the door of each segregation cell or a tier roster posted giving the name of the occupant and stating when he was confined and for how long. Additionally a log-sheet should be maintained for each man. Whenever a senior official visits the isolation or the segregation group, he should make a notation on the log-sheet of the date and time of his visit and should initial it. The officer in charge should make appropriate entries such as medications, general behavior and attitudes or detail operations such as baths, shaves, or any unusual occurrences. When the prisoner is released from isolation or segregation, his card or log-sheet should be placed in the central file.

Health

A medical officer should visit every prisoner in segregation at least once a day. If there is a psychiatrist on the staff he should also make at least one daily visit. If only a visiting psychiatrist is available, he should be required to visit segregated inmates as often as possible and should give general advice as well as advice on specific cases. All such visits should be recorded on log-sheets in the manner specified above.

Punitive segregation must not occur under conditions or continue for periods which produce a detrimental effect on the physical or mental health of those segregated. If the medical staff recommends that a particular inmate should not be placed in segregation or recommends release, this advice should be carefully considered. Particular care should be exercised in cases of segregation with restricted diet. Mental and emotional health are as important as physical health; therefore, attention should be given to a program of therapy and/or group or individual counseling for men in segregation. It is not enough to provide the other things mentioned unless some attempt is made to change the attitudes which bring about the cases of the assignments to these sections.

Clothing

It is advisable to strip and search inmates placed in segregation for punishment and give them felt slippers and loose-fitting clothing. A cover-all is a satisfactory type of garment. Underwear without an outer garment should not be used for this purpose.

Exercise

Inmates in segregation should be given a daily exercise period, preferably in a special yard or in the main yard at a time when not occupied by other inmates.

Diet

A fundamental rule of good custodial management is that the diet should always be sufficient in calories and properly balanced as to food elements. Therefore, prisoners who have been segregated should be on a regular diet, but with the amounts reduced because they are not working; 2,100 calories per day have been determined to be sufficient to maintain health and vigor in a person so confined. If they misbehave while in segregation, inmates may be placed on a restricted diet of a special type, such as the "monotonous diet" prescribed by the United States Bureau of Prisons for prisoners undergoing punishment in federal institutions. After experimenting with the monotonous diet, some states have eliminated it entirely, and the regular institution diet is fed in all segregation sections. In any event, the menu must be adequately prepared and consist of sufficient calories and properly balanced as to food elements so that the health of those undergoing segregation will not be impaired.

No inmate should be placed on a restricted diet without approval of the institution physician. A regular menu every third day, at least, should be provided. To make the diet more unpalatable, some institution officials mix several types of food together in a dish so that the prisoner's fare closely resembles a meal set out for an animal to eat. There is no justification for this undesirable practice.

CONCLUSION

The discipline of a prison is measured most readily by over-all morale. This is the result of the entire institutional program and the interpersonal relationships of the staff among themselves and with the inmates. If the discipline is good, this is not due to any one part of the program alone, such as the methods of punishment or the desirable activities of the Disciplinary Committee. Many practices and procedures give the inmate better insight into his attitudes and actions and help him to control his behavior. The helpful and understanding line officer, the shop supervisor, correctional officers, the professional personnel, psychiatrists, psychologists, chaplains and teachers, social case workers and others who have special aptitude or training in the study of human behavior and techniques of counseling all play their part.

It cannot be reiterated too often that the desirable program leading to good discipline in the prison must be well-balanced. Proper emphasis needs to be given to security, to care and welfare, as well as to the therapeutic procedures recommended by professional specialists in human behavior. All factors in the administration of a prison dovetail and are of equal importance. All play an important part in its morale. If the custodial provisions, medical service, educational and vocational training, work, recreation, religion, and the social services are well-organized, have trained personnel and are executed properly, each becomes a potent factor in the development of self-understanding and self-discipline. When good discipline is achieved, the institution is better able to accomplish its basic purpose, the rehabilitation of those sent there by society.

BIBLIOGRAPHY

California Department of Corrections, *Correctional Progress in California*, State of California, 1961-62.
California Department of Corrections, *Minimum Jail Standards*, Part I and Part II, State of California, 1963, 365 pp.
"Corporal Punishment," *Report of the Advisory Council on the Treatment of Offenders*, Her Majesty's Stationery Office, London, England, 1961, 58 pp.
Cressey, Donald R., *The Prison*, Holt, Rinehart & Winston, San Francisco, 1961, 392 pp.
"Crime and The American Penal System," *The Annals of the American Academy of Political and Social Science*, January, 1962, 237 pp.
Eaton, Joseph W., *Stone Walls Not a Prison Make*, Charles C Thomas, Springfield, Illinois, 1962, 212 pp.
Johnston, Norman; Savitz, Leonard; Wolfgang, Marvin E., *The Sociology of Punishment and Correction*, John Wiley & Sons, New York, 1962, 349 pp.
Klare, Hugh J., *Anatomy of Prison*, Hutchinson of London, 1960, 156 pp.
Korn, Richard R. and McCorkle, Lloyd W., *Criminology and Penology*, Holt-Dryden, San Francisco, 1959, 645 pp.
Lifton, Walter M., *Working With Groups*, John Wiley & Sons, New York, 1961, 238 pp.
McCleery, Richard H., "Authoritarianism and the Belief System of Incorrigibles," in *The Prison*, Cressy, Donald R.; Holt, Rinehart & Winston, 1961, 260-306 pp.
The Pennsylvania Prison Society, "Custody vs. Treatment, Can They Be Integrated?" *The Prison Journal*, Vol. XLIII, No. 2, 1963, 45 pp.
Ragen, Joseph E. and Finston, Charles, *Inside the World's Toughest Prison*, Charles C Thomas, Springfield, Illinois, 1962, 927 pp.
Scott, Robert H., "The Therapeutic Community in Prison," *Corrective Psychiatry and Journal of Social Therapy*, Vol. 7, No. 4, 1962, 197-203 pp.
Sutherland, Edwin H. and Cressey, Donald R., *Principles of Criminology*, J. B. Lippincott Co., Philadelphia, 1960, 624 pp.

REFERENCES

1. Tappan, Paul W.: *Contemporary Correction*, p. 167.
2. Jones, Maxwell, et al.: *The Therapeutic Community*.
3. Position Number 6, *Proceedings, American Correctional Association*, p. 414-415, 1963 and *Minutes*, American Correctional Association Board of Directors Meeting, 2-4-64.

4. Lifton, Walter M.: *Working With Groups,* p. 10.
5. Ibid, p. 19.
6. Sutherland, Edwin H. and Cressey, Donald R.: *Principles of Criminology,* p. 471.
7. McCleery, Richard H.: Authoritarianism and the belief system of incorrigibles. In Cressey, Donald R. (Ed.): *The Prison,* pp. 301, 299, 298.
8. See Chapter 10, *Personnel Management.*
9. Erickson, G. A.: *Warden Ragen of Joliet,* p. 143.
10. Pate, F. J.: *Discipline—Punitive and Preventive,* pp. 4-5.
11. Ibid., p. 5.
12. Tappan, P. W.: *Contemporary Correction,* Chapter XIII.
13. Principle XVIII, Declaration of Principles of the American Correctional Association.
14. See Chapter 15, *Legal Rights of Probationers, Prisoners and Parolees.*
15. Leiderman, P. Herbert: Sensory deprivation and behavioral change. *Corrective Psychiatry and Journal of Social Therapy,* Vol. 8 No. 2, 2nd Quarter, 1962.
16. See Chapter 26, *Health and Medical Service.*
17. Cook, Allen; Fenton, Norman; and Heinze, Robert: Methods of handling the severely racalcitrant inmate. American Correctional Association . . . Proceedings, p. 148.
18. Principle XX, Declaration of Principles of the American Correctional Association.
19. Tappan, Paul W.: *Contemporary Correction,* p. 169.

SECTION THREE

DILEMMAS and ALTERNATIVES

CHAPTER 8

THE DIVERSION OF OFFENDERS

By Robert M. Carter*

Diversion is increasingly being suggested as a viable alternative to traditional processing of offenders through the criminal justice system. This article is in two parts. The first segment attributes the current emphasis on diversion to three factors: (1) increasing recognition of deficiencies in the nonsystem of justice, (2) rediscovery of the ancient truth that the community itself significantly impacts upon behavior, and (3) growing demands of the citizenry to be active participants in the affairs of government. The second section identifies major unresolved problem areas in the diversion process such as the absence of guidelines for diversion, fiscal complexities, political and social issues, inadequate and uneven community resources, lack of assessment or evaluation of diversion programs, and the need for redefining traditional roles.

ORIGINS OF DIVERSION

Although there is considerable discussion and writing by academicians, administrators and researchers about the system of criminal and/or juvenile justice, the United States does not have a single system of justice. Each level of government, indeed each jurisdic-

---
*Reprinted from *Federal Probation,* Dec. 1972.

tion, has its own unique system. These many "systems"—all established to enforce the standards of conduct believed necessary for the protection of individuals and the preservation of the community—are a collectivity of some 40 thousand law enforcement agencies and a multiplicity of courts, prosecution and defense agencies, probation and parole departments, community-based organizations. It is clear that our approach to criminal and juvenile justice sacrifices much in the way of efficiency and effectiveness in order to preserve local autonomy and to protect the individual.

The many systems of justice in existence in the United States in the early 1970's are not the same as those which emerged following the American Revolution. Indeed this 200-year evolution has not been uniform or consistent; some of the innovations and changes in our systems have been generated by judicial decisions and legislative decrees; others have evolved more by chance than by design. Trial by jury and the principle of bail, for example, are relatively old and date back to our European heritage in general and the English Common Law in particular. Probation and parole began in the nineteenth century and the juvenile court is a twentieth century innovation.

Coupled with the numerous criminal and juvenile justice arrangements in the United States and their uneven development is the separation of functions within the systems. There are similar components in all systems ranging from apprehension through prosecution and adjudication to correction. Although in fact interwoven and interdependent one with the other, these components typically function independently and autonomously. This separateness of functions, which on one hand prevents the possibility of a "police state," on the other leads to some extraordinary complex problems. Not the least of these is that the systems of justice are not integrated, coordinated and effective entities, but rather are fragmented nonsystems with agencies tied together by the processing of an increasing number of adult and juvenile offenders. These nonsystems are marked by an unequal quality of justice; inadequate fiscal, manpower and training resources; shortages in equipment and facilities; lack of relevant research and evaluation to provide some measure of effectiveness; and, until recently, a general indifference and apathy on the part of the public which the systems were designed to serve.

Society Itself Contributes to Criminal Behavior

Society deals with crime in a manner which reflects its beliefs about the nature and cause of crime. Many centuries ago, for example, when crime was believed to be the product of the possession of the mind and body by an evil spirit, the primitive response was simple: drive the devil out of the body by whatever means were available for such purposes. The American tradition as relates to the etiology of crime has focused, until recently, upon the individual as a free agent—able to choose between good and evil and aware of the differences between right and wrong. Our "treatment" of crime accordingly reflected the simplistic notion that criminality was housed solely within the psyche and soma of the offender. Regardless of whether the prevalent philosophy was revenge, retaliation, retribution or rehabilitation, the individual was seen as being of primary importance.

We have long assumed that the criminal or delinquent either willfully disregards legitimate authority by his illegal acts or suffers from some personal defect or shortcoming. There is much to learn, however, about the mysteries by which a society generates abnormal responses within its own circles. But this has become increasingly apparent: Society itself contributes significantly to such behavior. Indeed, it is the self-same social structure expressing its force and influence in an ambivalent manner which helps create on one hand the conforming individual—the person respectful of the social and legal codes—and on the other the deviant and lawbreaker who are disrespectful of the law. We have only recently become aware that crime and delinquency are symptoms of failures and disorganization of the community as well as of individual offenders. In particular, these failures may be seen as depriving offenders of contact with those social institutions which are basically responsible for assuring the development of law-abiding conduct.

Note, for example, that it has become increasingly common to discuss the "decline in respect for law and order." In every quarter, and with increasing intensity, we hear that the citizenry, for reasons as yet unclear, is not only failing to honor specific laws, but also displays a mounting disregard for the "rule of law" itself as an essential aspect of the democratic way of life. But even as this concern is echoed, it is not clear that we are all agreed as to what is meant by "decline in respect for law and order" or precisely to whom or to what we are referring. It may be that a large amount of what we observe and label as "disrespect for law" in a wide range and diversity of communities is in fact a normal reaction of normal persons to an abnormal condition or situation.

As knowledge expands to recognize the role of society in the creation of deviance, justice systems themselves will be modified. The implementation of knowledge, of course, always lags behind the development of knowledge.

Mass Disaffection by Large Segment of Population

Concurrent with the recognition that (1) the justice system is but a nonsystem, and (2) the community itself has an enormous impact upon the crime problem, there has been—particularly within the past decade—the emergence of mass disaffection of a large segment of our population. This disaffection with the American system is often described in terms which suggest that citizens are not involved in decision-making and are acted upon by the government rather than impacting upon government. The disaffection has been manifested in many communities and in various ways.

We have, for example, been witness to mass civil disorder unparalleled in recent times. We have seen our young people in revolt against the war in Vietnam, the grape industry, selective service, marihuana laws, prison administration, Presidential and Congressional candidates, Supreme Court nominees, and Dow Chemical. We have observed rebellion against the establishment ranging from burning ghettos and campuses everywhere to looters in the North, freedom riders in the South, and maniacal bombers from East to West. Young and old, black and white, rich and poor have withstood tear gas and mace, billy clubs and bullets, insults and assaults, jail and prison in order to lie down in front of troop trains, sit-in at university administration buildings, love-in in public parks, wade-in at nonintegrated beaches, and lie-in within legislative buildings.

The establishment has been challenged on such issues as the legal-oriented entities of the draft, the rights of blacks to use the same restrooms and drinking fountains as whites, the death penalty, and free speech. Young people have challenged socially-oriented norms with "mod" dress and hair styles, language, rock music, and psychedelic forms, colors and patterns. We have seen the emergence of the hippy and yippy; the youthful drug culture; black, yellow, red, and brown power advocates; and organizations such as the Panthers, Women's Lib, the Third World Liberation Front, and the Peace and Freedom Party.

But this disaffection or unrest is not restricted to youth alone. Increasingly, adults are rebelling against the system. One need look no further than the recent slowdowns, work stoppages, and strikes of such tradition-oriented groups as police and fire officials, military personnel, social workers, schoolteachers, and indeed even prison inmates. Adult participation in protest has generally been more moderate than that of youth; some have been through membership in political organizations of a left wing orientation; others have joined conservative right wing organizations such as the Birch Society or Minutemen. Millions of Americans protested against the political establishment by voting for a third or fourth party or not voting at all in the last Presidential election.

Movement Toward Diversion

These three phenomena — recognition that the community impacts significantly upon behavior, the uncertainty as to the effectiveness or quality of justice in the nonsystem of justice, and the growing desire of the citizenry for active, relevant and meaningful participation in every area of governmental affairs and community life—are moving the responses to the challenge of crime in a new direction. This direction is typically referred to as "diversion" and relates specifically to movement away from the justice system. It is most likely a prelude to "absorption" . . . a process in which communities engage a wide variety of deviant behavior without referral to or only minimum interaction with the traditional establishment agencies.

Diversion is justice-system oriented and focuses upon the development of specific alternatives for the justice system processing of offenders. The diversion model and its application have been generated from a belief that the control of crime and delinquency would be improved by handling criminals and delinquents outside the traditional system. Diversion is also predicated upon the reported effects of the "labeling" process and the impact of the "self-fulfilling prophecy." Whether diversion, at long range, is more effective than the established justice systems and whether the "labeling" and "self-fulfilling" phenomena are operationally significant is unclear. These uncertainties do not dictate against diversion models, but rather should serve to restrain unbounded enthusiasm based upon belief and emotion rather than fact.

Absorption may be defined generally as the attempts of parents, peers, police, schools and neighborhoods to address social problems —including those of crime and delinquency—by minimizing referral to or entry into one or more of the official governmental agencies designated to handle those manifesting deviant behavior. If there has already been a referral, absorption involves the removal of the transgressor from the official processes by offering solutions, techniques or methods of dealing with him outside of the usual agency channels. Absorption is not restricted to the criminal offender or delinquent. It is, for example, equally applicable to deviants within the educational process. Absorption is adaptive behavior within the community in which alternative strategies are developed for coping with social problems. These involve the extensive use of community and personal resources.

DIVERSION: SOME PRACTICAL/OPERATIONAL ISSUES

There are issues about diversion—involving both philosophy and practice—which demand in-depth examination. Failure to address these completely interwoven issues is likely to result in diversion efforts which are every bit as fragmented and disjointed as those justice system practices which, in some measure, led to the diversion movement. Rather clearly, there is a need to explore operational aspects of diversion; examine the community, its role and resources; and determine the latent and manifest impact of diversion on the justice system. These requirements are, in fact, mandates for assessment and evaluation. There is an explicit need to (1) determine the guidelines and standards which define those eligible or ineligible for diversion, those agencies which are appropriate to receive those who are diverted, and programmatic activities of the agencies which receive diverted cases; (2) identify or develop, and mobilize, resources in a community, determine techniques for increasing community "tolerance" levels, enhance the system for these resources, and make more equitable the availability of resources to diverse types of communities; (3) determine the impact of diversion practices on the justice systems overall as well as their component parts and examine the need for possible administrative, organizational and legal changes; (4) prepare a complete methodology for evaluating the effectiveness of diversion, keeping in mind that being "progressive" is not synonymous with being "successful."

The need for diversion guidelines is critical. Without some minimum standards for practice and procedure and general consensus or agreement on philosophy, there is a distinct possibility that diversion may become the source of continuing and substantial inequities. Basic questions—such as who is (or is not) to be diverted, by whom, on what basis, and to what programmatic activities—should be answered by some shared understandings. Without such common understandings, the justice system—through increased use of nonsystematic diversion—may become more confused, autonomous and fragmented.

Some minimum standards are needed, for example, to guide the *selection of individuals* for diversion. Diversion practices may be exclusionary and identify types of offenders who are deemed ineligible, such as those with a history of violence or felony offenders. Or practice may be permissive and allow that all offenders who will benefit from nonjustice system treatment are to be considered eligible, regardless of other considerations. Diversion may be restricted to adjudicated offenders, or it may include nonadjudicated offenders. If the former, diversion is from the system after entry; if the latter, diversion is an alternative to entry into the system. Both raise substantial legal issues.

Determinations as to time frames are required, i.e. the optimum time for diversion, the length of time or duration of diversion, and so on. Guidelines are also needed as to actions to be taken if the person diverted fails to comply with the actual or implied conditions of diversion or if it appears that the diversion plan is inappropriate.

Meaningful standards are necessary for the *selection of agencies* to receive those who are diverted. Diversion need not necessarily be made to private agencies; it may be appropriate for there to be diversion to those public agencies which normally have been either minimally or not at all concerned with the offender population. And it may be appropriate for diversion to be to individuals rather than agencies. The selection of agencies requires community inventories which in turn may indicate the need for new private and/or public agencies or combinations/consortiums/conglomerates of established agencies which address needs of offenders.

Of equal significance is the complex and politically sensitive problem of sifting through a wide variety of potential diversion agencies including those with "unusual" or nontraditional characteristics such as those with an ex-offender or ex-addict staff. Underlying many of these guidelines are fiscal considerations—including possible requirements for subsidies to agencies which handle those who are diverted. A delicate issue arises from public support of private agencies in terms of performance objectives and standards, constraints and expectations. The subsidy issue is made even more complex as the need arises to determine which public agency at what level of government pays the subsidies to these new partners in the justice system.

There is, of course, a requirement to examine the *programmatic activities* of the agencies which receive diverted offenders. While an inventory of these various programs and some estimate of their effectiveness are essential to rational diversion practice, a basic question emerges as to whether offenders should be diverted if appropriate (or at least similar) programs exist within the justice system. And if such programs already exist in the justice system, the advantages, if any, which accrue by transfer to these programs and clientele to community-based, nonjustice system organizations must be established.

The movement of programs and offenders to nonjustice system organizations will require new roles for justice and nonjustice system personnel. As an example, the probation or parole officer realistically might be required to become a catalyst and seek to activate a community and its caretakers to absorb the offender as a member of that community. This would require a complete knowledge of community resources and diagnosis of clientele needs. There would be an emphasis on reducing the alienation of the offender from his community by impairing the continued maintenance of a criminal identity and encouraging a community identity. The officer would no longer find employment for the offender, but instead direct him into the normal channels of job seeking in the community. Residential, marital, medical, financial or other problems would be addressed by assisting the offender in engaging those community resources which deal with these problem areas. This new role, then, might be one of insuring a process of community, not correctional, absorption. Again illustrating interrelationships of these issues, note that the "new role" phenomenon itself raises questions about training for and acceptance of the role and methods or techniques of implementation.

Imbalance in Community Resources: A Problem

Other issues arise as one examines the role and resources of the community. Not at all insignificant is the complex issue of imbalance among communities to accept cases which are diverted and to provide necessary services and resources. Some communities have distinct economic advantages over others—and it is clear that diversion has an economic, as well as a motivation base. Middle- and upper-class communities and their citizens, socially and economically secure, often have internal financial resources available to mobilize a wide range of agencies of diversion or specialized service ranging from psychiatric care through private schools. The differences in resource levels need scrutiny, for it would be socially disastrous to deny diversion to those who are economically disadvantaged; diversion cannot be restricted to the affluent. Without action to balance resource requirements with the capacity of delivering services, the poor and the disadvantaged will continue to flow into and through the justice agencies.

A parallel community-based problem occurs where there is a low community tolerance for diversion. How is community tolerance to be increased? A simple demonstration of need may be insufficient. Numerous examples of low or nontolerance may be cited ranging from open to latent resistance and hostility directed against self-help groups and agency halfway houses. Besides the very difficult "how," there is the related question of "who" is responsible for dealing with community fears and axieties. Is every justice agency seeking to divert offenders responsible for its own resource development or is some overall plan among cooperating justice agencies more rational? And again, as one question leads to another, if a plan is necessary, who designs and implements it, and how are activities financed and monitored?

Diversion Will Result in Significant Changes

Although changes in justice systems are inevitable consequences of an increased use of diversion, there is a distinct probability that the changes will be both unplanned and unsystematic. These changes may range from administrative and organizational restructuring and modification in procedure and policy on one hand to major changes in the populations which are serviced by the justice system on the other.

As justice agencies become partners with communities, there may be requirements in all agencies for organizational change to include new bureaus or divisions of "community service." This would require new personnel or reassignment of personnel, development and acceptance of new roles such as those of diagnostician and/or catalyst, innovative training, perhaps additional funding and different kinds of facilities, and new understandings within the agencies and communities themselves. Permanent linkages with community organizations may be required. Traditional pyramid, hierarchical organizational models may have to be flattened. New information systems will be required, and continuing involvement or monitoring of diverted cases may be desirable.

The large scale diversion of offenders—either from or after entry into the justice system—may have other consequences for the justice agencies. If, for example, substantial numbers of offenders are diverted by local law enforcement to community-based agencies, there will be, in all likelihood, reduced inputs to prosecution, adjudication and correctional agencies. Lessened inputs will alleviate some of the backlog in the judicial system and reduce caseload pressure in probation and parole, and size of institutional population. While these occurrences are desirable, at some point in time the bureaucratic instinct for survival may be threatened. Reactions protective of the establishment may set in. Of greater significance, however, is that increased diversion may leave the justice system with a unique clientele of hardened, recalcitrant, difficult offenders who seem unlikely to "make it" in the community. These offenders may have complex problems requiring long-range treatment, and they may represent a major threat to and be rejected by their communities. In addition to creating major management problems, these offenders will require new and different programs, facilities and staff for treatment. In short, extensive diversion may not only "threaten" the justice establishment, it may change the justice system population and alter the system itself.

Planning and Evaluation Necessary

There are yet other important aspects of diversion which require attention—planning and evaluation. A lack of mid-range and strategic planning and systematic evaluation has long been a major defect in justice operations from law enforcement through corrections. The movement toward diversion of offenders mandates that planning and evaluation not be "tacked in" to operational processes, but rather be built-in, continually updated, constantly reviewed. The questions about planning and evaluation are familiar—criteria must be established; funds must be made available; personnel, software and hardware must be obtained; methodologies developed; responsibilities delineated. Without such planning and evaluation, it appears certain that diversion practices will produce more confusion and chaos than clarity and consistency.

CONCLUSION

This article has explored the origins of diversion and identified some of the major operational and philosophical problems associated with the movement. Diversion is seen as an outgrowth of a fragmented justice system which has been neither just nor efficient, the increasing demands of our citizenry to be participants in the affairs of government including the justice system, and recognition that the community is an appropriate base for many justice operations. But even as there is increasing momentum toward diversion, there is a pressing need for guidelines, standards and shared understandings, examination of the role and resources of the community, study of the long range impact of diversion on the justice system and society, and planning and evaluation.

Diversion is both a challenge and an opportunity. As a potentially major mechanism of the justice system, diversion requires considered attention. Although changes in our justice systems are indicated, rapid movement to untested and ill-defined alternatives is inappropriate.

CHAPTER 9

"DOING TIME" IN THE COMMUNITY

JOHN D. CASE*

A NY PRISON'S WORK-RELEASE PROGRAM has as its primary aim allowing selected prisoners to hold normal, productive, paying jobs and returning to the prison for all nonworking hours. In addition, men so employed have an opportunity daily for renewed contact with the society to which they eventually return, and through such contact may attain a much more realistic attitude toward their part in the everyday life of the average, law-abiding citizen.

WORK RELEASE MUST INCLUDE TREATMENT

There is a danger in work release if the sole end is to make money for the county. If this is the case, work-release centers can become nothing more than government-supported flophouses. We believe at the Bucks County Rehabilitation Center that with our treatment program we are avoiding this danger. Our whole approach is aimed toward problem solving and the acculturation of the man to the society to which he will return. By a combination of work release and treatment we believe we are not only seeing to it that the inmate pays his debt to society but that society also meets

---
*Reprinted from *Federal Probation*, March 1967.

its obligation to the inmate. Edwin Markham said: "We drew a circle that took him in." Too often the inmates in county jails have been kept out of the "circle" of a happy, satisfied, and opulent society. We believe the "circle" we are drawing will return the inmate to society outside as a respected person and help him to keep out of jail in the future.

HOW DID IT START?

Moral and physical deterioration of inmates through idleness has always been a problem in any prison system. In a report made by the Wisconsin State Board of Charities and Reform in 1873, the following declaration was made:

> Here are scores and hundreds of men, some of them young and in vigorous health, who are compelled to spend from a few days to a year, and sometimes two years, in absolute idleness, while the taxpayers of the various counties are supporting them. What a waste of labor! What an unwise expenditure of public funds!

In 1913 the Wisconsin State Legislature enacted a law that offered at least a partial solution to this problem. Sponsored by Senator Henry Huber and since known as the "Huber Law," this legislation was the first to authorize work release programs in county jails and similar institutions. Laws passed later to permit work release in other states were patterned after the Huber Law.

Actually, a New Hampshire sheriff whose name is lost to history, tried shortly before the Huber Law was passed in 1913 a plan of releasing prisoners to work in the community by day and to serve time nights and weekends in the jail. His actions were extra-legal and he received considerable publicity as a result. In Europe, a number of nations have experimented with private prerelease work programs during the past twenty years.[1] Professor Stanley E. Grupp of Illinois State University reports that by 1964, twenty-four states had formally provided for some form of work release including several which have extended it to both misdemeanants and felons.[2]

North Carolina started using work release in 1957 and since then has been able to close a number of prisons due to the reduced recidivism rates of men who had taken part in the work-release program. In the same year the California State Legislature enacted the Work Furlough Rehabilitation Law which gained little acceptance until George K. Williams, an ex-Navy commander who had worked with de-Nazifying German prisoners of war, was appointed rehabilitation officer of Santa Clara County and initiated a work-furlough program at Elmwood Rehabilitation Center, the success of which prompted a number of other counties to adopt work-release programs of their own.

On October 13, 1963, Public Law No. 774 established a work-release program for county jails in Pennsylvania. A month later, judges, prison board, and prison authorities of Bucks County had a work-release program under way, and inmates of Bucks County Prison had their first opportunity to work under the provisions of this legislation. The outstanding work of Warden Jack Tracey of Lancaster County, Pennsylvania, who had used such a program with success for years, was instrumental in bringing about a work-release law in the Keystone State.

WORK RELEASE IN BUCKS COUNTY PRISON

Because of special precautionary measures required in a maximum-security institution, the county prison proved to be an unsatisfactory place from which to base such a program; it required constant strip-searching and segregating work releasees from other inmates. Before the program had been in operation a year, the Bucks County Rehabilitation Center opened in August, 1964. Constructed at a cost of approximately $150,000, the Center was conceived by a group of interested citizens led by the late J. Augustus Cadwallader, and a dedicated prison board whose members realized the importance of rehabilitation in the county jail and wished to relieve the crowding in the old jail.

Like any new venture, the establishment of such a program was not without its pitfalls; setting it up involved some "playing by ear." There was opposition, naturally, from ultraconservatives who were prepared to say, "I told you so," if the project flopped, and crepe hangers who were saying, "It'll never work." Those prepared to condemn work release, however, were outnumbered, fortunately, by farsighted citizens who saw the value of work release despite its setbacks and early falterings. In a statement entitled "No Time for Panic," published in the Bristol *Courier-Times,* April 29, 1964, the writer had this to say when a hue and cry was set up after one of the first work releasees walked away:

> It would be unfortunate indeed if public clamor should be raised against the relatively new "work release" program of the Bucks County Jail because of the peccadilloes of the prisoner who this week failed to live up to the terms of his agreement. Such clamor, if it should be whipped up, could militate against extending or even continuing the program and would result in a loss to the taxpayer and to so many other prisoners more deserving than this one. The program is being tried in several other counties and several other states with marked success. Two instances in Bucks County are not enough to condemn it.

An article in the May 3, 1964, Bucks County *Times-Advertiser* said:

> Prisoners under a relatively new Pennsylvania law are permitted to hold daytime jobs. They are able to hold their jobs and support their families even while serving a jail sentence. The family benefits because it still has an income. The benefit to the taxpayers is twofold. First, the prisoner is paying his own keep at the prison; secondly, he is keeping his family off the welfare rolls.

Recently a feature writer for the Camden, New Jersey, *Courier Post* recorded the following conversation with a New Jersey inmate at the Bucks County Rehabilitation Center:

> I wasn't worth a damn when they brought me here, but I feel I've accomplished a lot. I feel I have a future. Before, I would usually look for the first bar and sit around drinking. It wasn't the booze I wanted so much as company. When they first lock you up and you see the bars and guards—wow! Just to show you about this place, my parents came to see me not too long ago. You can imagine what they thought—their son in jail and all.
>
> But when they saw this place and found I actually have a job on the outside and everything—well, they just couldn't get over it. To tell you the truth, I think they're glad I was put in jail. Here I am making $2.50 an hour while serving time.
>
> I tell you one thing, this is my first time in jail and it will be my last. I know I can make it now.

In the more than two years that the work-release program has been in effect in Bucks County, similar comment from the press and public has been typical. While all of it has by no means been favorable, we can almost take the attitude that, in regard to work release, no publicity is bad publicity. Citizens—taxpayers—need to know how their tax money is being spent, and it is well that the public be informed of the progress of work release.

GOALS OF WORK RELEASE

Just what is the extent of our program, and what are its goals?

In addition to enabling the prisoner to leave the prison during necessary and reasonable hours for the purpose of working at the place of his employment, work release also allows him to leave the institution to work at his own business or other self-employment. Inmates on work release may also be released to seek employment, attend an educational institution, or obtain medical treatment. In the case of a woman, work release may include housekeeping and attending to the needs of her family.

As the law now stands, only those prisoners who have already been sentenced and whose sentence is for one year or less are eligible to participate in the program. Any inmate may be sentenced initially to work release, or the warden may later request the judge by letter to make the inmate eligible because of his satisfactory conduct in prison.

A prisoner working on work release must, according to law, turn over his full pay, including any tips, to the warden. The pay thus turned over will be divided to cover the cost of the inmate's board at the prison, his travel expenses, support of his dependents, court costs, and judgments.

The amount remaining after deductions are made is placed in a special account to be turned over to the inmate upon his release. Often this amounts to a considerable sum, enough to tide the former inmate over until he can get settled as a full-time member of society. One inmate at the Center, imprisoned for nonsupport, was released on parole with about $500 in savings he had amassed while on work release. Another who was present at the time said: "Al, you sure you want to go out on parole? You're making more money in jail than you did on the outside!"

The rules of work release are explicit. In signing a work-release agreement, the prisoner agrees to "travel to and from work by the quickest route, with no stops; not to visit family or friends; not to drink any intoxicating beverages; nor to make any telephone calls while away from the prison." Men on the program are warned that they are to observe the provisions of the law *exactly*, because any violation will bring removal. The law definitely states that a court order for work release may be rescinded at any time, "with or without notice to the prisoner." Prison authorities may remove a man from work release temporarily for up to five days "for any breach of discipline or other violation of jail regulations." Only a small proportion of men have been suspended for this reason.

The sum and substance of this law is the legal foundation on which Bucks County has built its particular brand of work-release program. And since the worth of the program has been substantially demonstrated in the two years since its inception, it is well at this time to consider the whys and wherefores of work release, its benefits to the man in prison, his family, to the community, and to the county and its citizens.

WHY WORK RELEASE?

Keeping a man in prison is an expensive proposition. In 1965 it cost Bucks County $6.12 a day to keep a man in jail. At the same time, in many instances his wife and children, with no one at home to earn wages, go on the relief rolls. If the man had a job, it is not likely that it will be waiting for him when he is released, so relief payments will continue even after he leaves the prison. At best, he will lose seniority and go back at reduced wages—hardly an encouraging outlook for a person who already had had difficulties adjusting properly to society.

What part has work release had in alleviating these conditions?

On the credit side of the balance sheet is the fact that from November 20, 1963, to April, 1966, a total of 223 men from Bucks County Prison have held work-release jobs, earning more than $117,900 in wages. Of this amount a total of $29,990 was turned back to the County to pay for board, at a rate of $2.50 a day. The amount paid for costs and fines, often difficult for the County to recover under ordinary circumstances, was $13,560. Voluntary support paid to dependents totaled $8,330. Both these latter items might have been borne by County and State agencies otherwise.

Besides the payments directly benefitting the County and families, these men have paid $2,460 in restitution and about $2,840 in other costs and obligations. After payments of $17,110 to cover travel and other incidental expenses, a total of $26,375 has been set aside in two years, for canteen expenses and savings. Men are encouraged to save as much as possible from the amount left after payroll deductions are made, so that they will have enough funds to manage their affairs successfully until they are on a firm financial footing following their release from prison.

Well satisfied by the work performance of many work-release men, employers have been eager to retain many of them on their jobs after their release; this is a very significant morale factor.

"It is hard for an empty sack to stand upright," Benjamin Franklin once said, and this is nowhere more applicable than in the case of the jobless, penniless man just out of jail.

On the debit side of the work-release program, no provision has been made yet for a systematized accounting of the program, since it does not as yet seem warranted. But, running a work-release program does cost something. Our only tangible expense at this time is the preparation of box lunches. Out of about twenty-five men normally on work release in a given week, twelve can be expected to carry box lunches, averaging about 50 cents each—an expenditure beyond the normal prison food budget of about $30 per week.

Staff time involved can be considerable. One staff officer must spend a day each week in accounting connected with disbursing work-release wages. The kitchen officer must supervise the preparation of box lunches. These are not actual additional costs, however, as the twenty-five men on work release would have to be occupied otherwise if such a program were not in progress. This would require these officers to perform some other type of supervisory duty.

The largest cost involved in a work-release program is probably the cost of apprehending the small percentage who walk away from this open-door program. With all such costs combined, however, the County budget is still in an obviously more favorable position as a result of having the work-release program in effect.

In assessing the overall value of a work-release program, there is a nonfinancial gain. President Johnson, in advocating work-release legislation for the 1965 Federal prison program, deplored "the intolerable, endless, self-defeating cycle of imprisonment, release and reimprisonment." What can a work-release program do to prevent this cycle?

As has been pointed out, work release will permit a man to retain his skills and working habits, and sometimes the job itself. Through contacts with society, especially with responsible, genuinely interested persons who can help him gain a more healthy outlook toward the world he left behind, he can receive a better understanding of what he can expect from society, and what society expects from him on his return. Perhaps most important, it keeps the man involved in the normal decision-making experiences of daily living, as opposed to the detrimental effects of confinement where many of the decisions are made for him.

THE REHABILITATION CENTER

The Bucks County Rehabilitation Center, at which all work-release men are housed, offers through its program of work, training, education and treatment an excellent opportunity to work toward a reasonable reorientation. But it was through evolution rather than design that it became the "residence" for work-release personnel.

The Center was first conceived simply as an annex to the main prison, to relieve overcrowding in the old institution. When plans were later made to determine who would make up the population of the new building, it was decided that one wing of the structure would house alcoholics and the other wing youthful offenders whose problem was not basically that of alcohol. It was believed that the response of the inmate would be better in a minimum-security setting, where an intensive treatment program for alcoholism could be established in a "therapeutic community" environment.

In selecting a workable alcoholic program suitable for use at the Center, it was decided to employ, as closely as possible, methods successfully used by Chit Chat Farms Foundation at Wernersville, Pennsylvania, whose operation appeared adaptable to a prison setting. The president of the Foundation offered the services of his staff to help the Rehabilitation Center—then referred to as the "Prerelease Center"—through its "growing pains." The treatment program was scheduled as a thirty-day operation, since most commitments at that time averaged forty-five days.

Since the operation of a treatment center for alcoholic inmates necessitated having a staff trained in recommended procedure to be followed in such an institution's training program, it was essential that qualified correctional-counselor personnel be trained for the job of supervising the project. Two officers who had demonstrated an aptitude for counseling were sent to Chit Chat Farms Foundation for on-the-job training. Prior to the opening of the Center, they also attended a seminar on alcoholism at Elizabethtown (Pennsylvania) College and the Summer School of Alcohol Studies at Rutgers University. All officers who were to staff the Center attended, moreover, a course in group counseling technique at the Philadelphia Youth Center.

All officers who were to staff the Center also attended a five-day seminar on alcoholism conducted by the State Department of Health and had completed required courses in correctional training offered by the State Department of Corrections and the United States Bureau of Prisons.

A qualified educator was selected to direct the educational program, and a clinical psychologist's services were made available for counselor training, group counseling, and consultation with inmates.

Representatives of the local Alcoholics Anonymous group were consulted. They agreed to hold meetings twice weekly at the Rehabilitation Center. The work of this organization has been instrumental in helping a large number of inmates with long histories of alcoholism.

Since an estimated 50 percent of men in county jails have been found to have committed offenses either directly or indirectly because of the misuse of alcohol, and since alcohol contributes to unemployment, it was more a coincidence that the newly constructed Rehabilitation Center was selected for confinement of men eligible for work release. The Center's program of acculturation, together with education, retraining, and a positive approach to control alcoholism, made the addition of a work-release program a natural development.

Without a work-release program, we have no alternative after the span of a year or less required to complete a sentence, except to hand a prisoner back to society, saying, in effect, "He's all yours; take him, and you're welcome to the gamble."

By contrast, work release allows the prison to take the chance with the man. When he falls into the old antisocial habit patterns that led him to prison in the first place, the prison staff still is charged with the responsibility to offer guidance, discipline, and an incentive toward positive behavior.

NEED FOR "HABILITATION" IN MANY CASES

According to casework director Edward C. Boyle of the Los Angeles Salvation Army Family Service Department, "our legal offenders . . . have never truly been able to function adequately in a nondelinquent, free community . . .these men are in need of 'habilitation'—that is, not of retraining, but of the initial training itself toward a productive frame of mind and action missed in their preadulthood."

It is from such "habilitation" that the benefits of the work release are most apparent. Though our minimum-security building is officially named the Bucks County Rehabilitation Center, we feel that its mission is actually habilitation. In its correct use, rehabilitation means to return to a former condition; thus, to "rehabilitate" an inmate we could simply keep him in custody until the expiration of his sentence, and return him to his home neighborhood—usually located in a section whose residents are all members of a lower socioeconomic stratum. In so doing, we accomplish nothing other than protecting society from the individual while he is in prison.

Through our training—not retraining—programs, combined with work release, we offer each man a definite opportunity to work toward a higher standard of social behavior and tangible means by which he may become an acceptable citizen. Under such a flexible program we have been able not only to send men to work, but also to have young inmates go back to high school in a few instances. We have even had narcotic addicts going to Philadelphia for treatment on their own.

SELECTION FOR WORK RELEASE

The basic qualifications for work release selection are determined as follows:

The sorting out process starts with the judge whose sentence determines whether the man is eligible for work release. If he is sentenced to a maximum term of one year or less he then can be placed on work release if the judge so orders. In Bucks County, the judge sometimes will specify work release at the time of sentencing. In most instances the judge will state that "work release is recommended and will then receive recommendations from the warden as to whether the man is a good candidate for this program.

The warden's recommendations are made on the basis of certain primary considerations: Is the man a security risk? Has he a record of "running away" from home, school, or juvenile institutions? Is he an alcoholic? Has this problem been arrested? Are there now some built-in controls? Should he attend AA meetings in the community as part of his work-release program? Does he need education more than work at this time? Should he go back to high school instead of back to work? Does he need treatment for narcotics addiction or alcoholism? Can this be combined with work release so that he can work outside and also receive treatment at a recognized treatment facility?

Reward of good work or accomplishment while in jail awaiting trial must be considered. Like parole, work release should be earned by the inmate. Inmates of the Bucks County Prison are well aware that their conduct, attitude, and work record will be reported in writing to the sentencing judge prior to trial and before sentencing. A man who is intractable soon learns that work release is not for him until his conduct, attitude, and work record improve. Of course, unsentenced men cannot be forced to work. However, they may volunteer in writing—and all volunteer!

After a man is sentenced and approved for work release he is transferred to a Rehabilitation Center. A job must be found for this man before he can be placed on the program. It must be suitable employment at a reasonable distance from the Center, at wages sufficient for him to pay off any fines, costs, restitution, support or other obligations due within the time allowed by the length of his sentence. How is this accomplished?

In the beginning, men who were eligible for work release looked for job possibilities in the "Help Wanted" columns of the local or Philadelphia newspapers, telephoning possible employers from the Center. If told to report for an interview, they went to the prospective place of employment by their own or public transportation, or the potential employer might come to the Center.

As the number of men on work-release sentences increased, finding jobs for them required the services of a trained personnel worker. This post has been capably filled by Mr. Harry Patterson, counselor administrative officer, who was a purchasing agent for an industrial firm prior to assuming his present position.

Mr. Patterson interviews each man who is eligible for work release. He has him complete a short application form on which he gives his name, age, height and weight, education, date of sentencing, term and costs, and his former employer. It is a rather brief summary as employment applications go, but it supplies enough information to give an index to the man's educational level and skills and his past experience.

Potential jobs are located through the Want Ads columns, or by calling firms who have notified the Center that they have jobs or more vacancies for full- or part-time work. Or they may call employers of men already working on a work-release job, who have left word that one or more men are needed for job openings. If the man being interviewed believes he can get a job with a former employer, he may call his ex-boss and apply for work. If an interview is required, the counselor, depending on the circumstances, may or may not accompany the man for the interview. In approving employment, the distance from work, availability of transportation, amount of travel time involved, whether the job is seasonal or regular, or calls for unusual working hours, all have to be taken into account.

Before considering a man for employment, the potential employer is told that the applicant is an inmate of a minimum-security prison and is informed of the restrictions placed on the possible employee in regard to travel time and other requirements of the work-release program. Employers understand that work-release men are paid on the basis of their ability and performance, exactly as any other employee. Wages currently range from the $1.50-an-hour minimum to as high as $5 an hour, depending on the skills of the individual.

Inmates on work release have held a variety of jobs—laborers, kitchen helpers and cooks, maintenance men, highly skilled operators of construction machinery, carpenters, masons. Depending on the skills and experience of the men, there is no limit to the range of possibilities. On special approval from the judge, one responsible man was released to his employer overnight for a special, out-of-state job. Another was interviewed after being sentenced to work release; his application showed he had a Ph.D. A job was found for him too—operating a computer in an industrial plant, at night.

TIME CLOCKS REPLACE COUNTS

Once a man is hired, a time card is made out for him—a time card that differs from the usual kind only in that it contains much more detailed information. Besides the man's name, the card contains the following information: Employer's name, address, and telephone number; the hours he works, including starting and quitting times; and the time he is expected to leave for work and return.

There is another difference, also. The amount of money given the inmate for travel and incidentals is recorded when he goes to work, and the amount he brings back on his return is recorded when the man returns from work, plus the amount he may have received as pay that day. This is not only an accounting measure, but also serves as a check on how the inmate handles money, how much of a sense of responsibility he may have gained, and what his prospects are for the time when he will again be out on his own.

WORK RELEASE HAS ITS PROBLEMS

Having a work-release program creates problems, and the real problems are the day-to-day kind.

Transportation is one problem that is always with us. Even though a man may have a car, he may have lost his license as part of the judgment that sent him to prison. Many have no car or other means of getting to work. This would pose no problem if good public transportation were available, but many jobs otherwise accessible to inmates have to be bypassed because they are not located on routes covered by public conveyance. It is not at all unusual for a man on work release to start for work on a bus, transfer to a train, and complete the trip by walking or hitchhiking.

Another difficulty always present with a work-release program is interference with the planned prison schedule. Men may work any of the three eight-hour shifts, split shifts, or varying hours from day to day, yet these men are expected to attend educational classes, counseling sessions, AA meetings, and any other activities intended to improve their attitudes, skills and habits prior to release. Participation in such activities is an integral part of work release. If a man's working hours do not permit him to attend them at the times they are held, makeup or extra sessions must be arranged.

The Pennsylvania law has its own built-in problems. It restricts work-release men to those sentenced for one year or less. This makes for inequities inasmuch as county jails, as a result of state legislation recently passed, may hold men sentenced to as much as five years. Two men in Bucks County Prison, for example, may have committed the same offense and may have identical personal problems, yet one will be permitted to go on work release because his sentence is three months to one year (maximum one year) while the other, with a sentence of three to twenty-three months will be excluded because his maximum is *over a year* (twenty-three months).

Another sore spot in the law is that no provision is made for men sentenced by justices of the peace which will allow them work-release privileges. Since explicit permission is lacking under the law, it is the general opinion that justices of the peace cannot so sentence a man. Two men may receive equally short sentences, yet one may go on work release while another may not.

A FEW GO "OVER THE HILL"

Whatever problems may be anticipated in a minimum-security institution with a work-release program, the situation most feared by those unfamiliar with the system is that removing the bars from the prison will also remove the psychological bars, causing the prisoners to flaunt their freedom through undisciplined behavior. This has never materialized.

This is not to say that this sort of thing does not occur; it does, but not with alarming frequency. Since August 1963, 785 men have been transferred to the Rehabilitation Center and 223 have been placed on work release. Of this group, only seven men actually committed prison breach; and twelve, for various reasons, failed to return to the Center at the proper time. Men in the latter group either returned later voluntarily or called the Center and requested to be picked up. Thus, although about 9 percent of work releasees can be said to have actually been "over the hill" since the program has been operating, only 3 percent were "walkaways" serious enough to be considered escapees.

How do these men fall by the wayside?

One of these men reported for work on a Saturday morning, did a day's work for his employer, and went to a New Jersey town where, after a prolonged drinking bout, he left for Florida accompanied by his girl friend and her daughter. When apprehended, he was living with his girl friend in a trailer court at Daytona Beach. His Florida "vacation" was abruptly terminated, and he was permanently removed from the program.

One work releasee, a confirmed race track habitue, left the Center just as the racing season opened at the Philadelphia track. The township police in the area of Liberty Bell race track were alerted, as well as the police in Atlantic City. This man's only prior employment was pushing tourists around in chairs on the boardwalk. He was not found at either place, but in the meanwhile he became apprehensive, called the prison from a Philadelphia supermarket, and turned himself in. He was permanently removed from work release, not only because of his escape but also because he had not shown enough aptitude before the escape to warrant keeping him on the work-release program.

One man was on his way to work one morning and was toying with the idea of "taking a day off" when the fan belt broke on his 1955 car. Not having money enough to buy another fan belt, he begged one from a used parts dealer. Subsequently he picked up two girl hitchhikers whom he took to a town in the next county and got in an argument with their boy friends when he took the girls to their destination. He fled in his car and was chased to Norristown where he was arrested for speeding. After two weeks in Montgomery County Prison he was returned, much chastened, to Bucks County. This incident apparently helped the escapee gain some maturity. His attitude and outlook improved markedly, and he was later returned to the work-release program.

Other men have gone out for a few drinks at a nearby bar, or to visit a girl friend or wife, or any combination of the three, and then have come back voluntarily or called the Center or Prison, asking to be picked up. In many cases the man was suspended from work release for five days, and if during that time he could demonstrate that he was capable of going along with the program, he was allowed to continue on work release.

The rest of the failures are those who find the atmosphere of a minimum-security prison confusing and cannot adjust to the lack of regimentation found in the jail, and those who indulge in some sort of irresponsible behavior short of breaking a law or who are constantly wanting to change jobs. Or they may be like one inmate who charged $200 worth of merchandise at a local department store, making payments for a while from his travel money before being caught. The man was disciplined and the merchandise returned.

Such incidents, though, are occupational hazards of running a work-release program. After all, we would be somewhat hypocritical if we would not take risks with a man for a year or less, when society must take chances with the man on his release.

FUTURE OF WORK RELEASE

The 1966 edition of the American Correctional Association's *Manual of Correctional Standards* refers to the short-term institution of the future as a "Community Corrections Center." This in effect is what the Bucks County Rehabilitation Center is now. The next step, in my opinion, will be the establishment of residential centers in industrial areas as small satellite institutions legally and administratively part of the "parent" institution, but physically separated. Men in these residential centers could live there, work outside, and take part in a dynamic treatment program in which local professionals from various disciplines and citizens of the community would be greatly involved.

Another alternative would be to transport the work-release trainees each Monday morning to the residential center and return them to the parent institution Friday evenings in much the same fashion as is now done in Pennsylvania with forestry camps. Then, at the parent institution on weekends, treatment and training programs would be scheduled for these men.

It appears to me also, that in the future there will be closer daily supervision of work-release men while at work. It is a grave error to assume that all is well with a man because no one has complained about him and he himself has not asked for help. We find that frequent contact with the employer uncovers problems of which otherwise we would be completely unaware. We find, also, that these frequent contacts prevent trouble and make the employer a partner in the problem-solving process. For example, recently a trainee on work release failed to go to work and instead went to see his sick child in the hospital. He returned to the Rehabilitation Center on time as though he had been to work. However, his employer's relationship with us was such that he had called earlier to find out why the man had not been to work. The trainee was brought back to the prison but was very shortly returned to work release because his concern for his child was a very legitimate one. We had failed, to some extent, in our work with this inmate as he did not feel that a visit to a sick child in the hospital would be approved. It would have been if we had known about it. Our communications had broken down.

Most important for this man and for the work-release program was the attitude of the employer who voluntarily came to the prison and spent two hours of his working day with me and the trainee solving problems. The employer's remarks which helped me decide to try this trainee again on work release were as follows:

"Warden, this boy needs to learn to trust people like you and I, and he needs to learn a trade. If you'll give him a break I'll square him away and teach him a trade. He's a good worker."

I gave him a break and this very rough, not-too-articulate contractor is now the "agent of treatment" for this particular man.

Perhaps the greatest change in the future will be the training assignments in the community supplementing work for prisoners on work release. We are finding more and more that all resources and all kinds of community resources *are* available *for the asking* in the training of our men. For example, state and federal vocational rehabilitation laws provide for training of men who are physically, emotionally, or mentally handicapped. The Federal Manpower and Retraining Development Act through the Office of Manpower, Automation, and Training (OMAT) provides training programs for the unemployed and underemployed. The Federal

Equal Opportunities Act (antipoverty) under its various titles seems to have something for everyone, including many programs for the man on work release.

Finally, a "seed of the future" which will bloom very soon is the cooperation of labor, management and citizens as advisory committees to help "sell" and support work release. Without the efforts of our Bucks County Prison Citizens Committee, which includes representatives of labor, management and citizens, we might have had serious opposition of unions to prison competition, apprenticeship, etc. Instead, because of this committee, union representatives call me whenever one of their men is in trouble in order to be sure he is considered for work release.

THE CIRCLE THAT LETS HIM IN

The prison is part of the community, and the prison and community share in mutual responsibility to "habilitate" the offender. Work release, treatment, and training go hand-in-glove inside and outside the jail. Prison and community working together can reduce criminality by exposing offenders to the many ways of becoming positive and productive members of society. When we do this we are "drawing a circle that lets him in."

REFERENCES

1. See "Prisoners in German Institution Employed by Private Employers." *Federal Probation,* December 1960, p. 80. See also United Nations Department of Economics and Social Affairs, *Prison Labor* (ST/SOA/SD/5), 1955.
2. Stanley, E. Grupp: Work release and the misdemeanant. *Federal Probation.* June 1965, p. 6. Also see "Work Release," *The Prison Journal,* Spring 1964, pp. 4-25.

CHAPTER 10

COMMUNITY WORK
AN ALTERNATIVE TO IMPRISONMENT (PRINCIPLES AND GUIDELINES)

CORRECTIONAL RESEARCH ASSOCIATES*

INTRODUCTION
Definition

COMMUNITY WORK IS A PROGRAM which enables selected prisoners confined in a jail, prison or other correctional facility to leave the institution daily for employment at a regular job nearby. The prisoners then spend nonworking hours in confinement at the institution. In many jurisdictions, enabling legislation is broad enough to permit participation in community training programs and home visits for various purposes.[1]

History

Programs of Community Work in operation today have their origin in the 1913 Huber Law of Wisconsin which authorized judges and magistrates, in cooperation with the sheriffs in charge of local jails, to impose conditional sentences in certain misdemeanant cases which would enable selected offenders to retain their jobs and, at the time, fulfill the obligation of a jail sentence.

---
*A Monograph published by the United States Bureau of Prisons.

This 1913 concept was adopted in a few Wisconsin counties and has continued in practice off and on over the years.

It drew relatively little national attention until the past ten to fifteen years when the idea began to spread to other jurisdictions. In 1957, the legislature of North Carolina adopted the principles of the Huber Law and two years later became the first state to apply its provisions to felony offenders under limited conditions. Subsequently, Maryland and Michigan adopted legislation that included felons as well as misdemeanants. The broad provisions of the U.S. Prisoner Rehabilitation Act of 1965 brought community work opportunities to federal offenders, along with authority to grant furloughs for other purposes. Other jurisdictions have followed suit rapidly.

Variations

Several operating models of Community Work can be identified. Some jurisdictions have retained the original, rather limited, scope of the Huber Law: the program exists only for misdemeanants confined in local facilities, and it functions exclusively as a cooperative authority of the local institution or correctional facility.

A rapidly increasing number of jurisdictions have extended enabling legislation to felony offenders confined in prisons and reformatories. In some jurisdictions, management of the Community Work program is placed in the hands of correctional administrators, while in others, the statutes require a positive recommendation of the sentencing judge or concurrence of the parole board.

Community Work programs function in some places within the limitations of statutory safeguards which exclude certain types of offenders, and define the portion of a sentence that must be served before Community Work eligibility can be established in certain cases.

So far, the most flexible enabling legislation was passed by the Congress of the United States (and by the several states which have adopted the Prisoner Rehabilitation Act of 1965 as a model). Federal prisoners are sentenced to the custody of the Attorney General who, by delegation, designates the place of confinement where the sentence shall be served. In the language of the Act:

The Attorney General may extend the limits of the place of confinement of a prisoner as to whom there is reasonable cause to believe he will honor this trust, by authorizing him, under prescribed conditions, to . . .

(1) visit a specifically designated place or places for a period not to exceed thirty days and return to the same or another institution or facility. An extension of limits may be granted only to permit a visit to a dying relative, attendance at the funeral of a relative, the obtaining of medical services not otherwise available, the contacting of prospective employers, or for any other compelling reason consistent with the public interest; or

(2) work at paid employment or participate in a training program in the community on a voluntary basis while continuing as a prisoner of the institution or facility to which he is committed, . . .

The willful failure of a prisoner to remain within the time prescribed to an institution or facility, designated by the Attorney General, shall be deemed an escapee from the custody of the Attorney General . . .

Thus, it was the clear intent of the Congress that Community Work be a rehabilitative tool administered by the executive branch of government on a case management basis.

The Rationale of Community Work

Community Work is not a substitute for probation or parole. It is not part of an internal system of punishment and reward. Nor is it an obligatory means of offsetting the cost of public welfare payments to dependent families. It is intended to be a selective resource for the correctional treatment of certain offenders.

The tasks of corrections are only partly achieved when an offender begins to realize why he got into trouble in the first place and really decides to do something about it. He also must make a reasonable adjustment to the environment of the community in which he will eventually work and live. This implies that society—and particularly the correctional system—must extend its programming concerns beyond affecting changes in the offender himself. For the majority of offenders changes are needed in the opportunities, influences and ways of life accessible to him in the community. It is also essential, before correctional processes start, that there be a thorough-going diagnosis of each offender and the setting of realistic individual correctional goals as guides in decision-making and in evaluating the performance of offenders as they progress through the correctional system.

Just as all prisoners are not suitable candidates for Community Work, by any standard of selection, so Community Work, as a correctional treatment tool, has little or nothing to offer certain offenders. As a practical matter a gangster or other professional criminal is ordinarily not sentenced to imprisonment with any significant intent that he will be "corrected" or "rehabilitated." Rarely does the typical "white collar" offender need any of the rehabilitation services which a correctional system may offer, and his commitment, more often than not, is a reflection of public policy. In the light of present knowledge, there is grave doubt about how much can be done to change the ways of the chronic repeater who seems to "do life on the installment plan" with successive commitments to prisons and jails.

The predominant focus of correctional effort now and over the years ahead is on the younger offender who comes, typically, from a deprived economic, social and family background. He is most likely to be markedly deficient in educational attainment, without work skills and with little understanding or regard for the middle-class values upon which our society is based.

This is the context in which the potentials of Community Work are seen. Community Work will be an effective correctional tool only to the extent that it is used wisely for specific purposes and as a means toward the attainment of goals of treatment, training and control of selected offenders.

Multiple Uses

Community Work is a bridge between the institution and the community. Its particular usefulness, in some degree, depends upon where in the spectrum of correctional treatment and control it is applied.[2] It has many possible applications, for example, to both the intake and discharge ends of institutionalization.

At the point of intake, especially for short-term offenders who are not suitable for probation or some other disposition, Community Work may provide opportunity for:

    Continued employment, education or training.

Continued or resumed family responsibilities, as through contributions to family support.

Accumulating savings for release, to make restitution or pay legitimate debts.

Continuing or acquiring the self-respect that flows from self-support.

A practical way of demonstrating ability and trustworthiness to gain or regain employer and community acceptance.

Remaining or becoming a contributing member of society.

Oriented toward the discharge end of institutionalization, especially for longer-term prisoners and those in whom substantial investments have been made to overcome handicapping deficiencies, Community Work offers similar opportunities and at least the following in addition:

A prerelease transitional experience leading to increasing personal responsibility.

A valuable experience in actual work situations related to prior vocational or occupational training.

Furthering the education and training started at the institution.

Giving the paroling authority a means of testing suitability for parole before final decision is reached.

Reducing the risks and fears of both the offender and the community associated with the difficult period of adjustment immediately following imprisonment.

PLANNING A COMMUNITY WORK PROGRAM

Despite the reasonableness of the rationale for Community Work and indications of its effectiveness in jurisdictions that have gained experience with it, not everyone is ready to accept the premises upon which the program is based. There continues to be many who are convinced that only by locking offenders up can the ends of justice be satisfied. Neither can it be assumed that a Community Work program can be initiated without comprehensive planning nor that, once started, the program will continue to function by itself. Basic principles must be identified. Within the framework of enabling legislation, implementing policies must be formulated. A thorough job of community organization is absolutely essential. Operating procedures must be worked out with care.

Basic Principles

From the experience of many jurisdictions operating different kinds of Community Work programs, the following rules are commonly acknowledged as essential to a successful program.

1. Community Work should be utilized to the fullest extent that circumstances permit. However, there can be no compromise with essential safeguards, community acceptance and the careful selection of participating prisoners.

2. There must be assurance that the local employment situation is such that Community Work prisoners will not displace employed workers and will not be used when there is a surplus of community citizens with similar skills or trades.

3. It is imperative that exploitation in any form or degree be avoided, either as it might affect the community or Community Work prisoners. The compensation of Community Work prisoners should be no less than that of comparable workers, and offenders should not be employed under adverse working conditions or at less than prevailing standards. Conversely, Community Work prisoners should not be employed as strikebreakers or in situations that would evoke adverse public reaction directed either at the prisoner involved, the correctional system, or the unit of government.

4. All prisoners admitted to Community Work status remain in technical custody, and a prisoner who absconds should be treated as an escape.

5. Each job offer should be investigated to determine that it is bona fide, is consistent with Community Work policies and will fulfill the correctional objectives for the selected prisoner. While Community Work neither constitutes nor implies a contractual agreement between an employer and the correctional agency, it must be recognized that some mutual responsibilities exist. These derive from the fact that, although employed, the prisoner is still in custody, and his work release status is primarily for a correctional purpose.

6. Responsibility for decision-making with respect to admissions and removals should be vested in an appropriate official of

the agency which is accountable for the operation of the program. This may require the closest possible collaboration with judges and paroling authorities, especially in those jurisdictions where Community Work is recommended or ordered as part of the sentence or as a condition of parole.

7. Written procedures should be adopted and followed for the control, accounting and disbursement of salaries, wages or stipends received by Community Work prisoners. The distribution of earnings should be agreed to in advance and in writing by participating prisoners.

Community Organization

In no circumstances should a Community Work program be initiated until there is assurance that the local community has been adequately prepared for it. It is essential that correctional administrators and program managers promote public understanding and support for the program. In part, this is a matter of developing and maintaining communication networks for the purpose of imparting basic information, interpreting the aims of Community Work, and explaining its role in the total correctional process.

The public education effort should include:

1. Information to court, law enforcement and government officials: At least a consensus support of the program is required of the units representing the administration of justice and those components of the executive branch of local government that will be involved.

2. Use of community leadership: In any community there are particular individuals and organizations that are the major molders of public opinion. These may be found in business, in labor unions, among the clergy, in the legal profession, the news media and in a variety of civic organizations. Preliminary discussions, similar to those held with government officials, should be planned with the leaders of these groups.

3. Use of citizens advisory committee: An advisory committee composed of persons representing local community leadership can be an effective structure for utilizing this leadership. While such a group would not have operational responsibilities, it may be an

effective means of two-way communication as well as a sounding board for policy and program development. Members of such committees need to become actively involved beyond attending occasional meetings. Some may be prospective employers who can share responsibility for such functions as job development. In some localities, groups having an interest in corrections already exist and can help fill the role of citizen advisory committee.

Policy Formulation

The correctional administrator or program manager responsible for activating a Community Work program should, as part of his preliminary planning, develop a complete operating plan. In effect, this plan will be a detailed statement of operational policies and procedures.

The principles identified above, along with others that may be appropriate to particular situations, should be translated into definitive policy statements. The precise manner by which the program is to be administered must be fully outlined. Beginning with a statement of the purposes for which Community Work is to be used, attention should be given such matters as selection of prisoners, transportation arrangements, housing, disposition and control of earnings, clothing, supportive services, records, and reports. Staff assignments and responsibilities must be defined also.

The importance of advance detailed planning cannot be overemphasized. A successful program depends on the concerted, cooperative acts of many persons in diverse occupations and roles, both public and private. Such a joint endeavor cannot be "played by ear" but must have specific guidelines for all who are participants in the venture.

PROGRAM MANAGEMENT AND EVALUATION

Discussions of the program elements that follow are based upon the policies and operating experiences of a number of jurisdictions. To this extent they may be viewed, at least tentatively, as recommended minimum standards.

Selection

Any prisoner wishing to be considered for Community Work

must apply on forms prescribed. If a prisoner is to be held accountable for his behavior under conditions of extended custody he must fully understand and consent to those conditions.

Full minimum custody should be an obvious prerequisite to all cases and, as a matter of policy, the opportunity of Community Work should be available to prisoners in all offense categories on an as-needed basis. Necessary precautions center around the need to protect the community against further depredations and threats to safety and welfare; the need to protect the program from jeopardy arising from adverse public reaction toward the prisoner, the correctional system or the unit of government; and the need to avoid subverting the intent of criminal justice by allowing certain prisoners to escape the onus of a sentence to imprisonment. These precautions can be taken by careful prisoner selection and by judicious timing.[3]

The candidate for Community Work should be in good health and physically able to perform the tasks of the proposed job. This requirement should not preclude the use of Community Work as an unusual opportunity to aid a physically handicapped person in obtaining employment consistent with his capabilities or as part of a physical rehabilitation effort. Others who are mentally or emotionally handicapped and who are not dangerous may be considered when it is apparent that community employment will significantly aid their post-release adjustment.

Community Work is not intended as a program or status to be made available to all who may be technically eligible. There must be indicated need for the opportunities and responsibilities which the program provides. This type of decision is a case management judgment to be related to the prerelease family need or other individual circumstances for which the program is particularly appropriate. Further, it must be ascertained that a selected prisoner will benefit from the experience. Decisions in cases of family need, restitution and debt payment should be based on investigation so that official records will establish the prisoner's responsibility and verify that the claimed need exists.

Selection preference should be given candidates whose residence is in the vicinity of the institution or facility, or for whom release plans in this vicinity are reasonable and appropriate. Although this should not entirely exclude others, a number of factors should be carefully weighed:

1. It can be expected that many prisoners and their employers will want to continue their local employment after release from the institution or facility. Not infrequently, employers will make substantial investment in training Community Work prisoners for the jobs they hold, and numbers of prisoners will experience job satisfactions which they are reluctant to give up.

2. A community will not tolerate its becoming a "haven" for former offenders who "belong" elsewhere, even though they may be under parole supervision.

3. There will be circumstances in which sound correctional treatment involves relocating an offender from a home or community that is untenable or lacking in opportunity. Experience, indicates, however, that strong ties in the new community are needed. Relocating an offender solely because he thinks it is a good idea rarely works out. This is especially true of younger offenders.

4. Whenever relation is contemplated, the views and cooperation of those who will provide supervision after release must be obtained. This proposal should also be discussed with local officials and community groups who would be concerned.

There will be no general restrictions on the kinds of jobs for which candidates may be considered. The expectation is that the job selected will be legitimate employment and that which best fulfills the purpose of Community Work in each case, consistent with the fact that the employed prisoner is still in custody. Good employment placement will give reference to jobs that are related to prior training, work experience, institutional training, prisoner interest, and may be suitable as continuing postrelease employment. The "break even" point between wages and expenses will tend to eliminate temporary, part-time and intermittent employment.

When used for prerelease purposes for felony offenders, Community Work placements should be limited ordinarily to a period of not more than six months immediately preceding the probable release date. Although exceptions may be made when fully justified, present experience suggests the optimum period of program effectiveness to be from three to six months. Experience has also shown that the greatest number of in-program failures are likely to occur either during the first weeks on the program or after six months. The early failures seem to be associated with transitional adjustment difficulties. The late failures tend to be associated with the frustrations arising from the Cinderella-like existence of relative freedom on the job and returning to confinement each day.[4]

Transportation

All transportation arrangements should be approved by the correctional administrator or program manager in charge. As a practical matter, little can be accomplished if the travel time between the institution and the job exceeds one to one and a half hours each way. Within reasonable limits of convenience to the institution, jobs need not be restricted to "normal" work hours. When suitable transportation can be arranged, there should be no objection to work or overtime.

In nearly every jurisdiction, transportation becomes and remains the greatest single operating problem of Community Work programs. It is handled in many ways, depending upon agency policy and local circumstances. In some jurisdictions, transportation is provided by institution vehicles. In others, there is total reliance on public transportation. Not infrequently, car pool arrangements with fellow-workers are approved. Various combinations of these are common. In all instances the prisoner pays the costs of transportation. In some instances, prisoners are permitted to drive personally-owned or company vehicles, but this practice usually is not recommended because of additional problems related to licensing, insurance and liability.

Housing

There is no consensus whether Community Work prisoners should live within the confines of a main institution or in a separate facility outside the security perimeter of an institution. This decision is determined by many factors not central to the program itself—and no single pattern is necessarily preferable. Community work prisoners may live in a main institution, whether or not in specially designated quarters. On the other hand, they may live in outside quarters, although exclusive use of outside quarters is not always possible, nor is it necessarily desirable.

When Community Work prisoners live in a main institution, problems of contraband control are increased. This not only adds to staff concern but may require special admission and release procedures. The prisoners, themselves, are subject to additional pressures from fellow inmates to engage in contraband traffic. On the other hand, this arrangement enables regular institution staff to manage the program, and it makes essential supportive services more accessible to Community Work prisoners.

A number of institutions have reported vastly improved institutional "climate" and fewer disciplinary reports with the advent of Community Work, as the majority of prisoners become motivated and aspire to the program. The program is seen by personnel of these institutions as having a positive and significant impact upon traditional inmate culture and value systems.

The principal value of outside quarters is that management can become exclusively community oriented. This arrangement is likely to require additional staffing, and access to essential supportive services at the main institution may become limited.

Supportive Services

As previously stated, Community Work is intended to be a correctional program. To be effective, it cannot be divorced from other correctional programs and services. While in the institution during nonwork hours, participating prisoners should be encouraged, perhaps even required, to avail themselves of regular institutional activities, especially those which will improve work skills and increase their capacity to adjust in the community.

Case work, guidance and counseling services should be made available to Community Work prisoners to the fullest extent possible. Often there are special and immediate needs for such services arising from problems on the job and working conditions in addition to the usual range of personal and family matters. Counseling hours should be scheduled to permit no less than weekly contact with each Community Work prisoner.

For certain offenders, the full potentials of Community Work will be realized when regular employment and attendant job satisfactions become the means of an orderly, supervised transition to full community life. On the basis of individual needs and case management goals, correctional programming is aimed at the offender's progressive self-sufficiency in the community. Accordingly, participation in community religious, educational, social, civic and recreational activities may also be considered when there is reason to believe that such participation will contribute significantly to the offender's progress in learning and exercise of personal responsibility. Similarly, as statutes permit, occasional furloughs may be used as supplemental program resources.

Disposition of Earnings

All prisoners approved for Community Work or training who will receive salaries, wages or stipends should be required to execute an agreement for the disposition of such income. The agreement should provide the authority for all disbursements, whether they be payments to dependent families, reinmbursements to the institution for various required purposes, or other approved reasons.

In addition to paying the costs of their own transportation, Community Work prisoners in most jurisdictions, either by law or policy decision, are required to reimburse the institution for daily subsistence. Depending upon the jurisdiction, these payments are made at full per capita cost or on the basis of an adopted standard formula.

Participating prisoners need to carry cash with them while outside the institution to cover miscellaneous daily expenses. To make the prisoner fully accountable for such funds and to relieve the institution of additional responsibilities for contraband control, accounting, and daily receipts and disbursements, many institutions provide accessible lock boxes for which each prisoner holds the key. In some jurisdictions, it is permissible for local banks to handle all Community Work funds. In cooperation with the bank, the program manager controls all withdrawals and check issuances.

Many prisoners enter the program entirely without funds. In some jurisdictions, procedures exist enabling cash advances, usually not in excess of $100, to be used for the purchase of clothing, tools and payment of other necessary expenses until the first paycheck is received. The amount and purposes of such advances, as well as full reimbursements from initial pay checks, are carefully controlled.

As the Community Work prisoner is not a free agent, even though fully employed, most program managers will not permit charge accounts or contracting for installment buying.

Clothing

In the federal prison system and a few others, prisoners on Community Work are outfitted with clothing suitable for the kind of work or other placement at which they will be employed. For the longer-term prisoners this constitutes the "discharge outfit." Community Work prisoners are required to purchase, with their own funds, all supplemental and replacement clothing. This may be purchased through regular institutional sources or directly from outside cash commercial sources. So that civilian clothing will not be worn inside the institution by participating prisoners, special check-in—check-out arrangements are made for lockers, clothing change, and laundry service.

Laundry Services

Institutions which have laundries may provide this service for prisoners on the program, although special controls are required. Generally, this service is limited to the initial issue of clothing until the prisoner is established on his job and earnings are received. Typically, thereafter, arrangements are made with commercial laundries or nearby laundromats in accordance with the needs and services available.

Terminations

The removal of a prisoner from the program for willful negligence or misconduct is as much a case management decision as was the approval of his entering the program in the first place. He should be required to live up to the rules and expectations of the program. While a double standard of conduct is to be avoided within the institution, the status of a Community Work prisoner *is* different. As a general guiding principle, the judgments and standards which underlie disciplinary and removal decisions should be more closely identified with those decisions appropriate to the effective management and control of a parolee than with adherence to traditional prison discipline. This is a most difficult and challenging problem for the administrator. It tests the capacity of the correctional staff to truly practice individual correctional programming.

Reports and Records

The need to continually evaluate fully all aspects of work release cannot be overemphasized. This is more than a matter of learning by doing during early developmental stages. Wherever a Community Work program exists for a significant number of prisoners, its impact is felt in all areas of institutional operations, by the entire correctional system, by the paroling authority, and by those who are responsible for providing supervision after release. All officials must be alert to the impact of the program, must assess its meaning, and plan continuing adjustments that will insure a balanced and increasingly effective total correctional program. Feedback to institution staff of actual community experience provides a basis for intelligent reprogramming.

Especially needed for this purpose and to assure continued monitoring of program management are basic facts relating to the selection of prisoners and the jobs on which they are placed. Standard data on earnings and payments should be maintained. Termination reports should be prepared in all cases showing the reasons for removal from the program with explanations of removals for cause. Monthly or quarterly summaries prepared by program managers should carry basic statistics and include narrative observations of the adjustment of participating prisoners, acceptance of the program by employers and others, operating problems and the effects of Community Work on institutional operations and parole. Ideally, individual case records will evaluate the progress made by prisoners in the program, as in other institutional program areas, and will assess the relevance of this to original diagnostic findings, the correctional goals that were set, and the elements of release planning needed.

REFERENCES

1. Correctional administrators and program managers today are confronted with a growing problem of semantics. The terms "furlough" and

"release" tend to be too broad and to denote a status which can easily be misunderstood. There is also need for a generic, inclusive term referring to all kinds of extra-mural correctional programs, as distinguished from intra-mural institutional programs. There is further need to distinguish these actual programs from various community resources which are inputs to institutional programs. Such a term as "Community Correctional Programs," for example, is broad enough to include components of work, training, visits and others yet to be developed.

2. Variations of Community Work are emerging from bail reform programs in some jurisdictions. In some instances, employment is a critical factor in determining the conditions of release on personal recognizance. Community Work may be an essential component of a regime which permits defendants awaiting trial or disposition to be confined only at night and on weekends. At the other end of the correctional spectrum, some jurisdictions are experimenting with "open-ended parole" wherein the effective date is set after the offender is employed and other elements of an acceptable parole plan have been completed in the community.

3. Greatest care should be taken in authorizing Community Work for offenders identified with large scale, organized criminal activity; offenders convicted of crimes against the person, or whose records include such offenses; offenders with serious emotional or personality defects and those with histories of violent or assaultive behavior; prisoners whose offenses involved violations of financial trust.

4. This "rule of thumb" applies to prerelease use of Community Work. In some jurisdictions the Cinderella-like problem experienced by longer-term prisoners is partially alleviated by allowing occasional home visits and participation in company or community social activities. Prisoners authorized to participate in courses of education or training in the community normally remain in them for the duration of the courses.

CHAPTER 11

NEW DESIGN FOR CORRECTIONAL EDUCATION AND TRAINING PROGRAMS

By Sylvia G. McCollum*

CORRECTIONAL EDUCATION AND TRAINING has the special mission of upgrading the capacity of people found at varying points in the criminal justice system to cope more effectively (i.e. in legal and socially acceptable ways) with life's economic and social requirements. Some practitioners in the corrections field define this mission very narrowly; to them, education and training means primarily achievement of a high school diploma or a General Educational Development (GED) certificate and the acquisition of entry level job skills. Others increasingly define correctional education more broadly. This richer definition includes not only academic and career education, but also instruction in skills which stimulate and facilitate involvement in social, economic, and cultural pursuits and the ability to seek entry into and take advantage of available opportunity systems.[1]

The average daily population of offenders in institutions is estimated at approximately 400,000. Of these, around 150,000 are "detained" or serve sentences of such short duration that they can-

---
*Reprinted from *Federal Probation,* June, 1973.

not be educationally programmed. As a result, the potential daily student population in correctional institutions is estimated at about 250,000. Approximately 15 percent are youthful offenders (under age eighteen) and roughly 5 percent are females.

Characteristically, the student/prisoner comes from an economically and socially deprived background, lacks any stable work history, is a school pushout/dropout and has come in conflict with the law at an early age. He tends to be isolated from groups and organizations as well as from the kinds of situations and experiences which contribute to learning and maturation processes. The average prisoner's education and training needs are characteristically substantial and by any reasonable standards require intensive and diversified programming.

Despite these urgent needs, very few correctional institutions offer bona fide education and training programs. Most of the 4,000 county and local jails in the United States offer no programs at all. Some state institutions provide the opportunity to take high school equivalency and limited vocational training courses. Other state prisons and many Federal correctional institutions offer a wider range of educational opportunities. These broader programs include literacy education, instruction leading to a high school diploma or the GED, college level courses, varied skill training and job readiness programs as well as occupational counseling and related social education programs. In recent years structured leisure time and recreational programs and special cultural courses (Black studies, American Indian, Spanish American cultures, etc.) have been introduced. Drama, creative writing, the study of music and art and related arts, and crafts programs are still the exception rather than the rule.

THE FATAL FLAW

The fatal flaw in all correctional education programs stems from the assumption that people who happen to share a common address —a prison—share educational aptitudes, interests and needs which can be served by programs which are limited to high school equivalency courses, skill training in four or five vocational areas, and a few college level courses.[2] The age range of inmates in many state prisons and in some federal correctional institutions can be from fifteen to fifty years or older. Interests and aptitudes, past educational experiences and achievement levels cover a broad range and have brought each prisoner to an individual educational readiness which cannot reasonably be served by such narrow programming.

In addition, most correctional education and training programs imitate the worst of the public school models; the conventional classroom with students seated in orderly rows and the teacher safely isolated from the students by a large desk behind which he sits or stands most of the fifty-minute classroom hour are the rule in prison schools. Characteristically, instructors are white English-speaking men (except in women's prisons where teachers are generally women), and anyone who cannot read or write in the instructor's language, regardless of the person's literacy in any other language (Spanish for example), is regarded and programmed as an illiterate.

Vocational education programs are primarily in manual skill areas and are seldom, if ever, integrated with related academic courses. Math is math and learning to measure in carpentry class is something else again.

In some institutions, primarily those serving youth and young adults, classes are held during daylight "prime time" hours staffed by full-time, certified teachers; and in others, primarily adult institutions, classes are held during evening hours and staffed by part-time teachers who "moonlight" after a full day's teaching in a nearby public school. It is not uncommon to find a retired military or public school educator starting a second career teaching in a correctional institution. Many classrooms are makeshift, poorly lighted, inadequately ventilated, and drably furnished. In some, there is even a shortage of paper and pencils. There are, of course, outstanding exceptions to these general conditions, but we need to consider prevailing program levels rather than the exceptions. In view of these conditions "students" are predictably reluctant to enroll in prison schools despite the very real motivator of parole board interest in educational attainment as a factor to be considered at the time of parole review.

This negative overall picture persists despite continuing evaluations which urge that we regard correctional education and training as a priority area of concern.[3] It is also significant that inadequate education and training programs are increasingly being listed among the grievances for which prisoners' organizations are seeking redress.[4] Is not this sort of an educator's dream: students protesting that they want more and better education and training?

There needs to be a continuing and accelerating awareness among correctional administrators and educators that traditional methods are not working in prison education programs any more than they are in the "free world." Follow-up studies of prison education and training programs such as those reported by Abt Associates (1969), Spencer, et al. (1971), and Dickover, et al. (1971) reveal that postrelease jobs of prisoners are generally not related to training received in prison. In addition, Pownall (1969), Sullivan (1967) and others report that job loss after release from prison is generally not due to lack of specific skills but is due to other deficiencies such as poor attendance, hostile attitudes, overreaction to supervision and other nonjob content related issues.

On the other hand, Pownall (1969), McCabe and Driscoll (1971), and continuing reports from the Rehabilitation Research Foundation indicate that there is a positive relationship between a person's involvement in education and training programs while in prison, postrelease employment in some job, and "success" in staying out of prison.

THE NEED FOR NEW DELIVERY SYSTEMS

The challenge confronting creative educators concerned with using the correctional experience in positive ways is to structure an educational delivery system which takes into account the wide range of individual differences in age, levels of prior experience, aptitudes, interests, and learning styles of a group of people whose only common denominator is "serving time." Inherent in this challenge, also, is the problem of staff and public resistance to "rewarding" lawbreakers with genuine educational improvement opportunities, particularly if the education and training is purposefully designed to lead to job opportunities which pay as well or better than those held by the involved correctional staff.

Despite these many impediments, the time may be right to make significant changes in correctional education systems. Certainly the public is sensitive to the whole issue of prison reform. Prisoners themselves, either as individuals or in organizations, religious groups, community organizations, professional groups such as the American Bar Association, and, of course, correctional administrators and line staff are also keenly aware of the troubled situation and seem ready to talk about and accept significant changes. Ryan (1971) reports that 145 correctional staff members who participated in a series of in-service training programs during 1971 developed sixty-six different and innovative correctional education delivery systems, tailor-made to the specific conditions of their respective institutions, including special allowances for specific inmate profile data and institutional and community restraints.

Traditional approaches can be replaced, sometimes at no greater cost. Certainly the state of the art of education and training is such that we can structure models which have been found to offer hope with other groups of students who share some of the characteristics of prison populations. Educational decision-makers, both in and outside corrections, can profit from a careful examination of new designs which may prove particularly effective, not only with students found at varying places in the criminal justice system, but with their counterparts outside the walls.

EDUCATIONAL VOUCHER SYSTEMS

Many people seriously doubt whether it is possible to mount effective education and training programs within the constraints of prison environments. The primary purpose of all prisons is to physically restrain a person against his will. Very few prisoners would voluntarily remain in prison. Involuntary residence requires certain types of architecture, staffing patterns, rules and regulations, living arrangements, and deliberate withholding from community-based opportunities. In addition, in a prison environment, infractions of rules frequently result in disciplinary measures and physical separation from the main prison community which prevent sustained program participation regardless of consequences. Where program participation and the security of the institution come in conflict, almost without exception, security is the priority concern.

In addition, the historically low salaries, the exclusion of minority group members, and the geographic and social isolation of prison communities have resulted in correctional staff characteristics which are not always amenable to promoting education and training efforts. Long sentences, the practice of using prisoner labor to maintain the institution, "license plate variety" prison industries, and the antieducation prisoner subculture all take their toll. Add to all of this the fact that approximately five of every ten prison employees are guards, and it is not difficult to understand why some people conclude it is sheer sophistry to talk about providing meaningful education and training services in a prison environment.

One obvious alternative is to take correctional education out of the institution and separate it sequentially from the confinement period.

It may be possible to structure a system within which prisoners would be provided with individual educational vouchers, guaranteeing them access to educational services upon completion of specified time periods and upon meeting specified standards of conduct. This might mean that the individual prisoner would be involved in institutional maintenance work, prison industries, or some other appropriate range of activities for a specified portion of his sentence. He would then become entitled to full-time involvement in a carefully prescribed education and training program either at a nearby manpower skill center, a vocational-technical school, junior college, or other appropriate educational experience. A community-based approved apprenticeship program, a job which includes training, or some other approved work-study arrangement might also serve to meet individual needs. The educational commitment to particular prisoners might mean transfer to another correctional facility closer to the training opportunity. The details of individual arrangements would be less difficult to work out than acceptance of the basic concept, namely that fulfillment of certain requirements would bring with it entitlement to bona fide educational opportunities. Leiberg, et al. (1972) suggest that these educational vouchers could be in legally enforceable contract form, recognized by paroling authorities and the courts.

Some people react to this concept by insisting that it is very unrealistic; that since many "good people" who have never broken the law do not have corresponding opportunities, this idea can never really gain recognition and acceptance. This particular model, they argue, may have to await broader availability of education and training services to the population at large. Notwithstanding the merits of these arguments, the U.S. Department of Labor is in the process of funding experimental demonstration research projects to test the feasibility of using the educational voucher system for a selected number of prisoners.

Cost effective considerations are pushing the educational voucher idea faster than might otherwise be the case. It already costs more per year to keep a man in prison than it would cost to provide him with realistic education and training opportunities. The $3,000 per year it costs to keep a person locked up could buy first-class education and training services. In addition, we know that prison experience almost guarantees recidivism. We meet the young first offender many times; first in a "boys' home," later in a "youth center," then in a reformatory and finally in a penitentiary—sometimes with only a few months in between each step up (or down) the correctional ladder. It is not uncommon for one offender alone to cost society $100,000 in obvious costs and an incalculable amount in hidden costs over the span of his prison career.

THE PRISON AS A SPECIALIZED LEARNING CENTER

In the United States the institution to which a sentenced offender is sent is generally determined by his age, the nature of his crime, proximity to the legal jurisdiction of his offense or his home location. His education and training needs almost never are the basis for his assignment to a particular state or federal prison. Characteristically, therefore, if an institution is seeking to provide education and training services to its particular resident population it has the almost insurmountable task of providing a universal range of education and training opportunities. The required range of education and training programs is not necessarily smaller in an institution housing 200 prisoners than it would be in one housing 2,000. The need for services will depend *less* on the number of prisoners than on their age, educational attainment level when committed to prison, and their individual aptitudes, experiences, backgrounds, and interests. A relatively small prison housing 200 prisoners may require as wide a range of programs as one housing 2,000.

It is quite possible that the smaller the prison, the less able it will be to provide required programs, particularly from a cost effective standpoint. Under these circumstances, it becomes increasingly necessary to group prison populations by education and training requirements (all other factors being equal). One correctional facility could serve as a paramedical training center offering training in such high demand occupations as medical technicians and medical administrators. Proximity to a good hospital is important in such training programs, and this would be possible under the centralized training center concept.

Another prison might specialize in training for human service occupations sending forth certified occupational counselors, teachers, teacher-aides, and educational administrators. Regional specialized prisons could serve several states and coeducational populations. The combinations which could be developed to provide the much needed education and training services are limitless, depending only on the willingness and ability of managers and governmental jurisdictions to cooperate.

It is critical to remember when considering this approach that it is not as desirable as community-based programming and only makes economic and social sense when other delivery systems are not feasible.

EDUCATIONAL TECHNOLOGY CENTERS

Where it is not possible to centralize or specialize education and training programs, educational technology now makes it possible for us to provide a much wider range of educational and training offerings in the individual "all purpose" institution. Computer assisted instruction, dial access videotape systems, and programmed materials packaged and delivered in a variety of ways are now available to the correctional education program manager. While some of these systems appear to be relatively expensive, closer examination suggests that unit costs, amortized over reasonable periods of time, are lower than appear at first glance.

The use of educational equipment rather than live instruction makes possible not only a wider range of course offerings but also permits a greater degree of flexibility in scheduling student involvement. As a result, education programming can be more compatible with other institutional requirements.

Increased use of educational technology permits education staff to become program managers and educational counselors rather than talking textbooks before drowsy students. One important pitfall to avoid in these kinds of programs is over-assignment to machine education. It is important to maintain a balance between machine or programmed material and managed group discussions, involvement with "tutors," or other people-to-people contacts by students. It is apparently easy to forget that education and training are not limited to the mastery of information or skills, but rather embrace learning to live with and relate to people in mutually enhancing ways.

Dieuzeide (1970) summarized the purposes of educational technology as ". . . the systematic application of the resources of scientific knowledge to the process that *each individual* has to go through in order to acquire and use knowledge."

We need always to remember, particularly when working with troubled people, that the human encounter is one of our important educational resources.

ESTABLISHMENT OF CORRECTIONAL SCHOOL DISTRICTS

Several states, such as Texas, Connecticut and Illinois, have created statewide school districts which embrace correctional institutions in the state. This approach makes available budget, staff, materials and other resources normally provided to an operating school district in the state. Since many state correctional budgets make no provision for full-time teachers or other resources necessary to provide meaningful education programs, this new school district approach is very significant. In other states where correctional budgets include education funds, they must be fought for annually, and programs continually hover on the brink of disaster. The prison school district approach may offer some stability to these situations.

There are indications that other states are considering this approach and to the extent it represents a continuing commitment to education programs in prisons it is highly desirable. If, as a result of becoming a school district, however, programs and procedures imitate public school systems and make inadequate allowance for the special education needs of prison populations, they will not accomplish the high goals envisioned for this approach. In addition, if the educational services are provided primarily *inside* the institutions and ignore study-release and other alternatives, these new school districts will be going against the tide and will reduce the chances for new community-based models to emerge. It remains to be seen if the states embracing the school district concept will have the courage and the foresight to provide educational services outside the walls for appropriate individuals.

EDUCATIONAL DIAGNOSTIC AND REFERRAL CENTERS

Many correctional administrators are eager to tell visitors to prisons that a large percentage of the people in prison do not really belong there. If this is true there is a real need for more residential correctional facilities in which security is the last rather than the first priority. Such a center could serve as an education and training reception, diagnostic, and referral institution. The "students" would continue to be under the supervision of state or Federal authorities, but the primary goal of the institution would be to provide education and training diagnosis (testing), and prescriptive programming. It would also address location of appropriate education and training institutions, tuition and related financial support for "students," and if necessary intensive educational counseling and related services.

The kinds of people recruited to staff these correctional centers would be quite different from the kinds of people attracted to institutional work where the primary goal is security and/or maintenance of the institution. These institutions might be located near or could even be part of community college systems. Their primary purpose would be diagnosis and appropriate referral and provision of services necessary to bring the individual up to a level of readiness for education and training programming. Basic literacy, as well as industrial literacy, programs might be offered on-site, but beyond that level the individual would be referred to an already existing education or training opportunity. The institution could be residential or nonresidential depending on circumstances.

USE OF COMMUNITY COLLEGES

The nationwide chain of 1,100 community colleges offers another possible resource for relocating and redirecting correctional education efforts. Mensel (1972) has suggested that community colleges can serve as diagnostic and testing centers, developers of program plans for individual offenders, and effective referral agents to other community counseling, occupational or educational institutions. The American Association of Junior Colleges has indicated an interest in seeking out jurisdictions which might be willing to use community and junior colleges as precommitment diversionary centers. These colleges could serve as facilitators in the delivery of any services necessary to divert the first offender from commitment to a correctional institution.

Whether or not this concept can be implemented will depend to a large extent not only on the reaction of the professionals in the criminal justice and community and junior college systems, but also on the reaction of parents, students, and the public at large.

CONCLUSION

We need to start asking fundamental questions with respect to correctional education and training programs. The basic issue is: Do we agree that present systems are inadequate? If our answer to this important question is yes, we can then assemble some of the best theoreticians and practitioners in corrections and education to evolve new delivery systems. The broad conceptual models discussed in this paper are but a few of perhaps an unlimited number of combinations which could be developed.

The unanswered question is, of course, are the public and its elected representatives ready to encourage correctional administrators to test the water?

REFERENCES

Abt Associates. *Evaluation of MDTA Section 251 Inmate Training Programs—1st quarterly report.* Cambridge, Mass., 1969.

American Correctional Association Parole—MDT—Project Proceedings: *National Workshop of Corrections and Parole Administrators,* New Orleans, La., Feb. 20-23, 1972. (Leon Leiberg, Project Director)

Dickover, Robert M., Maynard, Verner E., and Painter, James A.: *A Study of Vocational Training in the California Department of Corrections.* Research Report No. 40, Research Division, Department of Corrections. Sacramento, Calif., 1971.

Dieuzeide, Henri: *Educational Technology and Development of Education.* UNESCO, Paris, 1970.

McCabe, Patrick, and Driscoll, Brian: *College Admission Opportunities and the Public Offender.* Project Newgate, Federal Correctional Institution, Ashland, Ky., 1971.

Mensel R. Frank: *Preliminary Proposal: College Probations to Rehabilitate Youth Under Criminal Sentences.* American Association of Community and Junior Colleges, Washington, D.C., 1972.

Pownall, George A.: *Employment Problems of Released Prisoners.* Prepared for the Manpower Administration, U.S. Department of Labor, 1969. (Available from the National Technical Information Service, 5285 Port Royal Road, Springfield, Va. 22151.)

Spencer, Carol, and Berecochea, John E.: *Vocational Training at the California Institution for Women: An Evaluation.* Research Report No. 41, Research Division, Department of Corrections, Sacramento, Calif., 1971.

Sullivan, Clyde E., and Mandell, Wallace: *Restoration of Youth Through Training.* Wakoff Research Center, Staten Island, N. Y., 1967.

Ryan, T. A.: *Experimental Training Program in Adult Basic Education in Corrections.* Education Research and Development Center, University of Hawaii, Honolulu, Hawaii, Final Report II, July 1971.

SELECTED ADDITIONAL RECOMMENDED READINGS

General Background

Glaser, Daniel: The Effectiveness of Correctional Education, *American Journal of Correction,* March—April 1966.

Joselson, M.: Prison education: A major reason for its impotence. *Corrective Psychiatry and Journal of Social Therapy,* Vol. 17, No. 2, 1971.

McCollum, Sylvia G.: Say have you got anything around here for a dummy? *Federal Probation,* September 1971.

McCollum, Sylvia G.: Education and training of youthful offenders. *A Report Based on the Princeton Manpower Symposium,* Princeton, New Jersey, 1968.

McCollum, Sylvia G.: Human relations problems in correctional systems. *California Youth Authority Quarterly,* Spring, 1971.

Evaluation of Programs

Adams, Stuart: *The San Quentin Prison College Project: Final Report, Phase I.* University of California, 1968.

California Department of Youth Authority: *Evaluation Summary of Compensatory Education in the California Youth Authority 1968-1969.* Sacramento, 1970.

Coty, Francis J.: Correctional education in the Northeast after a generation of effort. *American Journal of Correction,* November—December 1963.

Glaser, Edward M.: *An Evaluation of the Effectiveness of the Allen*

Teaching Machine at the Federal Correctional Institution, Lompoc, California. Final Report. Human Interaction Research Institute, Los Angeles, February 1970.

Hitt, William D. et al: *Final Report on an Analysis of the Education and Training Systems at Milan, Michigan, and Terre Haute, Indiana, to Federal Prison Industries, Incorporated, U.S. Department of Justice.* April 15, 1968. Battelle Memorial Institute, Columbus, Ohio 43201.

U.S. Bureau of Prisons: *To Help Men Change: A Report by Sterling Institute on Optimizing Training Potential in Federal Reformatories, Summary,* 1968.

U.S. Department of Labor, Manpower Administration: *The Draper Project.* 1969. (MDTA Experimental and Demonstration Findings No. 6)

Current Trends

National Committee for Children and Youth: *Project Challenge: An Experimental and Demonstration Program of Occupational Training, Counseling, Employment, Follow-up and Community Support for Youthful Offenders at the Lorton Youth Center.* Final report to the U.S. Department of Labor, Manpower Administration, and the U.S. Dept. of Health, Education and Welfare, Office of Education, 1968.

Rehabilitation Research Foundation: *The Experimental Manpower Laboratory for Corrections.* 1970-1971.

Rehabilitation Research Foundation: *An Individually Prescribed Instructional System.* (3 Manuals are included with the instructional material) R.R.F., Draper Correctional Center, Elmore, Ala., 1971.

Ryan, T. Antoinette: Program Director. *Collection of Papers Prepared for 1970 National Seminars Adult Basic Education in Corrections.* Education Research and Development Center, University of Hawaii, 1970.

Social Education Research and Development, Inc.: *A Survey and Plan of Action for Education and Training Services in the Maryland Correctional Training Center in Hagerstown, Md.* S.E.R. & D., Inc., Silver Spring, Md.

Sullivan, John C., and Bobo, Marvin O.: *Syllabus for Adult Education Tutoring Program in a Penal Institution, With a Look at the Past, Present, and Future of Institutional Education. An Independent Study and Research Paper, Developed and Compiled by Two Inmate Tutors at the U.S. Penitentiary, Marion, Illinois,* 1970.

U.S. Office of Economic Opportunity: Newgate: A Way Out of Wasted Years. O.E.O. Pamphlet No. 3400.

See also *Correctional Education: A Bibliography,* Federal Bureau of Prisons, Washington, D.C., Feb. 1972.

REFERENCES

1. Many correctional educators, like their counterparts in public schools

everywhere, make arbitrary and unnatural distinction between "academic" and "vocational" or "occupational" education. They operate under the false assumption that "academic" education is not job training despite impressive research data which establish that a high school diploma and a college degree impressively enhance lifetime occupational earning power.
2. Welding, food service, automotive maintenance and repair, and building construction trades are generally the vocational education offerings for men. A few institutions offer training as a computer programmer, dental technician, and draftsman. Women's institutions characteristically offer home economics and cosmetology training. Discrimination even follows women into prison: data processing and related keypunch training is sometimes offered women prisoners. Computer programmer training is reserved for men. As far as we have been able to determine, computer programmer training is not offered women prisoners inside correctional institutions anywhere in the United States.
3. The most recent official report (only one of many) to make this recommendation is the Report of the President's Task Force on Prisoner Rehabilitation. "The Criminal Offender—What Should Be Done?" Washington, D.C., April, 1970.
4. See for example "The Folsom Prisoner's Manifesto of Demands" and "Anti-Oppression Platform" as reported in *If They Come in the Morning,* Angela Y. Davis, New York, Joseph Okpaku Publishing Company, Inc., 1971.

CHAPTER 12

THE JAIL OMBUDSMAN

PAUL F. CROMWELL, JR.*

DESPITE STATE LAWS AND STANDARDS for operation for local and county jails, enormous discretion is left to administrators in defining the conditions of incarceration. They have far-reaching and exceptional powers in the day-to-day operation of the institution and in control over the activities of the inmate. This power is exercised in relative privacy behind institutional walls and away from the eyes of the public. It is exercised over persons whose individual power and means of redress is weak and over a group whose collective power is fragmented or completely atomized.

> This discretionary power determines how the jail inmate will live during the term of his confinement; how he is fed and clothed; whether he sleeps in a cell or a dormitory; whether he spends his days in a cell or in relative freedom;—whether he has access to mailing or visiting privileges. They define rules of conduct and penalties for violation of such rules.[1]

Traditionally, few external controls have been imposed on decisions in these areas. Legislation sets outside limitations but seldom provides guidelines for exercise of the vast discretion which remains. Courts have traditionally denied inmates petitions involving grievances on the grounds that institutional policy is generally beyond their jurisdiction.

---
*From *Federal Probation*, March, 1974.

But in recent years courts have been more ready to intervene.[2] The President's Commission on Law Enforcement and Administration of Justice reports:

> They have been more willing to consider on the merits, claims that prison authorities have denied prisoners decent medical care, or have imposed cruel and unusual punishment, or have violated prisoners' First Amendment Rights.[3]

However, there are limits to the extent to which courts alone can guarantee fair and humane treatment during incarceration. One means of creating external review of prisoner grievances and most likely reducing the necessity of court intervention would be the appointment of a jail ombudsman.

The ombudsman concept has gained favor and interest in corrections over the past several years, however, is not a "new" idea. In 1777, prison reformer John Howard suggested:

> Finally, the care of a prison is too important to be left wholly to a gaoler, paid indeed for his attendance, but often tempted by his passions, or interest, to fail in his duty. For every prison there should be an *inspector* appointed; either by his colleagues in the magistracy or by Parliament—The inspector should make his visit once each week, changing his days—HE SHOULD SPEAK TO EACH PRISONER, HEAR ALL COMPLAINTS, AND IMMEDIATELY CORRECT WHAT HE FINDS MANIFESTLY WRONG: WHAT HE DOUBTS OF, HE MAY REFER TO HIS BRETHEREN IN OFFICE, AT THEIR NEXT MEETING.[4]

Tibbles, in *Ombudsmen for American Prisons,* envisions the ombudsman as an independent, external, impartial and expert handler of citizen complaints against governmental agencies, who is easily accessible by the citizenry.[5]

> He is an individual . . . who, upon receiving a complaint from a citizen alleging governmental abuse or occasionally upon his own motion, investigates and intervenes on behalf of the citizen with the governmental authority concerned. He does not act in an adversary fashion, but remains independent of both the citizen and government as a mediator or intermediary. He attempts to see all sides of the dispute and bring a satisfactory resolution to the citizen's complaint.[6]

A jail ombudsman should have access to all inmates and should investigate all complaints which are not patently frivolous. Where, in his judgment, redress of grievances is warranted, he should seek the assistance of the appropriate official who can remedy the situation.

An ombudsman should not restrict his activities to complaints regarding conditions in the jail but rather act in his official capacity on all warranted complaints relating to inmates who by their circumstances are unable to act. An ombudsman could accomplish a great deal on behalf of inmates with a short telephone call to inmates' families, welfare agencies, public defender staffs, etc.

Many times the complaints of inmates stem from oversights and failures in communication. In these cases the ombudsman can simply bring the problem to the attention of the appropriate agency and have it corrected.

These services should create an atmosphere in which the emotional strain of incarceration and the feeling of helplessness by the inmate is reduced to a minimum.

THE OMBUDSMAN AND THE JUDICIARY

The authors of *Model Rules and Regulations on Prisoner Rights and Responsibilities* view the complaint mechanisms of the ombudsman and the judiciary as if it were an electrical circuit in parallel.

> You have the courts which carry some current of complaints, but which have a very high resistance, very low accessibility, high expense to the community; whereas, the ombudsman has a very low resistance, his accessibility is automatic, immediate and universal, and so you would be considering that a lot of complaints would be able to flow through that channel, and in so doing you're obviously going to protect the courts from being overburdened with a lot of trivial things.[7]

The ability of the ombudsman to separate legitimate grievances from unfounded complaints will be an invaluable service to the courts and other officials and agencies, and the fact that the ombudsman refers to these officials only cases which he has investigated and found meritorious will increase his credibility and chances for success.[8]

SELECTION OF THE OMBUDSMAN

The selection of an ombudsman is extremely important. His personal characteristics must include integrity and the ability to act impartially. His success or failure depends upon his ability to deal with both the inmate population and with the courts and other public officials.

Robert Force states, "The Prison Ombudsman needs the qualities of intelligence, persistence, maturity and tact. His success will relate directly to the extent he can gain the respect and confidence of the officials with whom he must deal. He must rely on an intelligent, persistent, quiet persuasion and not rabble-rousing."[9]

Kantz, et al., state, "Moreover, the viability as well as the credibility of his position is dependent upon his ability to remain independent, otherwise, his effectiveness is lost."[10]

Model Rules and Regulations on Prisoner's Rights and Responsibilities delineates the scope of the ombudsman's function into four categories:[11]

1. The ombudsman shall function as an information source for both inmates and corrections personnel.
2. His office shall primarily serve as a grievance-response mechanism.
3. The ombudsman may initiate his own investigations.
4. He will have a reporting as well as an investigative function.

Force suggests that the ombudsman have no enforcement powers. In order to redress grievances he would have to rely on his powers of persuasion and the good faith and sense of justice possessed by the various public support for his recommendations by exposing problems to the public.[12]

SUMMARY

The appointment by each metropolitan or large county jail of a jail ombudsman to act in behalf of jail inmates to redress grievances would serve to minimize the need for court intervention, to reduce tension among inmates by providing them with a grievance mechanism, and to create an atmosphere of fairness and humanity in the local correctional facilities.

The ombudsman is not an adversary, rather he is an intermediary and mediator between inmate and jail staff. As defined by Tibbles, he is . . . "an independent, external, impartial, and expert handler of complaints . . . who is easily accessible."[13]

REFERENCES

1. President's Commission on Law Enforcement and Administration of Justice: *Task Force Report: Corrections,* p. 84.
2. See generally Barkin, "The Emergence of Correctional Law and the Awareness of the Rights of the Convicted," 45 Neb. L.R. 699 (1966); Note, "Constitutional Rights of Prisoners: The Developing Law," 110 U. Pa. L. Rev. 985 (1962).
3. President's Commission, op. cit., p. 84.
4. Howard, John: *State of Prisons, 1777.*
5. Tibbles, "Ombudsman for American Prisons," 48 N.D.L. Rev. 383, 426-427 (1972).
6. *Ibid.,* p. 427.
7. Krantz, Sheldon, et al.: *Model Rules and Regulations on Prisoner's Rights and Responsibilities.* West Publishing Company, 1973, pp. 204-205.
8. Force, Robert: *Final Report on the Special Master. In Re* Orleans Parish Prison, 1972.
9. *Ibid.,* at p. 46.
10. Krantz, et al., *supra,* at 205.
11. *Ibid.,* p. 206.
12. Force, Robert: *op. cit.,* at p. 45.
13. Tibbles, *op. cit.,* at p. 426.

CHAPTER 13

DETOXIFICATION CENTER: A PUBLIC HEALTH ALTERNATIVE FOR THE "DRUNK TANK"

RICHARD J. TATHAM[*]

DURING THE PAST TWO DECADES alcoholism has broken away from its reputation as an "unmentionable" health problem and has become a household topic of considerable popularity. New definitions, proclamations, resolutions, legislation, and court decisions concerning alcoholism are appearing with increasing regularity. The average citizen is now quite familiar with the illness concept of alcoholism and readily accepts the claim that alcoholism is the nation's third major public health problem.

One might easily conclude from these observations that the alcoholic is now routinely accepted by all appropriate health facilities just as any other sick person. However, a quick look around promptly exposes this myth. In fact, alcoholics are excluded, by policy or practice, from most *general* health services; and *specialized* alcoholism treatment resources fall far short of meeting the existing need. Today, in an age of enlightenment and scientific achievement, it is a tragic fact that more alcoholics are "treated" in jails than in all the health facilities combined.

---

[*]Reprinted from *Federal Probation,* Dec., 1969.

TIME FOR CHANGE

A society that can solve the technological problems of space flight to the moon surely has the capability to solve its social problems at home. To do so may require a revision of outdated moralistic concepts and new directions of scientific inquiry, but with high priority and adequate support, it would be overly pessimistic to assume otherwise.

One serious social problem of mammoth proportions is public intoxication. As a facet of the alcoholism problem, it is long overdue for an objective study. Inebriety is viewed by society with ambivalence, irrationality or indifference, depending upon circumstances. As a result, laws and customs concerning intoxication often are unrealistic and in conflict. Are there ways to deal with insobriety which will more adequately protect and benefit both the individual and society? This is a central question which needs to be explored and one which was set forth in a 1966 proposal for a detoxification demonstration project submitted to the U.S. Justice Department's Office of Law Enforcement Assistance by the District of Columbia Department of Public Health.

A favorable climate had been set by various recommendations spanning many years. In 1966, two especially significant events occurred. On March 31, the U.S. Court of Appeals for the District of Columbia Circuit handed down a decision in the case of DeWitt Easter which held that alcoholics should be treated and not punished.[1] Then the *Report of the President's Commission on Crime in the District of Columbia* asserted that "persons who are so drunk that they cannot care for themselves should be taken into protective custody by the police and taken immediately to an appropriate health facility."[2]

A NEW APPROACH

It had been traditional in the District of Columbia for the police to assume the burden of arresting and holding intoxicated persons for court or bail until sober. Local laws concerning drunkenness dealt with the state of intoxication as a matter of antisocial behavior which was voluntary and therefore criminal. Notwithstanding the occurrence of nausea, hallucinosis, delerium tremens, seizures, and a variety of other medical symptoms, the police were expected to provide restraint and protection in what was almost universally known as the "drunk tank." This procedure served at least one purpose—it kept the streets, alleys, and other public places free from unsightly "drunks." There were few citizens or public servants who questioned the legal or ethical implications of the system. In an effort to probe alternatives to this procedure, the two-year Department of Justice grant permitted the Health Department to initiate a detoxification project.

Pending the construction of a permanent building, a temporary twenty-five-bed detoxification center was opened on the grounds of the District of Columbia General Hospital in November, 1967. Since there were no detoxification centers operating in the United States at the time the project was planned,[3] the European "Sobering-Up Station" served as a concept model. Based on review of the European experience, the D.C. Health Department made several early decisions:

1. A detoxification center should deal with simple intoxication only. Seriously ill patients, even though intoxicated, should be treated in a fully equipped hospital or other appropriate medical or psychiatric facility. To put it another way, the Center should function as an improvement over the police drunk tank for simple intoxication cases but not as a hospital substitute for inebriates who are seriously ill.

2. Efficiency of a detoxification center should be enhanced by the architecture of the building in order that the patients might be managed adequately at a cost considerably less than that of a general hospital.

3. The center should be located in an area easily available to both patients and police.

4. In order to encourage patients to cooperate and obtain the maximum benefit from their treatment, there should be nothing in the psychological or physical environment of a center reminiscent of jail.

5. A center should function as an integrated component of a comprehensive alcoholism treatment system rather than as an isolated facility.

6. Voluntary patients should be served as well as those brought in by the police.

These basic principles were accepted by the Justice Department and a two-year grant of $281,440 was awarded in 1966 to help fund the project.

THE PROGRAM

Under the Detoxification Center's director, who is a registered nurse, a staff of twenty-nine full-time and two part-time employees provide around-the-clock emergency care for inebriates. The maximum capacity of the Center is sixty patients. Patients arrive alone, under arrest, or with a friend, family member, or representative of Alcoholics Anonymous. Almost half of the patients admitted thus far have voluntarily applied without any formal referral. An additional 21 percent were brought in by the police either under arrest or informally. The remaining 29 percent were referred from various Health Department and other community agencies.

As a part of the admission screening, all patients are asked to cooperate with the staff and program. Neither the staffing pattern nor the facility are appropriate for unmanageable patients—these must be transferred elsewhere. Interestingly, very few patients have presented a problem in this regard.

Every effort is made to keep activities at the Center calm and well-organized in order to give the arriving patients a quiet welcome. Admitting procedures are brief and flexible. If a patient cannot answer all questions immediately, the admitting clerk checks back later. The shift nurse, who is experienced in working with alcoholics, quickly screens each patient for injuries or symptoms of problems which may be beyond the range of services offered at the Center. The patient is then toileted, bathed, and prepared for bed in an acute-care area. Medication is given from standing orders. The entire admission procedure rarely takes longer than twelve minutes.

When the patient is able, after three to twelve hours, he is moved into the self-care area. There he is free to move about, attend the dining room, visit the lounge, and have light refreshments. A physician is always on call and visits the Center each afternoon. He examines patients, prescribes medication necessary to avert withdrawal symptoms, and notes any medical problems needing further attention. A specially prepared high-protein diet, and vitamin and mineral supplements are provided.

Noncompulsory introductory meetings of Alcoholics Anonymous are held frequently and attended by up to 80 percent of the patients. Neighborhood clergymen conduct Sunday church services which also are well-attended.

A subprofessional social service worker determines the patients' immediate needs for clothing, food, lodging and funds. Those items judged to be beneficial to the patients' well-being are secured whenever possible. The entire staff tries to impress the patients with the desirability of entering or re-entering a psychiatrically oriented alcoholism aftercare program as in- or outpatients. For those who are interested, transfers are made to the Department's Rehabilitation Center for Alcoholics at Occoquan, Virginia, or to one of four community mental health centers. On the recommendation of the physician, referrals are also made for necessary medical-surgical care.

Patients are encouraged to stay at the Detoxification Center up to five days, but are permitted to leave earlier if they insist. The average stay is 3.78 days. When they do leave, their clothes have been washed and pressed in the patient laundry area, or replaced from a supply of used clothing kept at the Center. Pride in appearance is an almost universal trait of patients being discharged.

The demonstrated advantages of the Detoxification Center over a "drunk tank" include:

1. Better medical and nursing care;
2. More positive environment in which to motivate patients to do something about their drinking and related problems;
3. Greater emphasis on good nutrition;
4. More encouragement for patient utilization of supportive community health and social welfare resources upon discharge.

STATUTORY REVISION

Fortunately, the Detoxification Center was in operation and had accumulated considerable experience when the District of Columbia Alcoholic Rehabilitation Act of 1967 (P.L. 90-452) was signed into law on August 3, 1968. This Act repealed some existing statutes and required that:

> . . . any person who is intoxicated in public (and who is not conducting himself in such a manner as to endanger the safety of

himself or of any other person or of property) (1) may be taken or sent to his home or to a public or private health facility or; (2) if not taken or sent to his home or such facility under paragraph (1), shall be taken to a detoxification center. (Sec. 4)

This new law comes to direct grips with drunkenness and its relationship to the criminal system by unequivocally defining simple intoxication as a public health responsibility. Thus, the very procedure being demonstrated in the Detoxification Center became a legal requirement even before the demonstration project was completed!

Under the new law, drunkenness, *per se,* is no longer against the law. A "happy drunk," as the local police have labeled him, is simply taken into protective custody and delivered to the Detoxification Center. A "dangerous drunk," i.e. one whose situation endangers the safety of himself, another person, or property, is subject to arrest, but is also taken to the Detoxification Center for treatment before further legal action (release or civil commitment for alcoholism treatment) is taken. Finally, at the discretion of the police, any intoxicated individual arrested for any misdemeanor or felony charge may be taken to the Detoxification Center before proceeding through the normal criminal route.

Without ambivalence or equivocation, intoxication in the District of Columbia is now viewed as an acute medical problem entitled to prompt treatment in lieu of or prior to criminal prosecution. Without a doubt, this represents a major social change in our community.

These new procedures do much more to protect and benefit the individual than the ambivalent, irrational or indifferent approaches of the past. In addition, society seems to be no less protected under the new procedures and may well benefit from the change also. The latter observation is mere conjecture at this point in time and should be subjected to careful program evaluation. If more alcoholics can be motivated efficiently to come to grips with their problems, succeed in arresting their uncontrolled drinking, and become more productive citizens, society will ultimately benefit.

CONCLUSION

Various groups in the District of Columbia have made studies and recommendations concerning drunken offenders over a rather prolonged period of time without noticeable results. Then a combination of events—a high status crime commission report, a favorable court decision, a new Federal funding program, an aroused public, and an interested health department—suddenly converged. This resulted in dramatic changes in local criminal and public health responsibilities and procedures.

While the ultimate impact of these changes has not yet been fully evaluated, the short-term results are benevolent and seem beneficial to both patient and community.

REFERENCES

1. U. S. Court of Appeals for the District of Columbia Circuit, No. 19365, *DeWitt Easter, Appellant,* v. *District of Columbia, Appellee,* March 31, 1966.
2. *Report of the President's Commission on Crime in the District of Columbia,* 1966, p. 494.
3. Detoxification Centers in St. Louis, New York City, Baltimore, and elsewhere were not yet in existence.

CHAPTER 14

WHY PRISONERS RIOT

VERNON FOX, PH.D.*

FINDING VALID, CONSISTENT and reliable information as to why prisoners riot defies most standard methods of gathering data on human behavior. Official reports and most articles on the subject focus on overcrowding, poor administration, insufficient financial support, political interference, lack of professional leadership, ineffective or nonexistent treatment programs, disparities in sentencing, poor and unjust parole policies, enforced idleness of prisoners, obsolete physical plant, and a small group of hard-core and intractable prisoners.[1] Psychological viewpoints focus on aggression and acting-out personalities in the prison population.[2] Yet, while all the conditions mentioned in the sociological approaches exist in most prisons, the majority have not experienced riot. Further, all major prisons hold aggressive, hostile, and acting-out people. This leads to concern as to why these factors have been identified as causes of riot when riots have occurred in a small minority of prisons.

An examination of official reports following riots discloses a similar propensity for generalities and platitudes regarding causes of riots. These same conditions are consistently identified as causes of riots almost anywhere. The purpose of official reports, of course,

---

*Reprinted from *Federal Probation*, March, 1971.

is political in the sense that they give assurance to the general public after a riot that the remaining power structure in the prison has analyzed the causes, taken corrective measures, and merits the confidence of the public in that their interests will be protected. Investigating committees from governors' offices, legislatures, or other political directions seek simplistic answers that seem to structure their interpretations in accordance with the best interests of their own identifications. Reinterpretation of the situation has to occur frequently. Sometimes the focus is on the predisposing causes, such as poor morale among inmates fostered by poor food or injudicious or misunderstood paroling policies. Sometimes, it is more aimed at the precipitating causes, such as a confrontation between an officer and some inmates. Sometimes, it has been explained as an attempted mass escape that the administration successfully contained.

Many consultants who are invited from outside the jurisdiction as impartial experts tend to protect the person or group who invited them, which is ethical and logical. Diplomatic writing is a consultant's art. Other consultants invited from outside generally are not sufficiently well acquainted with the nuances and underlying intricacies of the power structure to understand as well as they might all the factors entering into a local situation. Whether the governor or the legislative committee chairman of an opposite political party was the source of the invitation seems to make a difference in the tone of the report. An impartial investigator must be aware of the political climate and what will and what will not be accepted in some political settings. Some reports have been rejected by political leaders, others have been used for political purposes, while many have just been shelved. In any case, the use of these reports for finding the real causes of riots must be tempered pending corroboration from other sources. Frequently, though, these reports may set the tone for further interpretation by the news media, political leaders, and writers of documentaries.

Identifying the causes of riot, then, is tenuous when official reports or statements *after* the riot are considered alone. Clearer vision can be obtained from news reports written *during* the riot. In decreasing order of validity and reliability, the materials that comprise this presentation are from (1) news stories during twenty serious riots since 1940 as reported in *The New York Times* during the action, (2) this writer's experience during the Michigan prison riot in 1952, (3) lengthy discussions with inmates involved in four prison riots, (4) conversations with prison personnel involved in seven prison riots, (5) literature concerning prison riots, (6) official reports and official statements *after* the riot, and (7) general literature on aggression, civil disturbances and violence.

Causes must be divided into *predisposing* causes and *precipitating* causes. Just as in civil disobedience, there has to be a "readiness" to riot. Then, there has to be a "trigger." Too frequently, the predisposing causes have been used as causes for prison riots and the precipitating causes have ben identified as causes for civil disorder. Neither is a cause in itself. The total social situation, with emphasis on the interaction or lack of it between dominant people and subjugated people, either in the prison or in the ghetto, must be evaluated to determine why people riot. It cannot be based simplistically in overcrowding, political interference, lack of treatment programs, or any other simple answer.

PATTERNS OF RIOT

The way to make a bomb is to build a strong perimeter and generate pressure inside. Similarly, riots occur in prisons where oppressive pressures and demands are generated in the presence of strong custodial containment. Riots are reported more frequently from custodially oriented prisons. Even the riot in 1962 in the progressive and relatively relaxed District of Columbia Youth Center at Lorton, Virginia, involved suppression, real or imagined, of the Black Muslims.

Riots are spontaneous—not planned—detonated by a spontaneous event. The inmates know who has the weapons and who has the force. The inmates know that no administration ever has to negotiate with them. Planned disturbances end in sitdown strikes, slowdowns, hunger strikes, and self-inflicted injury. Escapes do not begin with disturbances unless they are planned as a distraction, though the disturbance may end in escape attempts. The spontaneous event that detonates the riot may be almost anything from a fight in the yard that expands, someone heaving a tray in the dining hall, to a homosexual tricking a new officer to open his cell, as happened in the Michigan riot in 1952. Violent riots must happen spontaneously. Otherwise, they would not happen. There has to be pressure, though, that builds up the predisposition or readiness to riot and a spontaneous precipitating event to trigger or detonate the riot.

Riots tend to pattern in five stages, four during the riot and one afterward. First, there is a period of undirected violence like the exploding bomb. Secondly, inmate leaders tend to emerge and organize around them a group of ringleaders who determine inmate policy during the riot. Thirdly, a period of interaction with prison authority, whether by negotiation or by force, assists in identifying the alternatives available for the resolution of the riot. Fourthly, the surrender of the inmates, whether by negotiation or by force, phases out the violent event. Fifthly, and most important from the political viewpoint, the investigations and administrative changes restore order and confidence in the remaining power structure by making "constructive changes" to regain administration control and to rectify the undesirable situation that produced the riot.

The first stage of the riot is characterized by an event that triggered the unbridled violence. The first stage is disorganized among the prisoners and, too frequently, among the prison staff as well. It is at this point that custodial force could alter the course of the riot but, in most instances, custody is caught by surprise and without adequate preparation so that there is little or no custodial reaction other than containment. As a result, the riot pattern is permitted by default to move to the second stage.

The second stage is when inmate leaders emerge and the administrative forces become organized. Inmate leaders who emerge from this violence are people who remain emotionally detached sufficiently so that they lend stability to the inmate group. They "don't panic." They "keep their cool." As a result, they attract around them lesser inmate leaders or "ringleaders" who, similarly, do not panic but need to be dependent upon "the boss." In this manner, an inmate leader can gather around him probably two to six "lieutenants," each with some delegated authority, such as watching hostages, preparing demands, and maintaining discipline in the rest of the inmate group. Further, the inmate leader, like most political leaders, takes a "middle-of-the-road" position where he can moderate the extremes and maintain communication. In a prison riot, some inmates want to kill the hostages. Other inmates want to give up and surrender to the administration. The inmate leader controls these two extremes in a variety of ways and stabilizes the group into a position in the center.

The third stage is a period of interaction between inmates and prison officials. It has taken several forms, though they can be classified generally into (1) negotiation and (2) force or threat of force. No administration has to negotiate with prisoners, but the chances for negotiation are greater when the prisoners hold hostages. The chances for force or threat of force are greater when the prisoners do not have hostages. In either case, the decision on the part of the inmates to surrender is subject to the general principles of group dynamics. When the inmate group is cohesive and their morale is good, the prisoners will maintain the riot situation, whether faced with force or negotiation. When the group cohesion begins to disintegrate by some inmates wanting to surrender, others wanting to retaliate, and the leadership wanting to maintain the status quo, the administration may manipulate it for an early surrender. This disintegration of group cohesion may be promoted by negotiation or by force or threat of force, depending upon the situation. In case of negotiation, the group cohesion is diminished by the administration's demonstrated willingness to negotiate and by the personality of the official negotiators who convey a feeling of trust and confidence. The group can be disintegrated, also, by gas, rifle fire, and artillery shelling, all of which have been used recently in American prison riots. The less destructive approach, of course, is to await disintegration of cohesion by periods of inaction that places strain to hold the group together on the leadership by fatigue and impatience. Faced with this situation, the leadership frequently has to look for an honorable way out of a disintegrating situation.

The fourth stage, or surrender, may be the inmates' giving up after being gassed and shot at, or they may surrender in an orderly way either after force or threat of force or by negotiation. Political interference at the wrong time in the prison riot can affect the total situation in terms of negotiation, surrender, and subsequent investigations and administrative decisions.

The fifth stage, that of investigations, consolidation of the remaining power structure, personnel and policy changes followed by political fall-out, is really the most important stage, since it sets policy for the prison and the system for years to come. Editorials and news commentators suggest solutions and interpretations. Administrators have to respond satisfactorily to pressures from interest groups. This is why "get tough" policies become important after riots, even though they tend to intensify the problems.

Riots do not occur in prisons or correctional institutions with exceedingly high morale. Neither do they occur in prisons where the morale is so low that the prisoners endure penal oppression in a docile manner or break their own legs and cut their own heel tendons. Riots occur in prisons where inmates have medium to high morale and where some conflict appears in the staff, probably between treatment and custodial philosophies, and probably when the program is in a state of transition from one type of procedures and objectives to another.

Riots occur in prisons where there is a tenuous balance between controlling behavior and changing behavior. If there is a full commitment to either, riots do not occur. The riot itself, however, results in a political decision to *control* behavior. Consequently, the behavior changing in treatment forces always loses in a riot, at least in the immediate future.

There is also a direct relationship between news coverage by the mass media and the incidence of demonstrations, riots, and civil disturbances.[3] This is one reason why riots tend to cluster in terms of time.

One of the factors that contributed to the prison insurrections of 1952 was the decision of the administration to reverse the drift toward greater inmate control.[4] Abuses of official rules were curbed, preferential treatment for favored prisoners was eliminated, and the social system of the prison was "reformed" in the direction of the image of what the free community thought a maximum-security institution should be.

DURING THE RIOT

Guidelines for action during the riot are important. The custodial staff is frequently untrained and the administration is just as frequently caught by surprise. Action during the riot has to be planned ahead of time and modified according to the situation.

During the first stage of a riot, the disorganized inmates could well be effectively faced with force. As a matter of fact, most riots appear to have been vulnerable to custodial force in the early stages because of the disorganization on the side of the inmates. If disorganization occurs on both sides, however, then the riot cannot be contained early. Immediate custodial action could have altered the course of several riots. The lack of training, preparation, or even expectation of riot has resulted in disorganization on both sides for hours.

During the second stage, after the inmates have organized and their leadership begins to emerge, there is the question as to whether force should be used. No prison administration ever needs to negotiate with rioting prisoners. The prisoners know this. If hostages are held, then negotiation becomes a real possibility, depending upon other factors. If the inmates holding the hostages are young, reformatory-type people with short sentences and have not already demonstrated their capability to kill, if they are psychiatric patients who cannot organize into a team, or if their majority can see parole sometime in the future, then negotiation is not necessary. In the Michigan riot of 1952, the decision to negotiate was not made until after the files of the inmates holding the hostages in fifteen-block had been reviewed. In that situation, negotiation was apparently the only way to save the lives of the hostages. This was supported by subsequent reports by inmates, nationally known clinical psychologists, and consultants brought in for impartial investigation.

The third stage of the riot is determined by the nature of the situation. If no hostages are held or if the prisoners holding hostages are not hardcore intractables with nothing to lose, then force or threat of force is appropriate. If the hostages are considered to be in serious danger, the administration is placed in a real dilemma in determining action because lives have to be considered in relation to public and internal reaction and consequences. If waiting for fatigue to reduce the cohesion of the rebellious inmate group will accomplish the objective, then force is not necessary.

The fourth stage of the riot is the surrender. The regaining of custodial control is all that is needed. Any further action beyond the basic need has to be for public consumption or for the satisfaction of the prison administration.

The fifth stage of the riot is the aftermath where investigations, reinterpretations, and scapegoats are involved. There is not much the prison administration can do about this because the real power lies in the political structure. Free movement of newsmen and free access to information, both inmates and staff, is the only logical approach to take during this period. In this way, the administration can demonstrate that it is attempting to hide nothing, that it recognizes it has problems, and is openly and honestly seeking the best solutions.

In summary, official reaction to riot is dependent upon the situation. As in judo, the reaction is determined by the action of the adversary. No negotiation is needed where no hostages are held or where they might be held by short-term prisoners not considered to be dangerous. Out-waiting might be an approach in doubtful situations. An overshow of force is becoming decreasingly effective in American society and it invites unnecessary derision from some segments of the public.

ADMINISTRATIVE DO'S AND DONT'S

Discretion, rather than negotiation or force, is at issue while handling a riot. A basic principle of police work or any other type of social control in a democratic society is to use the minimum amount of force and destruction needed to accomplish the objectives.[5]

Discretion is based on knowledge. Consequently, the first approach for a correctional administrator to improve his program is to increase the educational level of his staff by more selective recruitment and by in-service training. In modern democratic society, in-service training should be directed toward the social and behavioral sciences. This can be achieved by bringing neighboring junior colleges and universities into the educational program of the prison.[6] An understanding and knowledgeable prison staff from the custodial employee to the warden is important in the discretionary or decision-making process. It is this staff that determines whether a confrontation occurs or is avoided and, if it occurs, how it will be handled or accommodated. This is why they need to know social problems, personality development and problems, criminology and correctional procedures, as well as the law, particularly as it relates to civil rights.

The correctional officer is the key to riot prevention, although a rough and harsh custodial lieutenant, captain, or deputy warden can use policies and behavior to neutralize the good work of a hundred officers. The entire custodial force has to be treatment-oriented, just as the entire treatment staff has to be aware of custodial problems, in order to emerge with an effective correctional program.

Readiness to riot results from the predisposing causes, such as bad food, oppressive custodial discipline, sadistic staff quick to write disciplinary charges against inmates, and general punitive attitude by administration and line personnel. The precipitating cause that "triggers" the riot is very seldom the real cause. As previously mentioned, a bomb is made by constructing a strong perimeter or casing and generating pressure inside. It blows at its weakest point, but it has to be detonated. The detonation is not the "cause" of the explosion, although it "triggered" it.

During the riot, the inmates want to smash the system that keeps them hopeless, anonymous, and in despair, and they will destroy at random.[7] They become so alienated from society that they regard violence as right and proper. Good treatment programs and an accepting custodial staff tend to reduce this problem. A relaxed atmosphere in a prison that avoids this alienation is most important for the eventual correctional objective and to avoid riots.

How to achieve a relaxed atmosphere is sometimes difficult for the administrator because it appears that he is "taking sides." Custodial personnel are generally concerned with good discipline, which is sometimes interpreted as "nipping problems in the bud" and is translated into overreaction to minor offenses and oppressive custodial control. Many treatment personnel, on the other hand, are in a relaxed atmosphere because it tends to lower the inmates' defenses and permit casework and psychotherapy to be better achieved. The inmates, of course, find the relaxed atmosphere more comfortable, so they favor it. This places the treatment staff "on the side of the inmates," although for different reasons. It is sometimes difficult for an administrator to interpret to the custodial staff the reasons for promoting a relaxed atmosphere in the prison. This is another reason for providing education and in-service training in behavior and social problems to all staff.

Good food, plentiful and well-prepared, is important to maintaining a prison. Napoleon's famous remark that an army marches on its stomach could be applied to any group of men. Food becomes a primary source of pleasure to men deprived of many of the comforts of normal life. Consequently, the prison administration cannot realistically compute food costs on the basis of nutritional needs alone. The emotional needs are important. An institutional program can make a lot of mistakes if it has a good kitchen that provides plenty of food. Conversely, food is a tangible item on which can be focused all the discontents and deprivations of the prison. Many riots have begun in or near the dining room. Food simply becomes a tangible substitute target for other complaints. Consequently, an administrator should spend a little extra time and effort to find a good steward to handle food services and pay special attention to the food budget.

Despite the other abuses, riots do not occur in prisons that are essentially run by inmates. There are some Southern prisons where selected inmates carry guns and guard other inmates. All the generalities attributed to riot causation exist, but no riots have occurred in these prisons. This is because the inmate leaders have a vested interest in the status quo and will protect it.

Inmate leadership is present in all prisons, as leadership is present in all groups of people. The constructive use of inmate leadership is an obvious way to avoid riots. Some type of inmate self-government that involves honest and well-supervised elections of inmate representatives to discuss problems, make recommendations, and, perhaps, even take some responsibilities from the administration could be helpful. Possibilities might be some control of those activities related to formalized inmate activities like manuscripts sent to potential publishers, pricing hobbycraft items for sale, or processing inmate activities like Alcoholics Anonymous or chess clubs. In an era when movements to unionize prisoners appear, such as in West Germany and Sweden, and when litigation initiated by inmates result in court rulings that change conditions and procedures within the prisons, it is in the interest of the administration to know the inmates' thinking and their action. In any case, downward communication is not enough.

The pattern could be taken from student government functioning under a university administration. It could be taken from a civilian government operating under military occupation by the victors after a war, such as those civilian governments in Germany and Japan after World War II. The pattern in the Federal Bureau of Prisons and some other systems has been the inmate council, where elected inmates discuss problems and appropriate policies with the prison administration, making recommendations and suggestions. A suggestion box system for inmates might be instituted if other approaches appear to be too innovative. Regardless of how it is organized, it should promote upward and downward communication between inmates and prison administration, and it should provide the inmate leadership with a vested interest in the status quo.

In summary, good communication can avoid the predisposing causes of riot. Whether by inmate council, inmate self-government programs, suggestion boxes, or free up-and-down communication of any type, knowledge by the inmate leadership of situations and their reasons can eliminate most predisposing causes. Establishment of the therapeutic community where inmates take responsibility for the improvement of other inmates, such as in the Provo Experiment in Utah in 1958-1964, the Minnesota State Training School at Red Wing, and some other places, would also provide a vested interest for the inmates in the institution and its program, as well as a constructive attitude. Raising the educational level of the prison staff, especially the correctional officers, would reduce the predisposing causes. Their better understanding of personality development and social problems would provide them with the capacity for discretion that would, in turn, reduce the precipitating causes. Prison riots can be eliminated when upward and downward communication, combined with discretionary use of authority, reduces the probability of serious confrontation that should not have to occur in a democratic society.

REFERENCES

1. A succinct and comprehensive review of the literature is found in Clarence Schrag, "The Sociology of Prison Riots," *Proceedings of*

the American Correctional Association, 1960. New York, 1961, pp. 136-146.
2. For example, see the late Dr. Ralph Banay's excellent articles on causes of riots in *The New York Times,* July 26, 1959, sec. VI, p. 8; August 9, 1959, sec. VI, p. 2; August 16, 1959, sec. VI, p. 72.
3. Lange, David L., Baker, Robert K., and Ball, Sandra J.: *Violence and the Media.* Washington, D.C., United States Government Printing Office, November 1969, p. 614.
4. Sykes, Gresham M.: *The Society of Captives.* Princeton, Princeton University Press, 1958, p. 144.
5. See George E. Berkley, *The Democratic Policeman.* Boston, Beacon Press, 1969.
6. For suggested curricula, see Vernon Fox, *Guidelines for Correctional Programs in Community and Junior Colleges,* American Association of Junior Colleges, Washington, D.C., 1969, and "The University Curriculum in Corrections," *Federal Probation,* September 1959. Also see *Criminology and Corrections Programs,* Joint Commission on Correctional Manpower and Training, Washington, D.C., 1968.
7. "Violence and Corrections," *The Correctional Trainer,* Southern Illinois University, Carbondale, Vol. I, No. 4, Spring, 1970, pp. 56-91.

SECTION FOUR

LEGAL RIGHTS OF PRISONERS AND MINIMUM JAIL STANDARDS

CHAPTER 15

THE EVOLUTION OF JUDICIAL INVOLVEMENT

Mike Place and David A. Sands*

THE TRADITION OF NONINTERVENTION

UNTIL VERY RECENTLY, federal courts had steadfastly and unanimously refused to redress the grievances of inmates in state penal institutions.[1] It was apparently felt that acting on prisoners' complaints would involve the courts in the "internal management" of the state's penal system—something which the courts thought they should avoid for many reasons.[2] First was the "separation of powers" principle, i.e., since penal institutions are administered under authority of the executive branch of government, the judicial branch should not interfere. One court stated it this way: "The prison system is under the administration of the Attorney General ... and not ... the district courts."[3] Derived from separation of powers were two other rationalizations for noninvolvement. One was the court's lack of expertise in penology. The other, perhaps more fundamental, was the fear that judicial intervention in this area would subvert prison discipline and undermine the authority of prison officials.[4] Additional difficulties were presented when federal courts were faced with complaints from state prisoners,

---
*Reprinted by permission of the *Buffalo Law Review*, Spring, 1972. (Copyright ©1972 by *Buffalo Law Review*.)

because intervention by federal courts was thought to violate fundamental principles of federalism.[5] These principles proscribed federal intervention in matters solely the concern of the state, as prisons and jails were thought to be. Less often articulated, but probably just as influential on the thinking of the courts, was the fear of being deluged with prisoners' complaints which could absorb far too much judicial time and attention.[6] Probably underlying this overworked justification for a court's unwillingness to grapple with difficult problems was a belief that many, if not most, complaints by prisoners would be overstated if not completely baseless in fact. Though these reasons were seldom if ever scrutinized for their cogency and force, they were asserted time and time again until this judicial tendency was dubbed the "hands-off" doctrine by a document prepared for the Federal Bureau of Prisons.[7] Thus, the courts stated the position this way: "We think that it is well-settled that it is not the function of the courts to superintend the treatment and discipline of prisoners in penitentiaries, but only to deliver from imprisonment those who are illegally confined."[8] Solace in this position was taken from a statement by the Supreme Court in *Price v. Johnston:* "Lawful incarceration brings about the necessary withdrawal or limitation of many privileges and rights, a retraction justified by the considerations underlying our penal system."[9] Thus, complaints about violations of rights were dismissed as being the necessary consequence of incarceration, and the only question left for judicial determination was the legality of that incarceration. Prisoners' remedies were consequently limited to seeking writs of habeas corpus.

A good example of the ineffectiveness of the habeas corpus remedy was *Ex Parte Pickens,*[10] decided in 1951. Pickens, along with forty other prisoners, thirty-six of whom were being held for trial, was confined to a room twenty-seven feet square, heated by an ancient coal stove, with fewer than twenty bunks, virtually no ventilation, and one unsanitary latrine. Pickens, one of those being held for trial, sought a writ of habeas corpus, on grounds that his imprisonment was illegal, being in violation of the eighth amendment's prohibition against cruel and unusual punishment. Recognizing "that the protection of the Eighth Amendment extends not only to those convicted but to those held for trial,"[11] the court nevertheless denied the writ of habeas corpus. And though the conditions were "rightly to be deplored and condemned by all people with humane instincts,"[12] it did not constitute cruel and unusual punishment because: (1) solving the problems was beyond the authority of those responsible for the jail; (2) those responsible had tried unsuccessfully to get additional funds from the legislature in order to make improvements; (3) the jail was the only holding facility near the place of trial; and (4) the conditions imposed would not be deemed cruel and unusual punishment by every other civilized society—the then most commonly employed standard in judging the bounds of acceptable punishment under the eighth amendment. We have enumerated these reasons because they repeatedly arise as the most frequent obstacles to effective court action. The inadequacies of the habeas corpus remedy and the protection afforded by the eighth amendment are readily apparent.

THE EROSION OF "HANDS-OFF"—RECENT DEVELOPMENTS

The abrogation of the hands-off doctrine began with the Supreme Court's ruling in *Monroe v. Pape*[13] that exhaustion of state remedies was not a condition precedent to a federal court's accepting jurisdiction under the federal Civil Rights Act of 1871. Shortly thereafter, in *Robinson v. California*,[14] the Court ruled that the eighth amendment did apply to the states through the fourteenth amendment. Finally, *Cooper v. Pate*[15] dispelled any remaining doubt that a prisoner in a state institution could bring an action in federal court under the Civil Rights Act. This history was traced and relied upon in *Wright v. McMann*[16] to reverse and remand the dismissal of a complaint by a state prisoner that various conditions and treatment constituted cruel and unusual punishment.

By 1967, the hands-off doctrine, though still surviving, had been weakened. Exceptions to the doctrine could now exist, and the reformulation was stated as follows:

> The matter of the internal management of prisons or correctional institutions is vested in and rests with the heads of those institutions operating under statutory authority, and their acts and administration of prison discipline and overall operation of the institution are not subject to court supervision or control, *absent most unusual circumstances or absent a violation of a constitutional right.*[17]

This is a significant departure from the rule as previously stated.

Rather than limiting the inquiry to the legality of the incarceration, the federal courts could now, in certain circumstances, take action to correct flagrant abuses or violations of constitutional rights.[18] It is hardly surprising, then, that many avenues were explored in an attempt to establish violations of the constitutional rights of prisoners.

Following the lead of *Wright v. McMann*,[19] the cruel and unusual punishment clause of the eighth amendment was a logical place to begin. At least one reason why the eighth amendment approach appeared productive was because, "[t]he Amendment must draw its meaning from the evolving standards of decency that mark the progress of a maturing society."[20] It was further recognized that the words of the amendment are "not precise, and that their scope is not static."[21] Thus, what was not cruel and unusual punishment for Pickens in 1951 might be cruel and unusual punishment today.

The eighth amendment approach was taken by inmates of the Arkansas penitentiary system in *Jackson v. Bishop*,[22] where an injunction was sought to bar use of a strap as a disciplinary measure. Then Circuit Judge Blackmun, in delivering the opinion of the court, repeated the standard litany in support of the hands-off doctrine, but then stressed that the federal courts will not hesitate to grant relief where violations of fundamental rights are asserted and proved.[23] Here, the court found that the factual showing of cruel and unusual punishment established the violation of a constitutional right, and therefore, the injunction was issued.

A similar eighth amendment approach was used by prisoners of the Arkansas state prison again when they sought to have various other practices and *conditions* declared unconstitutional. Ruling in favor of the inmates, the court said: "However constitutionally tolerable the Arkansas system may have been in former years, it simply will not do today as the Twentieth Century goes into his [sic] eighth decade."[24] Importantly, it was the living conditions themselves which were being found unconstitutional. The court put it this way:

> In the Court's estimation *confinement itself* within a given institution may amount to a cruel and unusual punishment prohibited by the Constitution where the confinement is characterized by conditions and practices so bad as to be shocking to the conscience of

reasonably civilized people even though a particular inmate may never personally be subject to any disciplinary action.[25]

Thus, the rights of these prisoners were being violated by simply subjecting them to the filth and other indignities which characterized the Arkansas prisons.

Given this approach, the logical, indeed mandatory, next step had to be taken—to apply this standard to state jails. Not only were conditions in the state jails just as bad if not worse than in the prisons, but the people in the jails were, for the most part, pretrial detainees—presumably innocent under our system of justice. For them, punishment of *any* kind, whether it be cruel and unusual or not, is totally unjustifiable. If some punishment must be considered a necessary, to some even desirable, part of our penal system, and thus may be justifiable for convicted criminals, it is certainly not appropriate for innocent people who are only awaiting trial in jail probably because they could not afford bail. This was recognized in *Hamilton v. Love*,[26] an action brought by the inmates of Arkansas' Pulaski County Jail. Though the state challenged maintenance of the suit in federal court, they were overruled. The jail was inspected by the court, and the utter inadequacy of the facilities was then stipulated by the parties. Noting the irony that the lot of those awaiting trial appeared to be worse than those convicted and serving sentences, the court stated that the conditions for pretrial detention must not only be equal to, but superior to, those permitted for convicted prisoners, and that, generally, the holding function, which is constitutionally permissible, must be accomplished in the least restrictive way possible.[27] Furthermore, the equal protection clause of the fourteenth amendment prohibited classifying detainees with those who had already been convicted of a crime. After opening up this special avenue for detainees, the court issued orders setting a maximum inmate capacity for the jail and requiring the correction of the specified conditions. It sought to insure compliance by threatening to entirely prohibit detention if it could not be done in accordance with minimum constitutional standards.[28]

Many of the same considerations prompted the Fifth Circuit Court of Appeals to find in favor of a group of pretrial detainees in *Anderson v. Nosser*.[29] Here, plaintiffs were arrested for parading without a permit. After arrest, they were transported over 200 miles to the Mississippi State Penitentiary where they were forced to strip naked, consume a laxative, and were then confined eight men to a cell for up to thirty-six hours in temperatures of sixty to seventy degrees. The bunks in each cell were without mattresses or bedding of any kind; neither towels nor soap were provided. When the prisoners were finally released, they brought an action for damages under section 1 of the Civil Rights Act of 1871.[30] Defendants' primary defense [was] that the matter of plaintiffs' treatment . . . was one of internal prison discipline, not reviewable by the courts."[31] The court rejected this argument, after discussing the hands-off doctrine and the reason for it, and found serious violations of plaintiffs' constitutional rights under the eighth amendment.[32] In so finding, the court stated:

> We should be even more alert where one of the basic underpinnings of the "hands-off" policy is absent. Incarceration after conviction is imposed to punish, to deter, and to rehabilitate the convict. . . . Some freedom to accomplish these ends must of necessity be afforded prison personnel. Conversely, *where incarceration is imposed prior to conviction, deterrence, punishment, and retribution are not legitimate functions of the incarcerating officials. Their role is but a temporary holding operation, and their necessary freedom of action is concomitantly diminished*[33]

The implications of this statement and these rulings are significant for both the hands-off doctrine and the constitutional rights of pretrial detainees. The hands-off doctrine will have very limited application to actions brought by pretrial detainees because what the incarcerating officials may do is restricted to what is required to perform their "temporary holding function." Any deviation from this will be considered a violation of the pretrial detainee's rights, and therefore actionable. Constitutional rights and their violation are more easily established: their eighth amendment rights are violated by the imposition of conditions which are cruel and unusual; "even if that punishment were not cruel and unusual, it would still be proscribed for them, since it is imposed as a matter of form and routine, and without any semblance of due process or fair treatment",[34] and their rights to equal protection are violated when they are treated in the same way convicts are. Thus, "they are not to be subjected to any hardship except those absolutely requisite for the purpose of confinement only, and they retain all the rights of an ordinary citizen except the right to go and come as they please . . . ."[35] Accordingly, due process rights—the right not to be punished except by due process of law—can be added to those constitutional rights available to pretrial detainees as they seek to redress their grievances and escape the burden of horrendous living conditions.

Given the practices of and conditions in the vast majority of our nation's jails, there are important developments, a long way indeed from the *Pickens* case. The boundaries of legitimate action by penal officers have changed from freedom to impose any burden or restriction or maintain any condition under the guise of internal management, to permission to do only what is minimally necessary to hold a person for trial and maintain the order of the institution. One must hope that these legal advancements will begin to bring real improvements in the actual conditions which exist in jails, for they have not been significantly upgraded since the days of *Pickens*.

BLUEPRINT FOR INVOLVEMENT—THE EXAMPLE OF WAYNE COUNTY

If the courts can overcome the self-imposed restraints of the hands-off doctrine, there is good reason to believe that they can remedy some, though certainly not all, of the ills of our jails. Correcting abusive treatment by injunction, as was done in *Jackson v. Bishop*, is a straightforward judicial remedy. The more difficult questions regard conditions—the overcrowding; the unsanitary and unhealthy, deteriorating facilities; the lack of medical care and recreational facilities; and all the rest. Previously, these were considered to be part of the "internal management" of the institution, and therefore the exclusive province of the institution's officials—beyond the jurisdiction or the competence of the courts. It is understandable that the courts did not want to assume responsibility for the day-to-day running of the state's penal institutions. That concern was expressed as follows:

> It is hard to believe that persons . . . convicted of crime are at the mercy of the executive department and yet it is unthinkable that the judiciary should take over the operation of the places of detention and prisons. There must be some middle ground between these

extremes. The courts have proceeded very slowly toward defining it.[36]

Recently, such efforts have been made, and the boundaries of court action are being defined.

With the erosion of the hands-off doctrine came a recognition that when jail conditions deteriorate so that they become violations of laws or rights under the Constitution, they do become matters for the court, and the court should not shun the responsibility to fashion appropriate orders to remedy the situation. This was recognized and stated by the Fifth Circuit Court of Appeals in remanding the dismissal of a complaint about various conditions by prisoners on "Death Row": "Although federal courts are reluctant to interfere with the internal operation and administration of prisons, we believe that the allegations appellant has made go beyond matters exclusively of prison discipline and administration . . . ."[37] It hardly needs restating that leaky, unsanitary toilets; filthy food trays, dishes and utensils; lack of heat, bedding and medical facilities; and all the other ills have no relationship to maintenance of discipline and order within the institution. If anything, these are the very conditions which breed discontent and turmoil. They thus warrant judicial intervention when a demand for relief is properly made.

One method of relief, admittedly rather extreme, is the outright release of all pretrial detainees. The presumption of innocence protects the detainee from punishment of any kind. Thus when conditions of incarceration are so severe that they can only be considered punishment, incarceration becomes illegal. In this situation, courts have threatened the widespread use of habeas corpus—the traditional judicial remedy for illegal incarceration[38]—to release all pretrial detainees, or at least those in excess of a judicially fixed limit).[39] The repercussions for both the community and the court may be undesirable, however. Serious doubt must be entertained as to whether any amount of legal explanation could justify to the community the wholesale release of inmates awaiting trial. Further, habeas corpus has most commonly been a remedy sought by individual prisoners, on a case by case basis. Certainly hearing hundreds of pleas for habeas corpus on an individual basis could prove an awkward and burdensome form of relief. For these reasons, a more palatable method needs to be found.

One such method might base relief upon the standards set in state or city housing and sanitation codes. Recent litigation has determined that these standards apply to penal institutions and may be appropriate grounds upon which to base judicial relief.[40] A class action was brought by the inmates awaiting trial in Detroit's Wayne County Jail alleging various violations of their constitutional rights and alleging that the jail conditions were illegal as not conforming to state housing laws. Defendants, certain county and jail officials, set up the standard defenses: that they had no control over crowded conditions because the sheriff was required by law to accept all those referred to him; that appropriation of funds necessary to make needed repairs was beyond their control; that state or city housing, health or safety laws did not apply to the jail. The court rejected each of these contentions.

First. "The prisoners at the Wayne County Jail have a legal right to be housed in a physical facility which complies with the laws of our state and nation. This right is being infringed upon by the Defendants."[41] The court found that state housing laws establish minimum floor and air space requirements for all rooms, including those in jails,[42] and that the jail did not meet these requirements. Likewise, the plumbing, heating, ventilation, fire and sanitation facilities were found not to comply with minimum statutory standards. In fashioning a decree to remedy the situation, the court employed a unique approach. With regard to the overcrowding, it differentiated between the "rated capacity" of 1240 inmates, which included placing several men in single cells; "design capacity" of 813 men, the number for which the structure was designed and built; and "lawful inmate capacity" which was "clearly less" than 813, or the maximum number the jail could hold to meet all state and city statutory requirements.[43] Noting "that instant compliance with overcrowding laws could result in the release of roughly half of the prisoners now confined," and that doing this was probably inimical to the public interest, the court adopted a three-stage approach to reaching "lawful inmate capacity."[44] Thus, the court ordered that "rated capacity" had to be reached in ninety days: "[t]hree men to an undersized one-man cell has created an explosive situation which needs immediate defusing."[45] Nine months was given to achieve "design capacity," and two and a half years to reach "lawful inmate capacity." The court suggested numerous ways in which this could be done, including temporary use of federal or state facilities, leasing of additional facilities, greater use of pretrial release programs, and refusal to accept prisoners in excess of "rated capacity."[46]

Second. The court recognized that compliance with these decrees would cause inconvenience and require the expenditure of funds. But, on balance, the court thought the "considerations of convenience and thrift do not outweigh the rudiments of human decency. Inconvenience and expense are the inevitable price to be paid for many years of callous neglect. . . . As always, convenience and thrift must yield to the mandate of the law."[47] This statement represents an increasing awareness by the courts that they should not hesitate to order the expenditure of funds necessary to avoid the imposition of illegal or unconstitutional burdens. A federal court strongly stated the position as follows:

> Inadequate resources can never be an adequate justification for the state's depriving any person of his constitutional rights. If the state cannot obtain the resources to detain persons awaiting trial in accordance with minimum constitutional standards, then the state simply will not be permitted to detain such persons.[48]

Just as the courts will order cessation of abusive physical treatment by jail authorities, so should they correct conditions which are equally harmful to the inmate's health and well-being. The fact that correcting conditions will require expenditure of funds should not bar appropriate judicial relief.

Recently, in *Commonwealth ex rel. Carroll v. Tate*,[49] the Pennsylvania Supreme Court held that the judicial branch can compel appropriation of monies "reasonably necessary" for its proper functioning. The Judges of the Court of Common Pleas in Philadelphia brought an action to compel the Mayor and City Council to appropriate additional funds, after their request had been turned down once following hearings before the city legislature. In deciding first whether the court could determine what is reasonably necessary for its operation and then if it had power to compel appropriation of funds, the court said that such a power must exist if it is in reality to be a coequal, independent branch of government. "[T]he deplorable financial conditions in Philadelphia must yield to the Constitutional mandate that the Judiciary shall be free and independent and able to provide an efficient and effective system of Justice."[50] The only difference of opinion on the court was in deciding what was "reasonably necessary." Justice Roberts, concurring and dissenting, would have included a bail project, the purpose of which was to avoid the injustices of the present bail system and the concomitant needless pretrial detention. "In sum," Justice Roberts writes, "the proposed bail project presents a rare and realistic opportunity to improve the administration of justice and minimize the social costs of pretrial imprisonment, all at a substantial savings to the taxpayers."[51] Even though the majority did not concur in this, all were agreed on the larger issue—that the judiciary could order monies spent in order to maintain the integrity and viability of the administration of justice. With the "reasonably necessary" standard, the opportunity is available for the courts to order the correction of other conditions which impede the administration of justice, including those found in jails.

Third. Just as responsibility for correcting terrible conditions cannot be shunned because of lack of funds, neither can jail authorities shun their responsibility to guarantee the health and safety of the inmates. "Under common law, bailees, including sheriffs, must take reasonable care of the chattels in their custody. No less is required of jailers who have custody of human beings."[52] This duty has been recognized and codified.[53] Thus, when a government deprives a person of his freedom to look after his own health and safety by imprisoning him, "no one should be surprised that the common law recognizes a duty on the part of the jailer to give . . . [him] . . . reasonable protection against assault, suicide and preventable illness."[54] In each instance, the court found the degree of risk in the Wayne County Jail unreasonably high. In the first eleven months of 1970, there were ninety-six assaults; forty-seven suicide attempts; there was a high incidence of infectious disease. The opinion of the court goes on and on, describing what is minimally required in order to meet fundamental standards set by law and human decency, and explaining how the situation in the Wayne County Jail failed in each case to meet these standards. In each case, the court ordered the inadequacy corrected or improved. Some things could be accomplished at once: scrubbing the floors and shower walls, ordering new mattresses, providing towels, toilet paper, and other sanitary items. For what could not be accomplished at once, the courts required submission of plans to solve the problem: plans for adequate vermin control; disinfecting all cells, and keeping them that way; recreation; treatment of drug addicts; adequate medical care; separating of the dangerous or mentally ill inmates; etc. Depending upon the complexity of the problem, from thirty to sixty days was allowed for submission of each plan.[55]

Although it is too soon to make any conclusive judgments about the effectiveness of the court action in *Wayne County,* there is no reason to believe that the consequences of the action will be undesirable for either the court or the jail. Ordering compliance with this comprehensive scheme to restore lawful operation of the jail certainly is a dramatic step, in the context of previous judicial unwillingness to become involved at all. But if the remedies seem dramatic it is only because the problems themselves are so great, and so many in number. With many jails, we are not concerned simply about the violation of one right, but with many rights being violated in many different ways. Applying state and city housing and health codes to jails is a significant step forward, because it may allow state courts to avoid (1) deciding complex constitutional issues; and (2) basing relief upon vague, generalized constitutional standards.

It is also important to realize that the action taken by the court is designed only to correct illegal and unconstitutional abuses and stops far short of assuming management of the jail. Good faith efforts by jail administrators to correct conditions and to comply with legal requirements are usually sufficient to stay[56] or end[57] close judicial supervision over the operational conditions in the jail. This is done in the realization that it will take time to rectify some matters. Thus a clear line of distinction is drawn between violative conditions which can be immediately corrected and those which are more long-range and which will require substantial reliance on the good faith efforts of the jail's administrators.

Furthermore, not every restriction placed on pretrial detainees will violate their rights. Once the decision to incarcerate is made, the person gives up only those rights, privileges and immunities necessarily or reasonably taken "for the security or good order of the penal institution."[58] For pretrial detainees, the court determined

The Evolution of Judicial Involvement

that the curtailment of liberties or the imposition of burdens is not punishment without due process of law if certain tests were met:

> 1. The purpose of the imposition or restriction must be the security or good order of the institution and not the exaction of a penalty for the offense charged.
> 2. The burden, hardship, or restriction must be reasonably related to the security or good order of the institution.
> 3. The burden, hardship, or restriction must not be overly broad in scope; that is, it must be no more onerous than is reasonably necessary to accomplish its institutional purpose.
> 4. The purpose or goal of the burden or restriction must not be the pursuit of some malicious or sadistic objective of the jailer.[59]

There can be little doubt about the propriety of the legal standards as established by these tests. Here, as in *Commonwealth ex rel. Carroll v. Tate,* the court relies upon a traditional common law formulation—"reasonable necessity." The court states that it will also inquire into the relationship between the burdens being imposed and the ends (security or good order) for which the burden is imposed. These formulations are highly suggestive of other tests for determining the constitutional validity of any exercise of the police power of the state. They place the action of the court, both now and in the future, squarely within the boundaries of appropriate judicial behavior. They give jail officials the leeway and flexibility needed to deal with a rowdy inmate, or to see that contraband is not smuggled into their jail. The court is simply telling the jail's officials that they must run their institution within the boundaries of the law and not use great force or action when a little will do. These concepts are by no means new to the law. Blackstone wrote in 1765:

> [T]his imprisonment, as has been said, is only for safe custody, and not for punishment: therefore, in this dubious interval between the commitment and trial, a prisoner ought to be used with the utmost humanity, and neither be loaded with needless fetters, or [sic] subjected to other hardships than such as are absolutely requisite for the purpose of confinement only . . . .[60]

If there is any newness at all, it is in their application to officials of penal institutions. And that was long overdue.

REFERENCES

1. Comment, *Beyond the Ken of the Courts: A Critique of Judicial Refusal to Review the Complaints of Convicts,* 72 Yale L.J. 506 (1963).
2. Goldfarb & Singer, *Redressing Prisoners' Grievances,* 39 Geo. Wash. L. Rev. 175, 181 (1970).
3. Powell v. Hunter, 172 F.2d 330, 331 (10th Cir. 1949).
4. *See, e.g.,* Golub v. Krimsky, 185 F. Supp. 783 (S.D.N.Y. 1960).
5. United States *ex rel.* Atterbury v. Ragen, 237 F.2d 953 (7th Cir. 1956), *cert. denied,* 353 U.S. 964 (1957).
6. Barnett v. Rodgers, 410 F.2d 995, 1004 (D.C. Cir. 1969) (Tamm, J., concurring).
7. *See* Fritch, Civil Rights of Federal Prison Inmates 31 (1961).
8. Stroud v. Swope, 187 F.2d 850, 851-52 (9th Cir. 1951).
9. 334 U.S. 266, 285 (1948).
10. 101 F. Supp. 285 (D.C. Territory of Alaska, 1951).
11. *Id.* at 288.
12. *Id.* at 289.
13. 365 U.S. 167 (1961).
14. 370 U.S. 660 (1962).
15. 378 U.S. 546 (1964).
16. 387 F.2d 519, 522 (2d Cir. 1967).
17. Douglas v. Sigler, 386 F.2d 684, 688 (8th Cir. 1967) (emphasis added).
18. Support by implication is derived from language in Johnson v. Avery, 393 U.S. 483 (1969), in which the Supreme Court seems to have rejected the position that the exigencies of prison discipline are always sufficient to restrict human liberties. *See also* Lee v. Washington, 390 U.S. 333 (1968), in which racial segregation to maintain good order and discipline of the prison was constitutionally prohibited.
19. 387 F.2d 519 (2d Cir. 1967).
20. Trop v. Dulles, 356 U.S. 86, 100-01 (1958).
21. *Id.*
22. 404 F.2d 571 (8th Cir. 1968).
23. *Id.* at 577.
24. Holt v. Sarver, 309 F. Supp. 362, 381 (E.D. Ark. 1970), *aff'd,* 442 F.2d 304 (8th Cir. 1971).
25. *Id.* at 372-73 (emphasis added).
26. 328 F. Supp. 1182, 1191 (E.D. Ark. 1971).
27. *Id.* at 1191-92.
28. *Id.* at 1194.
29. 438 F.2d 183 (5th Cir. 1971).
30. 42 U.S.C. § 1983 (1970):

    Every person who, under color of any statute, ordinance, regulation, custom, or usage, of any State or Territory, subjects, or causes to be subjected, any citizen of the United States or other person within the jurisdiction thereof to the deprivation of any rights, privileges, or immunities secured by the Constitution and laws, shall be liable to the party injured in an action at law, suit in equity, or other proper proceeding for redress.

31. Anderson v. Nosser, 438 F.2d 183, 189 (5th Cir. 1971).
32. *Id.* at 194.
33. *Id.* at 190 (emphasis added).
34. Jones v. Wittenberg, 323 F. Supp. 93, 100 (D. Conn. 1971).
35. *Id.* at 100.
36. United States *ex rel.* Yaris v. Shaughnessy, 112 F. Supp. 143, 144 (S.D.N.Y. 1953).
37. Sinclair v. Henderson, 435 F.2d 125, 126 (5th Cir. 1970).
38. *See* Stroud v. Swope, 187 F.2d 850 (9th Cir. 1951).
39. *See* Hamilton v. Love, 328 F. Supp. 1182 (E.D. Ark. 1971).
40. Wayne County Jail Inmates v. Wayne County Bd. of Comm'rs, No. 173217 (Mich. Cir. Ct., May 25, 1971) (all paginations cite to the "slipsheet" opinion). This decision is summarized in 5 Clearinghouse Rev. 108 (1971).
41. *Id.* at 6.
42. The court refused to include the hallway in front of each cell in the computation of space requirements. *Id.* at 11-12.
43. *Id.* at 21.
44. *Id.* at 22.
45. *Id.* at 24.
46. *Id.* at 26-27.
47. *Id.* at 28 (footnotes omitted).
48. Hamilton v. Love, 328 F. Supp. 1182, 1194 (E.D. Ark. 1971).
49. 442 Pa. 45, 274 A.2d 193 (1971).
50. *Id.* at 56, 274 A.2d at 199.
51. *Id.* as 62, 274 A.2d at 206 (Roberts, J., concurring and dissenting).
52. Wayne County Jail Inmates v. Wayne County Bd. of Comm'rs, No. 173217, 30-31 (Mich. Cir. Ct., May 25, 1971).
53. *See e.g.,* N.Y. Correc. Law § 500(c),(d) (McKinney Supp. 1971).
54. Wayne County Jail Inmates v. Wayne County Bd. of Comm'rs, No. 173217, 31 (Mich. Cir. Ct., May 25, 1971).
55. A similar requirement for submission of plans was used by a federal court. *See* Holt v. Sarver, 442 F.2d 304 (8th Cir. 1971).
56. Rhem v. McGrath, 326 F. Supp. 681 (S.D.N.Y. 1971).
57. Holt v. Sarver, 442 F.2d 304 (8th Cir. 1971).
58. Wayne County Jail Inmates v. Wayne County Bd. of Comm'rs, No 173217, 66 (Mich. Cir. Ct., May 25, 1971).
59. *Id.* at 67.
60. 4 W. Blackstone, Commentaries *300.

CHAPTER 16

STANDARDS AND GOALS FOR LOCAL CORRECTIONAL FACILITIES

NATIONAL ADVISORY COMMISSION ON
CRIMINAL JUSTICE STANDARDS AND GOALS*

STANDARD 9.1

TOTAL SYSTEM PLANNING

STATE AND LOCAL CORRECTIONS systems and planning agencies should immediately undertake, on a cooperative basis, planning for community corrections based on a total system concept that encompasses the full range of offenders' needs and the overall goal of crime reduction. Total system planning for a particular area should include the following concepts.

1. While the actual methodology may vary, total system planning should include these phases:

   a. A problem definition phase, including initial demarcation of the specific service area, as determined by the scope of the problem to be addressed. Its identification results in a preliminary statement of the correctional problem.

   b. Data survey and analysis designed to obtain comprehensive information on population trends and demography, judicial

---
*Task Force: *Report on Corrections,* Wash., D.C., 1973.

practices, offender profiles, service area resources, geographic and physical characteristics, and political and governmental composition. Such information is needed to assess service area needs and capability to determine priorities.

c. A program linkage phase involving examination of various ways to meet the problems identified. The linkages should emphasize service area resources that can be used to provide community-based correctional programs as alternatives to incarceration. Identification and development of diversion programs by program linkage will have significant implications for a service area's detention capacity and program requirements.

d. A definition and description of the correctional delivery system for the service area developed on the basis of results of the previous phases. Facility and nonfacility program requirements should be included.

e. Program and facility design, which proceed from delivery system definition. The resulting overall community correctional system design will vary with specific service area characteristics, but it should follow either a regional or a network approach.

(1) A network service delivery system should be developed for urban service areas with large offender populations. This system should have dispersed components (programs and facilities) that are integrated operationally and administratively. The network should include all components necessary to meet the needs of clientele and the community. Court intake, social investigation, and pretrial release and detention programs should be located near the courts. Other residential and non-residential components should be located in the clients' communities or neighborhoods and should use existing community resources.

(2) A regionalized service delivery system should be developed for service areas that are sparsely populated and include a number of cities, towns or villages. Such a system may be city-county or multicounty in composition and scope. Major facility and program components should be consolidated in a central area or municipality. Components should include intake and social investigations service, pretrial release services, pretrial and posttrial residential facilities, special programs,

and resource coordination. Extended components, such as pre-release, work/education release, alcohol and narcotic addict treatment, and related program coordination units, should be located in smaller population centers with provision for operational and administrative coordination with the centralized components. The centralized system component should be located in close proximity to court services and be accessible to private and public transportation.

2. All correctional planning should include consideration of the physical, social and aesthetic impact imposed by any facility or network. Such consideration should be based on the National Environmental Policy Act of 1969.

3. All planning efforts should be made in the context of the master plan of the statewide correctional planning body.

4. Individual program needs, such as detention centers, should not be considered apart from the overall correctional service plan or the relevant aspects of social service systems (health, education, public assistance, etc.) that have potential for sharing facilities, resources and experience.

5. All community correctional planning should give highest priority to diversion from the criminal justice system and utilization of existing community resources.

STANDARD 9.2

STATE OPERATION AND CONTROL OF LOCAL INSTITUTIONS

All local detention and correctional functions, both pre-and post-conviction, should be incorporated within the appropriate state system by 1982.

1. Community-based resources should be developed initially through subsidy contract programs, subject to state standards, which reimburse the local unit of government for accepting state commitments.

2. Coordinated planning for community-based correctional services should be implemented immediately on a state and regional basis. This planning should take place under jurisdiction of the state correctional system.

3. Special training and other programs operated by the state

should be available immediately to offenders in the community by utilizing mobile service delivery or specialized regional centers.

4. Program personnel should be recruited from the immediate community or service area to the maximum extent possible. Employees' ties with the local community and identification with the offender population should be considered essential to community involvement in the correctional program. At the same time, professional services should not be sacrificed, and state training programs should be provided to upgrade employee skills.

STANDARD 9.3

STATE INSPECTION OF LOCAL FACILITIES

Pending implementation of Standard 9.2, state legislatures should immediately authorize the formulation of state standards for correctional facilities and operational procedures and state inspection to insure compliance, including such features as:

1. Access of inspectors to a facility and the persons therein.
2. Inspection of:
   a. Administrative area, including record-keeping procedures.
   b. Health and medical services.
   c. Offenders' leisure activities.
   d. Offenders' employment.
   e. Offenders' education and work programs.
   f. Offenders' housing.
   g. Offenders' recreation programs.
   h. Food service.
   i. Observation of rights of offenders.
3. Every detention facility for adults or juveniles should have provisions for an outside, objective evaluation at least once a year. Contractual arrangements can be made with competent evaluators.
4. If the evaluation finds the facility's programs do not meet prescribed standards, state authorities should be informed in writing of the existing conditions and deficiencies. The state authorities should be empowered to make an inspection to ascertain the facts about the existing condition of the facility.
5. The state agency should have authority to require those in charge of the facility to take necessary measures to bring the facility up to standards.

6. In the event that the facility's staff fails to implement the necessary changes within a reasonable time, the state agency should have authority to condemn the facility.

7. Once a facility is condemned, it should be unlawful to commit or confine any persons to it. Prisoners should be relocated to facilities that meet established standards until a new or renovated facility is available. Provisions should be made for distribution of offenders and payment of expenses for relocated prisoners by the detaining jurisdiction.

STANDARD 9.4
ADULT INTAKE SERVICES

Each judicial jurisdiction should immediately take action, including the pursuit of enabling legislation where necessary, to establish centrally coordinated and directed adult intake services to:

1. Perform investigative services for pretrial intake screening. Such services should be conducted within three days and provide data for decisions regarding appropriateness of summons release, release on recognizance, community bail, conditional pretrial release, or other forms of pretrial release. Persons should not be placed in detention soley for the purpose of facilitating such services.

2. Emphasize diversion of alleged offenders from the criminal justice system and referral to alternative community-based programs (halfway houses, drug treatment programs, and other residential and nonresidential adult programs). The principal task is identifying the need and matching community services to it.

3. Offer initial and ongoing assessment, evaluation, and classification services to other agencies as requested.

4. Provide assessment, evaluation and classification services that assist program planning for sentenced offenders.

5. Arrange secure residential detention for pretrial detainees at an existing community or regional correctional center or jail, or at a separate facility for pretrial detainees where feasible. Most alleged offenders awaiting trial should be diverted to release programs, and the remaining population should be only those who represent a serious threat to the safety of others.

The following principles should be followed in establishing,

planning and operating intake services for adults:
1. Intake services should be administratively part of the judiciary.
2. Ideally, intake services should operate in conjunction with a community correctional facility.
3. Initiation of intake services should in no way imply that the client or recipient of its services is guilty. Protection of the rights of the accused must be maintained at every phase of the process.
4. Confidentiality should be maintained at all times.
5. Social inventory and offender classification should be significant components of intake services.
6. Specialized services should be purchased in the community on a contractual basis.
7. The following persons should be available to intake service programs, either as staff members or by contract:
   a. Psychiatrists.
   b. Clinical psychologists.
   c. Social workers.
   d. Interviewers.
   e. Education specialists.

STANDARD 9.5

PRETRIAL DETENTION ADMISSION PROCESS

County, city or regional jails or community correctional centers should immediately reorganize their admission processing for residential care as follows:
1. In addition to providing appropriate safeguards for the community, admission processing for pretrial detention should establish conditions and qualities conducive to overall correctional goals.
2. Detention center admission staffing should be sufficient to avoid use of holding rooms for periods longer than two hours. Emphasis should be given to prompt processing that allows the individual to be aware of his circumstances and avoid undue anxiety.
3. The admission process should be conducted within the security perimeter, with adequate physical separation from other portions of the facility and from the discharge process.
4. Intake processing should include a hot water shower with soap, the option of clothing issue, and proper checking and storage of personal effects.

5. All personal property and clothing taken from the individual upon admission should be recorded and stored, and a receipt issued to him. The detaining facility is responsible for the effects until they are returned to their owner.

6. Proper record keeping in the admission process is necessary in the interest of the individual as well as the criminal justice system. Such records should include: name and vital statistics; a brief personal, social, and occupational history; usual identity data; results of the initial examination; and results of the initial intake interview. Emphasis should be directed to individualizing the record-taking operation, since it is an imposition on the innocent and represents a component of the correctional process for the guilty.

7. Each person should be interviewed by a counselor, social worker, or other program staff member as soon as possible after reception. Interviews should be conducted in private, and the interviewing area furnished with reasonable comfort.

8. A thorough medical examination of each person should be made by a physician. It should be mandatory that the physician's orders be followed.

STANDARD 9.6

STAFFING PATTERNS

Every jurisdiction operating locally based correctional institutions and programs should immediately establish these criteria for staff:

1. All personnel should be placed on a merit or civil service status, with all employees except as noted below assigned to the facility on a full-time basis.

2. Correctional personnel should receive salaries equal to those of persons with comparable qualifications and seniority in the jurisdiction's police and fire departments.

3. Law enforcement personnel should not be assigned to the staffs of local correctional centers.

4. Qualifications for correctional staff members should be set at the state level and include requirement of a high school diploma.

5. A program of preservice and in-service training and staff development should be given all personnel. Provision of such a

program should be a responsibility of the state government. New correctional workers should receive preservice training in the fundamentals of facility operation, correctional programming, and their role in the correctional process. With all workers, responsibilities and salaries should increase with training and experience.

6. Correctional personnel should be responsible for maintenance and security operations as well as for the bulk of the facility's in-house correctional programming for residents.

7. In all instances where correctional personnel engage in counseling and other forms of correctional programming, professionals should serve in a supervisory and advisory capacity. The same professionals should oversee the activities of volunteer workers within the institution. In addition, they themselves should engage in counseling and other activities as needs indicate.

8. Wherever feasible, professional services should be purchased on a contract basis from practitioners in the community or from other governmental agencies. Relevant state agencies should be provided space in the institution to offer services. Similarly, other criminal justice employees should be encouraged to utilize the facility, particularly parole and probation officers.

9. Correctional personnel should be involved in screening and classification of inmates.

10. Every correctional worker should be assigned to a specific aspect of the facility's programming, such as the educational program, recreation activities, or supervision of maintenance tasks.

11. At least one correctional worker should be on the staff for every six inmates in the average daily population, with the specific number on duty adjusted to fit the relative requirements for three shifts.

STANDARD 9.7

INTERNAL POLICIES

Every jurisdiction operating locally based correctional institutions and programs for adults should immediately adopt these internal policies:

1. A system of classification should be used to provide the basis for residential assignment and program planning for individuals. Segregation of diverse categories of incarcerated persons, as well

as identification of special supervision and treatment requirements, should be observed.

   a. The mentally ill should not be housed in a detention facility.

   b. Since local correctional facilities are not equipped to treat addicts, they should be diverted to narcotic treatment centers. When drug users are admitted to the facility because of criminal charges not related to their drug use, immediate medical attention and treatment should be administered by a physician.

   c. Since local correctional facilities are not proper locations for treatment of alcoholics, all such offenders should be diverted to detoxification centers and given a medical examination. Alcoholics with delirium tremens should be transferred immediately to a hospital for proper treatment.

   d. Prisoners who suffer from various disabilities should have separate housing and close supervision to prevent mistreatment by other inmates. Any potential suicide risk should be under careful supervision. Epileptics, diabetics and persons with other special problems should be treated as recommended by the staff physician.

   e. Beyond segregating these groups, serious and multiple offenders should be kept separate from those whose charge or conviction is for a first or minor offense. In particular, persons charged with noncriminal offenses (for example, traffic cases) should not be detained before trial. The state government should insist on the separation of pretrial and posttrial inmates, except where it can be demonstrated conclusively that separation is not possible and every alternative is being used to reduce pretrial detention.

2. Detention rules and regulations should be provided each new admission and posted in each separate area of the facility.

3. Every inmate has the right to visits from family and friends. Each facility should have at least fourteen regular visiting hours weekly, with at least five between 7 and 10 p.m. Visiting hours should be expanded beyond this minimum to the greatest extent possible. The environment in which visits take place should be designed and operated under conditions as normal as possible. Maximum security arrangements should be reserved for the few cases in which they are necessary.

4. The institution's medical program should obtain assistance from external medical and health resources (state agencies, medical societies, professional groups, hospitals, and clinics). Specifically:

   a. Each inmate should be examined by a physician within twenty-four hours after admission to determine his physical and mental condition. If the physician is not immediately available, a preliminary medical inspection should be administered by the receiving officer to detect any injury or illness requiring immediate medical attention and possible segregation from other inmates until the physician can see him.

   b. Every facility should have a formal sick call procedure that gives inmates the opportunity to present their request directly to a member of the staff and obtain medical attention from the physician.

   c. Every facility should be able to provide the services of a qualified dentist. Eyeglass fitting and other special services such as provision of prosthetic devices should be made available.

   d. Personal medical records should be kept for each inmate, containing condition on admission, previous medical history, illness or injury during confinement and treatment provided, and condition at time of release.

   e. All personnel should be trained to administer first aid.

5. Three meals daily should be provided at regular and reasonable hours. Meals should be of sufficient quantity, well-prepared, served in an attractive manner, and nutritionally balanced. Service should be prompt, so that hot food remains hot and cold food remains cold. Each facility should also have a commissary service.

6. The inmates' lives and health are the responsibility of the facility. Hence the facility should implement sanitation and safety procedures that help protect the inmate from disease, injury, and personal danger.

7. Each detention facility should have written provisions that deal with its management and administration. Proper legal authority, legal custody and charge of the facility, commitment and confinement rules, transfer and transportation of inmates, and emergency procedures are among the topics that should be covered.

8. The use of an inmate trusty system should be prohibited.

STANDARD 9.8

LOCAL CORRECTIONAL FACILITY PROGRAMMING

Every jurisdiction operating locally based correctional facilities and programs for adults should immediately adopt the following programming practices:

1. A decision-making body should be established to follow and direct the inmate's progress through the local correctional system, either as a part of or in conjunction with the community classification team concept. Members should include a parole and probation supervisor, the administrator of the correctional facility or his immediate subordinates, professionals whose services are purchased by the institution, representatives of community organizations running programs in the institution or with its residents, and inmates. This body should serve as a central information-gathering point. It should discuss with an individual inmate all major decisions pertaining to him.

2. Educational programs should be available to all residents in cooperation with the local school district. Particular emphasis should be given to self-pacing, learning programs, packaged instructional materials, and utilization of volunteers and paraprofessionals as instructors.

3. Vocational programs should be provided by the appropriate state agency. It is desirable that overall direction be provided on the state level to allow variety and to permit inmates to transfer among institutions in order to take advantage of training opportunities.

4. A job placement program should be operated at all community correctional centers as part of the vocational training program. Such programs should be operated by state employment agencies and local groups representing employers and local unions.

5. Each local institution should provide counseling services. Individuals showing acute problems will require professional services. Other individuals may require, on a day-to-day basis, situational counseling that can be provided by correctional workers supervised by professionals.

6. Volunteers should be recruited and trained to serve as counselors, instructors, teachers, and recreational therapists.

7. A range of activities to provide physical exercise should be

available both in the facility and through the use of local recreational resources. Other leisure activities should be supported by access to library materials, television, writing materials, playing cards, and games.

8. In general, internal programs should be aimed only at that part of the institutional population unable to take advantage of ongoing programs in the community.

9. Meetings with the administrator or appropriate staff of the institution should be available to all individuals and groups.

STANDARD 9.9

JAIL RELEASE PROGRAMS

Every jurisdiction operating locally based correctional facilities and programs for convicted adults immediately should develop release programs drawing community leadership, social agencies, and business interest into action with the criminal justice system.

1. Since release programs rely heavily on the participant's self-discipline and personal responsibility, the offender should be involved as a member of the program planning team.

2. Release programs have special potential for utilizing specialized community services to meet offenders' special needs. This capability avoids the necessity of service duplication within corrections.

3. Weekend visits and home furloughs should be planned regularly, so that eligible individuals can maintain ties with family and friends.

4. Work release should be made available to persons in all offense categories who do not present a serious threat to others.

5. The offender in a work-release program should be paid at prevailing wages. The individual and the work-release agency may agree to allocation of earnings to cover subsistence, transportation cost, compensation to victims, family support payments, and spending money. The work-release agency should maintain strict accounting procedures open to inspection by the client and others.

6. Program location should give high priority to the proximity of job opportunities. Various modes of transportation may need to be utilized.

7. Work release may be operated initially from an existing jail

facility, but this is not a long-term solution. Rented and converted buildings (such as YMCA's, YWCA's, motels, hotels) should be considered to separate the transitional program from the image of incarceration that accompanies the traditional jail.

8. When the release program is combined with a local correctional facility, there should be separate access to the work-release residence and activity areas.

9. Educational or study release should be available to all inmates (pretrial and convicted) who do not present a serious threat to others. Arrangements with the local school district and nearby colleges should allow participation at any level required (literacy training, adult basic education, high school or general educational development equivalency, and college level).

10. Arrangements should be made to encourage offender participation in local civic and social groups. Particular emphasis should be given to involving the offender in public education and the community in corrections efforts.

STANDARD 9.10

LOCAL FACILITY EVALUATION AND PLANNING

Jurisdictions evaluating the physical plants of existing local facilities for adults or planning new facilities should be guided by the following considerations:

1. A comprehensive survey and analysis should be made of criminal justice needs and projections in a particular service area.

    a. Evaluation of population levels and projections should assume maximum use of pretrial release programs and post-adjudication alternatives to incarceration.

    b. Diversion of sociomedical problem cases (alcoholics, narcotic addicts, mentally ill, and vagrants) should be provided for.

2. Facility planning, location and construction should:

    a. Develop, maintain and strengthen offenders' ties with the community. Therefore, convenient access to work, school, family, recreation, professional services, and community activities should be maximized.

    b. Increase the likelihood of community acceptance, the availability of contracted programs and purchased professional services, and attractiveness to volunteers, paraprofessionals, and

Standards for Local Correctional Facilities

professional staff.

c. Afford easy access to the courts and legal services to facilitate intake screening, presentence investigations, postsentence programming, and pretrial detention.

3. A spatial "activity design" should be developed.

   a. Planning of sleeping, dining, counseling, visiting, movement, programs and other functions should be directed at optimizing the conditions of each.

   b. Unnecessary distance between staff and resident territories should be eliminated.

   c. Transitional spaces should be provided that can be used by "outside" and inmate participants and give a feeling of openness.

4. Security elements and detention provisions should not dominate facility design.

   a. Appropriate levels of security should be achieved through a range of unobtrusive measures that avoid the ubiquitous "cage" and "closed" environment.

   b. Environmental conditions comparable to normal living should be provided to support development of normal behavior patterns.

   c. All inmates should be accommodated in individual rooms arranged in residential clusters of eight to twenty-four rooms to achieve separation of accused and sentenced persons, male and female offenders, and varying security levels and to reduce the depersonalization of institutional living.

   d. A range of facility types and the quality and kinds of spaces comprising them should be developed to provide for sequential movement of inmates through different programs and physical spaces consistent with their progress.

5. Applicable health, sanitation, space, safety, construction, environmental and custody codes and regulations must be taken into account.

6. Considerations must be given to resources available and the most efficient use of funds.

   a. Expenditures on security hardware should be minimized.

   b. Existing community resources should be used for provision of correctional services to the maximum feasible extent.

c. Shared use of facilities with other social agencies not conventionally associated with corrections should be investigated.

d. Facility design should emphasize flexibility and amendability to change in anticipation of fluctuating conditions and needs and to achieve highest return on capital investment.

7. Prisoners should be handled in a manner consistent with humane standards.

a. Use of closed-circuit television and other electronic surveillance is detrimental to program objectives, particularly when used as a substitute for direct staff-resident interaction. Experience in the use of such equipment also has proved unsatisfactory for any purposes other than traffic control or surveillance of institutional areas where inmates' presence is not authorized.

b. Individual residence space should provide sensory stimulation and opportunity for self-expression and personalizing the environment.

8. Existing community facilities should be explored as potential replacement for, or adjuncts to, a proposed facility.

9. Planning for network facilities should include no single component, or institution, housing more than 300 persons.

CHAPTER 17

RIGHTS OF OFFENDERS

The National Advisory Commission on
Criminal Justice Standards & Goals*

Increased assertion and recognition of the rights of persons under correctional control has been an insistent force for change and accountability in correctional systems and practices. Traditional methods of doing things have been reexamined; myths about both institutionalized offenders and those under community supervision have been attacked and often proved to be without foundation. The public has become increasingly aware of both prisons and prisoners.

Although the process by which the courts are applying constitutional standards to corrections is far from complete, the magnitude and pace of change within corrections as the result of judicial decrees is remarkable. The correctional system is being subjected not only to law but also to public scrutiny. The courts have thus provided not only redress for offenders but also an opportunity for meaningful correctional reform.

In theory, the corrections profession has accepted the premise that persons are sent to prison *as* punishment, not *for* punishment. The American Prison Association in its famous "Declaration of Principles" in 1870 recognized that correctional programs should

---
*Task Force, *Report on Corrections,* Wash., D.C. 1973.

reflect the fact that offenders were human beings with the need for dignity as well as reformation. The following selection of principles is instructive:

> V. The prisoner's destiny should be placed measurably in his own hands; he must be put into circumstances where he will be able, through his own exertions, to continually better his own condition. . . .
>
> XI. A system of prison discipline, to be truly reformatory, must gain the will of the prisoner. He is to be amended; but how is this possible with his mind in a state of hostility?
>
> XIV. The prisoner's self-respect should be cultivated to the utmost, and every effort made to give back to him his manhood. There is no greater mistake in the whole compass of penal discipline, than its studied imposition of degradation as a part of punishment. . . .

More recently, the American Correctional Association and the President's Commission on Law Enforcement and Administration of Justice issued warnings about respect for offenders' rights.

In 1966, the American Correctional Association's *Manual of Correctional Standards* declared:

> The administrator should always be certain that he is not acting capriciously or unreasonably but that established procedures are reasonable and not calculated to infringe upon the legal rights of the prisoners. . . .
>
> Until statutory and case law are more fully developed, it is vitally important within all of the correctional fields that there should be established and maintained reasonable norms and remedies against the sorts of abuses that are likely to develop where men have great power over their fellows and where relationships may become both mechanical and arbitrary. Minimum standards should become more uniform, and correctional administrators should play an important role in the eventual formulation and enactment of legal standards that are sound and fair.[1]

In 1967, the President's Commission on Law Enforcement and Administration of Justice emphasized the importance of administrative action.

> Correctional administrators should develop guidelines defining prisoners' rights with respect to such issues as access to legal materials, correspondence, visitors, religious practice, medical care, and disciplinary sanctions. Many correctional systems have taken important steps in this direction, but there is a long way to go.

Such actions on the part of correctional administrators will enable the courts to act in a reviewing rather than a directly supervisory capacity. Where administrative procedures are adequate, courts are not likely to intervene in the merits of correctional decisions. And where well thought out policies regarding prisoners' procedural and substantive rights have been established, courts are likely to defer to administrative expertise.[2]

Despite the recognition of the need for reform, abuse of offenders' rights continued. It remained for the judiciary to implement as a matter of constitutional law what the corrections profession had long accepted in theory as appropriate correctional practice.

EVOLVING JUDICIAL REGARD FOR OFFENDERS' RIGHTS

Until recently, an offender as a matter of law was deemed to have forfeited virtually all rights upon conviction and to have retained only such rights as were expressly granted to him by statute or correctional authority. The belief was common that virtually anything could be done with an offender in the name of "correction," or in some instances "punishment," short of extreme physical abuse. He was protected only by restraint and responsibility of correctional administrators and their staff. Whatever comforts, services or privileges the offender received were a matter of grace—in the law's view a privilege to be granted or withheld by the state. Inhumane conditions and practices were permitted to develop and continue in many systems.

The courts refused for the most part to intervene. Judges felt that correctional administration was a technical matter to be left to experts rather than to courts, which were deemed ill-equipped to make appropriate evaluations. And, to the extent that courts believed the offenders' complaints involved privileges rather than rights, there was no special necessity to confront correctional practices, even when they infringed on basic notions of human rights and dignity protected for other groups by constitutional doctrine.

This legal view of corrections was possible only because society at large did not care about corrections. Few wanted to associate with offenders or even to know about them. The new public consciousness (and the accompanying legal scrutiny) did not single out corrections alone as an object of reform. Rather, it was part of a sweeping concern for individual rights and administrative accountability which began with the civil rights movement and subsequently was reflected in areas such as student rights, public welfare, mental institutions, juvenile court systems, and military justice. It was reinforced by vastly increased contact of middle-class groups with correctional agencies as byproducts of other national problems (juvenile delinquency, drug abuse, and political and social dissent). The net result was a climate conducive to serious reexamination of the legal rights of offenders.

Applying criminal sanctions is the most dramatic exercise of the power of the state over individual liberties. Although necessary for maintaining social order, administering sanctions does not require general suspension of the freedom to exercise basic rights. Since criminal sanctions impinge on the most basic right—liberty—it is imperative that other restrictions be used sparingly, fairly, and only for some socially useful purpose.

Eventually the questionable effectiveness of correctional systems as rehabilitative instruments, combined with harsh and cruel conditions in institutions, could no longer be ignored by courts. They began to redefine the legal framework of corrections and place restrictions on previously unfettered discretion of correctional administrators. Strangely, correctional administrators, charged with rehabilitating and caring for offenders, persistently fought the recognition of offenders' rights throughout the judicial process. This stance, combined with the general inability of correctional administrators to demonstrate that correctional programs correct, shook public and judicial confidence in corrections.

The past few years have witnessed an explosion of requests by offenders for judicial relief from the conditions of their confinement or correctional program. More dramatic is the increased willingness of the courts to respond. Reflective of the new judicial attitude toward sentenced offenders is the fact that in the 1971-72 term, the U.S. Supreme Court decided eight cases directly affecting convicted offenders and at least two others which have implications for correctional practices. In all eight cases directly involving corrections, the offender's contention prevailed, five of them by unanimous vote of the Court.

The Court unanimously ruled that formal procedures were required in order to revoke a person's parole,[3] that the United States

Parole Board must follow its own rules in revoking parole,[4] that institutionalized offenders are entitled to access to legal materials,[5] and that offenders committed under special provisions relating to defective delinquents[6] or sexually related offenses[7] are entitled to formal procedures if their sentences are to be extended. With one dissent, the Court also ruled that prison officials are required to provide reasonable opportunities to all prisoners for religious worship,[8] and that prisoners need not exhaust all possible state remedies before pursuing federal causes of action challenging the conditions of their confinement.[9] The Court also held that a sentencing judge could not use unconstitutionally obtained convictions as the basis for sentencing an offender.[10]

Two additional cases have potential ramifications for the rights of offenders. In *Argersinger* v. *Hamlin,* 407 U.S. 25 (1972), the Court held that the state must provide counsel in criminal trials for indigent defendants regardless of the seriousness of the offense charged where a person's liberty is at stake. Throughout the correctional process various officials may make decisions which increase the time spent in confinement. This effect on the offender's liberty may require appointment of counsel and other procedural formalities.

In *Jackson* v. *Indiana,* 406 U.S. 715 (1972), the Court held that indefinite commitment of a person who is not mentally competent to stand trial for a criminal offense violates due process of law. The Court noted that the state had the right to confine such an individual for a reasonable time to determine if he could be restored to competency by treatment but, if he could not, he must be released. In the course of his opinion, agreed to by the six other justices hearing the case, Justice Blackmun commented: "At the least, due process requires that the nature and duration of commitment bear some reasonable relation to the purpose for which the individual is committed." The effect of such a rule if applied to correctional confinement is yet to be determined.

These cases demonstrate the distance the law has come from the older view that courts ought not intervene in correctional activities. However, the real ferment for judicial intervention has come in the lower courts, particularly in the federal district courts. Broadening interpretations of the federal civil rights acts, the writ of habeas corpus, and other doctrines providing for federal court jurisdiction have facilitated the application of constitutional principles to corrections. And it is in these courts that the "hands off" doctrine has been either modified or abandoned altogether.

Contemporaneously with the increased willingness of the courts to consider offenders' complaints came a new attitude toward offenders' rights. As first enunciated in *Coffin* v. *Reichard,* 143 F.2d 443 (6th Cir. 1944), courts are more readily accepting the premise that "[a] prisoner retains all the rights of an ordinary citizen except those expressly or by necessary implication taken from him by law." To implement such a rule, courts have found that where necessity is claimed as justification for limiting some right, the burden of proof (of the necessity) should be borne by the correctional authority. Administrative convenience is no longer to be accepted as sufficient justification for deprivation of rights. Additionally, correctional administrators are subjected to due process standards which require that agencies and programs be administered with clearly enunciated policies and established, fair procedures for the resolution of grievances.

A concomitant doctrine now emerging is that of the "least restrictive alternative" or "least drastic means." This tenet simply holds that, once the corrections administrator has demonstrated that some restriction on an offender's rights is necessary, he must select the least restrictive alternative to satisfy the state's interests.

This change of perspective has worked major changes in the law governing correctional control over sentenced offenders. By agreeing to hear offenders' complaints, the courts were forced to evaluate correctional practices against three fundamental constitutional commands: (1) state action may not deprive citizens of life, liberty or property without due process of law; (2) state action may not deprive citizens of their right to equal protection of the law; and (3) the state may not inflict cruel and unusual punishment. Courts have found traditional correctional practices in violation of all three commands. The standards in this chapter examine the various issues which have been—or in the future no doubt will be—the subject of litigation.

IMPLEMENTATION OF OFFENDERS' RIGHTS
Courts

The courts perform two functions within the criminal justice system. They are participants in the process of trying and sentencing those accused of crime; and at the same time they act as guardian of the requirements of the Constitution and statutory law. In the latter role, they oversee the criminal justice system at work. It was this function which inevitably forced the courts to evaluate correctional practices a decade before they subjected the police to constitutional scrutiny. Thus the courts have not only the authority but also the responsibility to continue to judge corrections against constitutional dictates.

It should be recognized, however, that the Constitution requires only minimal standards. The prohibition against cruel and unusual punishment has not to date required affirmative treatment programs. If courts view their role as limited to constitutional requirements, litigation will merely turn filthy and degrading institutions into clean but unproductive institutions. Courts, however, have a broader role. A criminal sentence is a court order and like any court order should be subject to continuing judicial supervision. Courts should specify the purpose for which an offender is given a particular sentence and should exercise control to insure that the treatment of the offender is consistent with that purpose. A sentence for purposes of rehabilitation is hardly advanced by practices which degrade and humiliate the offender.

On the other hand, litigation alone cannot solve the problems of corrections or of offenders' rights. The process of case-by-case adjudication of offenders' grievances inevitably results in uncertainties and less-than-comprehensive rulemaking. Courts decide the issue before them. They are ill-equipped to enter broad mandates for change. Similarly the sanctions available to courts in enforcing their decrees are limited. While some courts have been forced to appoint masters to oversee the operation of a prison, full implementation of constitutional and correctional practices which aid rather than degrade offenders requires the commitment of funds and public support. Courts alone cannot implement offenders' rights.

Correctional Agencies

Implementation of offenders' rights is consistent with good correctional practice. Corrections has moved from a punitive system to one which recognizes that 99 percent of those persons sentenced to confinement will one day return to the free society. This fact alone requires that offenders be prepared for reintegration into the community. An important precedent to successful reintegration is the establishment of personal rights prior to release. Thus the judicial philosophy which provides that offenders retain all rights of free citizens unless there are compelling reasons for restrictions is compatible with and supportive of the correctional philosophy of the reintegration of offenders into the community. And therefore correctional administrators have a professional interest in completing the implementation of the rights of the offender that is begun by the judiciary.

Additionally, correctional administrators are responsible for the welfare of offenders committed to their charge. Judicial decisions which improve the conditions under which an offender labors should be welcomed, rather than resisted, by correctional officers. Maurice Sigler noted in his address as retiring president of the American Correctional Association in 1972:

> In committing offenders to us, the courts have assigned us the responsibility for their care and welfare. All of us have acknowledged that responsibility. It is inconsistent and ill-advised for us to fight every case that comes along involving the rights of our clients. After all, who is supposed to be most concerned about their welfare?

The corrections profession has a critical role to play in implementing the rights of offenders. No statutory mandate or judicial declaration of rights can be effectively realized and broadly obtained without the understanding, cooperation and commitment of correctional personnel. Corrections will have to adopt new procedures and approaches in such areas as discipline, inmate grievances, censorship, and access to legal assistance. Traditions, schedules and administrative techniques will have to be reevaluated and in many instances modified or abandoned. Line personnel will have to be trained to understand the substance of offenders' rights and the reasons for enforcing them.

Corrections, at the same time, is provided with an opportunity for meaningful progress. Most prisons are degrading, not because corrections wants them to be but because resources for improvement have not been available. Judicial decrees requiring change should make available additional resources. In the last analysis, the Constitution may require either an acceptable correctional system or none at all.

Legislatures

Full implementation of offenders' rights will require participation by the legislature. The inefficiencies and uncertainties of case-by-case litigation in the courts over definition of offenders' rights can be minimized if legislatures enact a comprehensive code which recognizes the new philosophy regarding offenders. Legislatures have generally been slow in modernizing correctional legislation, but pressure from the courts should stimulate badly needed reform.

Legislatures may well discover that in the short run a constitutionally permissible system of corrections is more costly than the traditional model. Legislatures can insure that only the minimal dictates of judicial decrees are met, or they can utilize the opportunity provided to commit the resources necessary to provide an effective correctional system.

The Public

While the Constitution prescribes conduct by government rather than by private persons, the public has not only a stake in implementing offenders' rights but also a responsibility to help realize them. Most people think of corrections as a system that deals with violent individuals—murderers, rapists, robbers, and muggers. To them the philosophy of "eye for eye" seems correctionally sound. This attitude may account for public tolerance of deplorable conditions in correctional facilities and the rigid disabilities imposed upon released offenders. But even a philosophy of retribution does not require blanket suspension of constitutional rights.

On the other hand, many people believe minor criminal incidents should be dealt with compassionately, especially where youthful offenders are involved. They realize that most offenders are involved in crimes against property rather than against persons and thus present a smaller risk to community safety than those perceived as being violent.

To the extent that the community continues to discriminate on the basis of prior criminality, efforts toward reintegration will be frustrated. There must be recognition that society does not benefit in the long run from attempts to banish, ignore or degrade offenders. In part such a response is a self-fulfilling prophecy: if an offender is considered a social outcast, he will act like one. Removing legal obstacles is of little benefit if individual employers will not hire ex-offenders. Statutory provisions for community-based programs are for naught if no one wants a halfway house in his neighborhood. Efforts to improve the offender's ability to relate to others mean little if family and friends do not wish to associate with him.

Affirmative and organized efforts must be made by community leaders, correction officials, legislators, and judges to influence public opinion. Acceptance can be fostered by improving the public's understanding of offenders' problems and of correctional processes. This chapter's standards on visiting and media access aim at improving such understanding as well as removing limitations on the exercise of basic rights. Correctional institutions and programs should be opened to citizens' groups and individuals, not for amusement but so that citizens may interact on a one-to-one basis with offenders.

In the final analysis, the offender's social status may be the most important determinant of reintegration. Any person will respond with outrage, hostility and nonconformity to a community that continually rejects, labels, and otherwise treats him as an outlaw.

REFERENCES

1. American Correctional Association: *Manual of Correctional Standards.* Washington, ACC, 1966, pp. 266, 279.
2. President's Commission on Law Enforcement and Administration of Justice: *Task Force Report: Corrections.* Washington, Government Printing Office, 1967, p. 85.
3. *Morrissey* v. *Brewer,* 408 U.S. 471 (1972).
4. *Arciniega* v. *Freeman,* 404 U.S. 4 (1971).
5. *Younger* v. *Gilmore,* 404 U.S. 15 (1971) affirming *Gilmore* v. *Lynch,* 319 F. Supp. 105 (N.D. Cal. 1970).

6. *McNeil* v. *Director, Patuxent Institution,* 407 U.S. 245 (1971).
7. *Wilwording* v. *Swenson,* 404 U.S. 249 (1971).
8. *Cruz* v. *Beto,* 405 U.S. 319 (1972).
9. *Humphrey* v. *Cady,* 405 U.S. 504 (1972).
10. *U.S.* v. *Tucker,* 404 U.S. 443 (1972).

CHAPTER 18

TAYLOR v. STERRETT

344 F.Supp. 411 (N.D. Tex. 1972)

Sarah T. Hughes

MEMORANDUM OPINION AND JUDGMENT

This civil rights suit considers conditions of life experienced by prisoners at the Dallas County jail. The plaintiffs, Joseph Taylor, James Douglas Thompson and John Henry Woods, Jr., are inmates at the Dallas County Jail. They have brought this action for themselves and as representatives of a class comprising all the inmates of the jail.

The defendants are Dallas County officials charged with responsibility for the maintenance and supervision of the jail. W. L. Sterrett, County Judge; Mel Price, John Whittington, Jim Tyson, and Roy Orr, members of the Commissioners Court; Clarence Jones, Sheriff; Carl Rowland, Chief Jailer; and J. N. Pickard, M.D., Dallas County Health Officer. The Court acquired jurisdiction over this action pursuant to 28 U.S.C. 1343 which authorizes a federal district court to hear actions under 42 U.S.C. 1983 to redress any deprivation, under color of state law, of any right, privilege or immunity secured by the Constitution. The plaintiffs seek declaratory and injunctive relief under 28 U.S.C. 2201 against certain acts, practices, policies and conditions at the Dallas County jail.

Prior to the hearing on the merits of the complaint, this Court issued a permanent injunction concerning the practice of censorship of the mail by jail officials. The Court ordered the sheriff to cease opening or censoring mail transmitted between inmates of the jail and the following persons: courts, prosecuting attorneys, probation and parole officers, governmental agencies, lawyers and the press.

Also during the pendency of this suit, the Court entered a preliminary injunction against the jail officials enjoining them from destroying certain reading materials to which the prisoners attached importance and which they do not wish to surrender, provided that the prisoners maintain the material in good condition and do not create a fire or health hazard. These materials included law books, legal materials, legal documents, books, magazines, and newspaper clippings.

Before the trial on the merits, the Court visited the facilities of the Dallas County jail with the chief jailer and counsel for the plaintiffs and defendants. During these visits the Court became acquainted with the areas which are the subject of this suit. The Court's familiarity with the physical condition of the jail permits it to take judicial notice of certain matters presented during the trial.

Immediately prior to trial the case of *Perry v. Decker*, C.A.3-4138-C was consolidated with *Taylor v. Sterrett*. The Perry case complained of inadequacy of medical services and was brought by Julius Duane Perry, an inmate of the jail, for himself and as representative of the class of inmates similarly situated.

The plaintiffs have alleged in their complaint a long list of deprivations which they contend constitute individually and collectively a violation of their rights protected by the first, eighth and fourteenth amendments of the Constitution. In addition, the plaintiffs declare that the defendants have failed to comply with state law regarding the operation and supervision of the county jail. The constitutional questions raised by the complaint are substantial and require the intervention of the Court to assess the charges and to redress any infringement on the rights of the class. The Court takes cognizance of the strong pressures on it to abstain from reviewing matters involving prison administration and policy. "It is a rule grounded in necessity and common sense, as well as authority, that the maintenance of discipline in a prison is an executive function with which the judicial branch ordinarily will not interfere." (*Sewell* v. *Pegelow,* 291 F.2d 196, 197 [4th Cir. 1961]). Although the federal courts are reluctant to interfere with the internal operation of jails, the claims made by the plaintiffs in the present case do not involve mere matters of preference or convenience concerning administrative practices. The allegations raise basic questions of constitutionally protected rights.

The Court recognizes that the plaintiffs are prisoners held either for conviction of a crime or under charge of a crime. Although the courts have acknowledged that prisoners have obvious limitations placed on their privileges and rights, "it is well established that prisoners do not lose all their constitutional rights and that the Due Process and Equal Protection Clauses of the Fourteenth Amendment follow them into prison and protect them there from unconstitutional action on the part of prison authorities carried out under color of State law." *Washington* v. *Lee,* 263 F. Supp, 327, 331 (N.D. Ala.), *aff'd sub nom,* 389 U.S. 967 (1967). Furthermore, when the rights of those prisoners who are held as pretrial detainees are in question the courts have subjected the cases to even closer scrutiny (*Anderson* v. *Nosser,* 438 F.2d 183 [5th Cir. 1971]).

PHYSICAL FEATURES—CROWDING

The Dallas County Jail is located in two buildings referred to as the old jail and the new jail. The new jail is located in the new County Government Center. It was designed to accommodate 1220 inmates at capacity. The quarters now in use in the two buildings has a total capacity for 1370 inmates. During the first fourteen days of May, 1972, the peak number per day varied from 1491 on May 6th to 1693 on May 4th. The average peak number for the fourteen days was 1589. During 1971 the average daily number housed during three months of the year was more than 1700 and one month was more than 1800. The women's section located on one floor of the new jail consists of twenty-five cells containing 198 bunks. On the day of the trial there were ninety-two female inmates, leaving more than 100 bunks unoccupied. The failure to use all the bunks on this floor results from design problems which do not provide adequate segregation of male and female prisoners.

The vacancies on the women's floor increases the crowding of the cells reserved for men.

Most of the inmates are lodged in cells each with eight to twelve bunks which open into a "day room." The entire area is referred to as a "tank," the capacity of a tank varying from approximately twenty-four to thirty-six. In addition to ten tanks there are 168 cells without a day room each containing several bunks. These open into a corridor.

All tanks for men are overcrowded having approximately fifteen more inmates than the number of bunks. Those not assigned to bunks sleep on mattresses in the day room. The hospital ward for men is likewise overcrowded and it is common for men to sleep on mattresses in place of beds. Its capacity is forty-eight. On the day of the Court's visit there were sixty-two persons who had been admitted.

At the time the new jail was built in 1966 the old jail was abandoned and became unusable for the detention of prisoners. It soon became apparent that the new jail was inadequate, but no steps were taken to repair or remodel the facilities in the old jail until 1971. Early in 1972 a part of the old jail was opened and some prisoners transferred to it. Presently 150 inmates are lodged there. By remodeling and removing stored items an additional 550 men could be housed. In addition to the possibility of use of all quarters in the old jail the sheriff reported that the 100 extra bunks in the women's section could be used for men by changing the floor plan.

In addition to the tanks and cells without day rooms the jail has a number of solitary cells, which are completely inadequate, used for punitive segregation and insane prisoners. Six have dimensions of 4'3" x 5'1". The rest measure 6'11" x 5'1" and 7'1" x 6'. Only four have running water. None have drinking fountains. The only facility for excrement is a hole in the floor which is rarely flushed. There is no outside light, the inside electric globe burning twenty-four hours a day. Mattresses are used in place of bunks. The only place to sit is on the floor or mattresses. Insane persons are placed in the solitary cells without the benefit of padding on the walls or a hammock for sleeping.

MEDICAL FACILITIES

The medical care facilities consist of an infirmary for men with forty-eight beds and one for women with eighteen beds. There is provision for a nurse to be on duty twenty-four hours each day. In addition there is a doctor on call throughout the day. Previously, requests by inmates for the nurse have been ignored, but recently a policy has been inaugurated of sending a note, termed a "kite," to the nurse immediately. Until recently the only dental care has been tooth extraction. The program has now been expanded to include filling. Examination of inmates is not adequate—when admitted they are tested only for tuberculosis and for venereal disease if suspected. Food handlers receive no examination.

PRACTICES, POLICIES AND PROCEDURES

Censorship

Prior to the filing of this suit, the chief jailer enforced a policy of opening and reading each item of mail which was transmitted between prisoners and the outside. The stated purpose of this procedure was to insure security and to prevent the transmission of contraband. The jailer in charge of this procedure would read all of the inmate mail and had authority to refuse to send those letters which he found unacceptable for outside mailing. If there was matter in the letters which did not meet his approval, the jailer returned the letter to the inmate for rewriting. All letters had to be submitted to the jailer unsealed.

The first action taken in the present case was to enjoin the sheriff from continuing this procedure as it applies to certain categories of mail. The inspection of the mail between the inmates and the persons or agencies set out in the order is now limited to superficial examination for possible contraband.

The testimony of Chief Rowland revealed that since the first of the year his department has stopped the censorship of all mail and has limited its inspection to merely discovery of money or contraband which could be transmitted. In his opinion, the practice of censorship of the mail had little impact on the security of the jail.

Reading Matter

The inmates of the jail have access to periodicals and books by purchasing them off the commissary cart and through mail subscriptions. The reading matter sold from the cart is limited to a list of items approved by the sheriff. The alleged criteria for the periodicals are (1) that they contain no pictures of nude persons and (2) that there be no pictures of weapons. The sheriff or the chief jailer has the sole authority to decide what books or periodicals are admitted to the jail.

The plaintiffs presented at trial evidence of magazines which are sold from the cart, yet do not conform to the stated policy of the jail. There were several with pictures of nude women and guns and stories of crime. Furthermore, inmates have been refused permission to have magazines which do not violate the two criteria.

Jail Rules and Discipline

Previously there have been no written rules relating to conduct in the jail and inmates were not advised of any unwritten rules. Infraction of rules was punished by a supervisor on complaint of a guard or of a corridor boss who is merely an inmate chosen by the supervisor. It was not required that the inmate be advised of the charge, and he could be placed in solitary, without a hearing, for an indefinite time. There was no provision for review.

The sheriff testified that new rules have been promulgated and will be posted in each tank and in the corridors. New prisoners will likewise be given a copy. As of the date of the trial the rules had not been posted and even the chief jailer was unaware of their existence.

The sheriff has likewise proposed a formal procedure for handling infractions of the rules. Under this procedure the guard or other jail personnel who witnesses the infraction must submit a written statement of the offense which is directed to a supervisor who reviews the report and then assesses the punishment. The prisoner is presented with a copy of the charge and the disposition made by the supervisor. On the back of the report the sheriff has listed an appeals procedure which the prisoner may initiate after the supervisor has acted. There is no provision for notice of the charge prior to action by the supervisor and one member of the Appeals Board is the jail supervisor taking the punitive action. As of the trial this new procedure had not been put into effect.

Recreation and Exercise

There is no area or program for exercise and recreation for inmates in the jail. The prisoners are confined to their cells for the duration of their sentences or until their trial. While a prisoner is waiting on postconviction appeals, he remains in the jail, and it is not uncommon for prisoners to be in jail for several years while the appeal is being considered.

When a person is placed in jail he is forced to remain in a cell with no opportunity to engage in recreational activities other than reading and playing cards and dominos. The prisoners have no exposure to either sunlight or fresh air. In the new jail, the only outside light is transmitted through translucent windows. Artificial light is so poor that reading presents difficulties. The overcrowded cells, poor ventilation, poor lighting, and lack of exercise all contribute to the physical deterioration of the inmates, and these factors also tend to heighten their frustrations and anxieties. There is no opportunity to burn off surplus energy other than by mischievous conduct.

Rehabilitation and Counseling

Prior to the filing of this suit, there was no program of rehabilitation or education at the jail. There is no effort to influence the lives of the inmates in any positive manner. The county performs an exclusively custodial function of placing the accused and the convicted into crowded cells and letting them vegetate until their release. The county officials have completely ignored the rehabilitative role the jail should play in the criminal justice system.

In the past months the chaplain has begun a small pilot program of teaching selected prisoners some rudimentary educational subjects. There is, however, no established program of evaluating the needs of the inmates and then providing them with education, vocational training or counseling.

There are no trained counselors for the inmates other than the voluntary work done by the chaplains. Men do not have the privilege of attending religious services. The only religious service available is for the chaplain to come into the tank and speak. The practice of the jail is totally devoid of any constructive measures which might act on an individual prisoner to influence him to become a contributing member of society. The inmates are relegated to the dehumanizing existence of idle isolation in a cage. The fundamental objective of correctional institutions, that of rehabilitation, has been subordinated to the limited goal of punishment and security.

Classification and Segregation of Prisoners

The inmate population of the Dallas County Jail consists of arrestees, persons convicted of misdemeanors serving their sentence, convicted felons awaiting either a decision on appeal or transfer to the Texas Department of Corrections, and federal prisoners awaiting trial. The jail officials, however, have not made any attempt to segregate the various classes of prisoners in any meaningful way. The sheriff testified that he was instituting a system of classification based on a maximum, medium and minimum security risk standard. At the present time, however, this program has not been implemented. The inmates of the jail are assigned to cells on the basis of their name, that is, by alphabetical order.

The pretrial detainees in most instances experience treatment similar to that accorded convicted criminals, but in some respects they are in a worse position. They are not permitted to engage in the limited educational program at the jail, and they are not allowed to work in the relative freedom of the trusty job. Ironically, when one compares the opportunities for education, recreation and training at the Texas Department of Corrections to the total lack of any programs at the Dallas jail, the obvious conclusion is that these technically innocent individuals suffer worse punishment in the jail than the convicted in the penitentiary. Ostensibly, the chief purpose of placing the arrestee in jail is to guarantee his appearance at trial. His incarceration is, in most instances, because he cannot afford to pay a bondsman. The result is that pretrial detainees are subjected to the demeaning confinement in the jail without trial solely because they lack money.

The plaintiffs have alleged that the jail officials enforce a policy of racial segregation of the prisoners. The sheriff denies that there is a policy of racial segregation, but he admitted that there are a number of tanks which are all black or all white. In the visit of the

Court to the jail, there was almost complete segregation of blacks and whites.

Guards

The sheriff testified in the trial that one of the major restrictions on providing any meaningful programs for the inmates is the lack of adequate supervisory personnel. There are ninety-nine guards divided into three shifts. While the guards are on duty, they supervise the five floors of the new jail and the old jail which together house more than 1500 persons. On account of the high ratio of prisoners to guard, the role of the guard is limited to housekeeping and to security measures such as controlling inmate conduct and preventing escapes. According to the sheriff, the small staff has resulted in restrictions being placed on the privileges of inmates to use telephones and on coordinating visiting sessions and has likewise prevented the development and coordination of recreational, educational and vocational training programs.

The Cop-out System

During the trial of this action, the plaintiffs raised a constitutional question regarding the practice of admitting investigators into the jail to interview the inmates concerning their plea on the charges for which they are held. The investigators, called cop-out men, are individuals hired by the District Attorney and assigned to particular state courts. Their chief role is to work out an agreeable recommendation for punishment to be presented by the District Attorney if the inmate pleads guilty. As a matter of policy, the investigators will not discuss a plea or punishment with an inmate who has a lawyer unless the lawyer is present. If the inmate has no lawyer, the cop-out man interviews him, regardless of whether the inmate has requested the interview. Although the investigators are not part of the sheriff's staff, they are given relatively free access to the jail and the inmates. The plaintiffs have asked that the sheriff be enjoined to restrict the access of cop-out men to the prisoners except when the prisoner makes a specific request for an interview.

APPLICABLE LAW

This action is primarily a class action. While there was testimony relating to individual grievances this memorandum opinion and judgment relates only to the abuses and deprivations common to all inmates.

Texas Statutory Requirements

The Texas legislature has provided for certain minimum standards for county jail facilities.[1]

1. Article 5115 of the Texas Revised Civil Statutes Annotated provides in pertinent part as follows:

> The Commissioner's Court shall provide safe and suitable jails for their respective counties, and shall cause the same to be maintained in good sanitary condition at all times, properly ventilated, heated and lighted . . .
>
> SUITABLE SEGREGATION
>
> The term "safe and suitable jails," . . . shall be construed to mean jails which provide adequate segregation facilities . . . separating . . . first offenders, awaiting trial, from all classifications of convicted prisoners. . . .
>
> [F]or . . . temporary holding of each person suspected of insanity, or who has been legally adjudged insane, there shall be provided a special enclosure or room, not less than forty (40) square feet. . . . Furthermore, the floor and the walls of such enclosure shall be provided with a soft covering designed to protect a violent person, temporarily held therein, from self-injury or destruction. . . .
>
> SUITABLE SECURITY AND SAFETY
>
> For the purpose of this Act, the term "safe and suitable jails" is further defined to mean jails which provide adequate security and safety facilities by having separate cells or compartments, dormitories and day rooms, of varying dimensions and capacities for prisoners confined therein, except that, if practicable, no one such cell or compartment shall be designed for confining two (2) prisoners only. Cells or compartments shall be designed to accommodate from one (1) to eight (8) prisoners each, and furthermore, such dormitories and day rooms shall be designed to accommodate not more than twenty-four (24) prisoners each. . . . All cells, compartments and dormitories for sleeping purposes, where each such cell, compartment or dormitory is designed to accommodate three (3) or more prisoners, shall be accessible to a day room to which prisoners may be given access during the day. Cells for one (1) prisoner only shall have a minimum floor area of forty (40) square feet and all other cells, compartments, dormitories and day rooms . . . shall have minimum floor area equal to eighteen (18) square feet for each prisoner to be confined therein.

SUITABLE SANITATION AND HEALTH

The term "safe and suitable jails" is further defined to mean jails which provide adequate facilities for maintaining proper standards in sanitation and health. Each cell designed for one (1) prisoner only shall be provided with a water closet and a combination lavatory and drinking fountain, table and seat. Each cell, compartment or dormitory designed for three (3) or more prisoners, shall be provided with one (1) water closet and one (1) combination lavatory and drinking fountain for each twelve (12) prisoners or fraction thereof to be confined therein. Furthermore, all such cells, compartments and dormitories shall be provided with one (1) bunk, not less two (2) feet, three (3) inches wide and six (6) feet, three (3) inches long, for each prisoner to be confined therein. Furthermore, each day room for the confinement of three (3) or more prisoners shall be provided with one (1) water closet, one (1) combination lavatory and drinking fountain and one (1) shower bath for each twelve (12) prisoners, or fraction thereof, to be confined therein. Furthermore, each day room shall be otherwise suitably furnished.

In the statutes, the legislature has charged the Commissioner's Court with the ultimate responsibility for providing "safe and suitable jails." The laws also state that the sheriff is to be the keeper of the jail, with the right to delegate the responsibility to a jailer who will be under his supervision and control.

The statute requires that the jail provide for adequate segregation for the prisoners. The county must separate "first offenders, awaiting trial, from all classifications of convicted prisoners." As heretofore stated there is no segregation of pretrial detainees from other inmates in the Dallas jail. Although there is some segregation of those suspected of insanity from other inmates, the facilities for housing do not comply with the statute.

Article 5115 sets down the minimum standards on the dimensions and capacities of the cells in county jails. Solitary cells are to have a minimum of forty square feet, and larger cells must have a minimum of eighteen square feet per prisoner. The law prescribes that twenty-four is the maximum number of prisoners which may be placed in a "tank."

The sanitation and health requirements for jails include the provision of at least one water closet and combination lavatory and drinking fountain for each twelve prisoners or fraction thereof.

In addition, the law requires that there be a shower for each twelve prisoners and another water closet and fountain for each day room. Each inmate must be provided a bunk.

The defendants have been quite candid in their admission that the county does not provide facilities which conform to article 5115. Furthermore, they do not contest the pendent jurisdiction of this Court to adjudicate the state law question. The failure to provide the necessary space to house the prisoner population is one of the chief causes of the deprivations which the inmates experience. Living in the overcrowded cells with less than minimal sanitary facilities has a dehumanizing effect on the persons subjected to these conditions. Already this year the Dallas jail has witnessed a riot of inmates protesting the substandard and inhumane conditions.

The charges of inadequate medical treatment and the use of the solitary cells arise in large part from the deficiencies in the physical facilities. The overcrowding of the infirmary prevents the treatment of many who should be admitted, and the lack of space makes the proper care impossible. The use of the solitary cells is one of the significant challenges of the plaintiffs. The plaintiffs have charged that confinement in the small cells with no sanitary facilities or running water constitutes cruel and unusual punishment and a violation of due process. By the defendants' own admission, the cells do not meet the minimum requirements of the state statute. The Court, therefore, is not compelled to apply subjective criteria such as "unnecessary cruelty,"[2] "standards of fairness and justice,"[3] and "evolving standards of decency"[4] to decide the question of cruel and unusual punishment. The statute provides an objective basis for judging the jail facilities, and the Dallas jail does not withstand the test of the local law.

The County Health Officer testified that the inmates working in the kitchen did not have health certificates. Article 705d of the Texas Penal Code requires that food handlers have an examination by a licensed physician to detect the presence of communicable diseases.

Eighth Amendment

In addition to violating state statutes, the plaintiffs contend that the county officials subject them to cruel and unusual punishment prohibited by the eighth amendment because of the imposition of the following conditions: overcrowded cells and tanks necessitating sleeping in day rooms and corridors; the use of inadequate and unsanitary solitary cells; unclassified assignment to tanks and cells; lack of physical exercise and of a rehabilitation program; supervision of inmates by other inmates called corridor bosses; inadequate medical facilities; the lack of rules of conduct and rules for discipline procedures.

In the past the courts limited their review under the eighth amendment to isolated incidents involving physical brutality.[5] The focus has been on a particular practice and not on a broad view of the system as the cause of the punishment. Recently the courts have expanded their examination of the charges of cruel and unusual punishment giving consideration to the effect of a "combination of circumstances" upon the contested act, practice or system.[6]

They have placed emphasis on the role of the eighth amendment as it applies to overall prison conditions which have been found detrimental to the mental and moral well-being of inmates as well as being physically debilitating.[7] As early as 1910 the Supreme Court in *Weems v. United States,* 217 U.S. 349, held that the eighth amendment ". . . is not fastened to the obsolete but may acquire meaning as public opinion becomes enlightened by a humane justice." (*Id* 378.) The Court declared further that it was the intent of the drafters of the amendment that it cover " . . . exercises of cruelty by laws other than those which inflicted bodily pain or mutilation." (*Id* 372.) In *Robinson v. California,* 370 U.S. 660 (1962) the Court concluded that the eighth amendment applies to the states.

The emphasis on nonphysical concepts of cruel and unusual punishment gained impetus in the courts as it is applied in a correctional context in the case of *Jackson v. Bishop,* 404 F.2d 571 (8th Cir. 1968). Although this case considered the use of physical punishment on inmates, the Court condemned such punishment because of its lack of rehabilitative potential.

> Corporal punishment generates hate toward the keepers who punish and toward the system which permits it. . . . It frustrates correctional and rehabilitative goals. . . . Whipping creates other penological problems and makes adjustment to society more difficult (*Id.* at 580.)

of the Supreme Court, Warren E. Burger, has stated that recreation is a necessary concomitant with education in our prisons. He recognized that one of the more pervasive evils in our correctional institutions is idleness and gave this admonition concerning the lack of programs in our jails.

> Playing cards, watching television or an occasional movie (the Dallas jail has no video recreation), with nothing more, is building up to an expensive accounting when these men are released—if not before. Such crude recreation may keep men quiet for the time, but it is a quiet that is ominous for the society they will try to reenter.[8]

The lack of physical exercise has been considered by the Courts in the context of being cruel and unusual punishment. In *Sinclair v. Henderson,* 341 F. Supp. 1123 (E.D. La. 1971), the Court reviewed the charge that the failure to afford inmates confined on death row an opportunity for exercise was a violation of the eighth amendment. It noted the decision in *Morris v. Travisono,* 310 F. Supp. 857 (D.R.I. 1970), which required the state to provide outdoor exercise to prisoners and concluded that "[c]onfinement for long periods of time without the opportunity for regular outdoor exercise does, as a matter of law, constitute cruel and unusual punishment. . . ." 331 F. Supp. at 1131.

The plaintiffs have challenged the use of the punitive segregation cells as a violation of the eighth amendment. As heretofore stated in the discussion of the state law, most of the cells do not conform to the standards provided in the statute. In *Novak v. Beto,* 452 F.2d 661 (5th Cir. 1971) *rehearing denied en banc,* No. 31116 (5th Cir., Mar. 8, 1972), the Court considered the propriety of the use of solitary confinement at the Texas Department of Corrections. In that case the facility in question conformed to the physical requirements of the statute. In upholding the use of the solitary cells, the majority placed great weight on the fact that the cells were sanitary and there was no "deprivation of the basic elements of hygiene." (*Id.* at 665.) The *Novak* case is clearly distinguishable from the situation at the Dallas jail. Here there are no sanitary facilities, the cells are smaller than the statutory requirement, and there has been in the recent past the practice of placing the inmate in the cell nude and on bread and water diet.

The trend toward examining programs for rehabilitation in conjunction with physical abuses and inhumane treatment has been articulated in the decision of *Holt v. Sarver,* 309 F. Supp. 362 (E.D. Ark. 1970) which declared the entire Arkansas prison system violative of the eighth amendment constituting cruel and unusual punishment.

The Arkansas prison system displayed shocking practices of brutality and injustices perpetrated on prisoners. The Court was confronted with numerous practices which even in isolated use would have constituted cruel and unusual punishment. In spite of the obvious cruelty in the practices, the Court also placed emphasis on them in the context of the system's failure to offer any program of rehabilitation and to prepare inmates for release. In this connection it stated

> The absence of an affirmative program of training and rehabilitation may have constitutional significance where in the absence of such a program conditions and practices exist which actually militate against reform and rehabilitation. . . . The absence of rehabilitation services and facilities . . . remains a factor in the overall constitutional equation. . . . (309 F. Supp. 379).

Holt v. Sarver is a recognition of one of the most widely regarded theories of penology that restraint and retribution have a tendency to produce recidivism in the inmates upon their release. The report of the President's Commission on Law Enforcement and Administration of Justice, "The Challenge of Crime in a Free Society" (1967) had this to say with reference to our penal institutions:

> Life in many institutions is at best barren and futile, at worst unspeakably brutal and degrading. To be sure, the offenders in such institutions are incapacitated from committing further crimes while serving their sentences, but the conditions in which they live are the poorest possible preparation for their successful reentry into society, and often merely reinforce in them a pattern of manipulation or destructiveness (*Id.* 159).

Rehabilitation must be the overriding goal of our correctional institutions. Unless society subordinates all of the correctional purposes to the goal of rehabilitation, it faces the paradox of promoting the production rather than the reduction of crime.

Another important deficiency in the Dallas jail program is the lack of any program for recreation or exercise. The Chief Justice

The use of the substandard facilities at the Dallas jail for punitive segregation or any other purpose would constitute cruel and unusual punishment.

Fourteenth Amendment

The plaintiffs have asserted that the practices and policies of the jail in relation to discipline procedure for infraction of the rules, particularly with reference to pretrial detainees infringes on their civil rights protected by the fourteenth amendment. There are several recent cases bearing on this subject.

In *Landman v. Royster,* 333 F. Supp. 621 (E.D. Va. 1971) inmates of a Virginia prison complained of the manner in which punishment was inflicted. The Court held that in adjudicatory proceedings "certain due process rights are both necessary and will not unduly impede legitimate prison functions." (*Id.* 653.) Two of these requirements the Court declared were: "First, the decision must be made by an impartial tribunal—Second, there shall be a hearing." (*Id.* 653.)

Sinclair v. Henderson, 341 F. Supp. 1123 (E.D. La. 1971) was a case involving discipline of prisoners on death row in a Louisiana prison. The Court held (1) there must be rules officially promulgated and communicated to the prisoner; (2) the prisoner must be given official written notice of the specific charge against him; (3) before serious punishment, such as punitive segregation, can be imposed, the prisoner must be given a hearing at which he shall have an opportunity to be heard; (4) the imposition of punishment should be made by one other than the accusing guard.

These two cases deal with convicted felons confined in prison. The inmates of the Dallas jail in addition to those serving sentences for misdemeanors includes pretrial detainees and men whose sentences are on appeal. All are entitled to due process in the assessment of punishment.

It is, however, not necessary that the procedure for inmates in all institutions to receive exactly the same treatment in order for their rights to be protected. There is no question in this case or in *Landman* and *Sinclair* of the power of the person in charge to discipline the inmates. The proper operation of the institution requires order. It is recognized that when rules are violated there is need to act quickly and in a way that will not disrupt the security of the jail and the safety of the other inmates. It seems reasonable to place inmates in solitary for short periods of time without a hearing in case of certain violations and such action would not be a violation of rights under certain circumstances.

The procedure rules for discipline promulgated by the sheriff appear to be reasonable except that an inmate who is confined in a solitary cell for more than three days should have a hearing, and if an appeal is taken the person charging the inmate should not be on the board. The sheriff is likewise to be complimented for limiting the maximum time in solitary to fifteen days when heretofore it has been unlimited.

The recent en banc decision of *Anderson v. Nosser*, ____ F. 2d ____ (5th Cir. 1972) holds that confinement of arrestees under the conditions existing in a Mississippi prison were a violation of due process. Here conditions are not similar, and we do not hold that the mere confinement of the inmates in the Dallas County Jail is a failure of due process.

CONCLUSION

The correctional programs and facilities of the Dallas County Jail are in desperate need of upgrading and expansion. The county does not provide the minimum facilities required by law. The policy of the county has been to confine the accused and the convicted as inexpensively as possible, thereby preventing their circulation in society. Punishment results from the inadequate facilities and unpleasant experience. The present jail system serves no other purpose.

The local jail performs the unique role of being a misdemeanant institution, that is, an institution for persons charged with petty crimes with short sentences. The local jail is the only correctional institution to which the misdemeanant is associated, but the term correctional is a euphemism. Dallas County has shown complete indifference to its responsibility to attempt rehabilitation of those offenders charged to its care.

The sheriff and chief jailer in recent months made an effort to change some of the deficient conditions at the jail. For these efforts they are to be commended. The county has begun renovating the old jail; medical and dental programs have been upgraded; censorship of mail has been limited; punitive segregation has been limited to fifteen days; the disciplined prisoner is not deprived of his clothing; a pilot remedial education program is underway; and the inmates have increased telephone and visitation privileges.

The sheriff has stated that he is prepared to initiate more programs and to improve the jail, but he is handicapped by a small staff and small budget. There is no quantitative statement of the costs which the necessary improvements will require. This Court recognizes that enlarging the jail will be costly, but "inadequate resources can never be an adequate justification for depriving any person of his constitutional rights." (*Hamilton v. Love,* 328 F. Supp. 1182 [E.D. Ark. 1971].)

The injunctive order provided herein is, of course, only the minimal action which is required. The Court is encouraged by the apparent good faith and interest of the Sheriff's Department in providing a "safe and suitable jail." Although this Court does not invite judicial review of jail administration, it is hoped that public attention to jail conditions which this action has produced will stimulate interest in the community to do something about our jails. The recent events at Attica, New York, and the disturbance at the Dallas jail should be warnings of the need to re-examine and upgrade correctional programs. The costs for making the changes may be substantial. But the consequences of inaction are greater.

In view of the foregoing conditions at the Dallas County Jail, it is the judgment of this Court

1. The Commissioner's Court is enjoined from further violating the provisions of Article 5115 of the Texas Revised Civil Statutes and is directed to provide immediately as follows:

    a. Sufficient cells and tanks to accommodate a number of inmates equal to the largest number in the Dallas County jail during 1972 in any one day.

    b. Solitary cells of not less than forty square feet, provided with a bunk, water closet and a combination drinking fountain and lavatory.

    c. The capacity of the hospital ward for men shall be increased and bunks provided for all patients confined therein.

    d. Padded cells with hammocks for insane persons.

It is suggested in this connection that the old jail be renovated and the women's floor in the new jail be redesigned to accommodate both male and female inmates. A reasonable time for the completion of these improvements in the opinion of the Court is six months. Even with such remodeling and repairs the provisions of Article 5115 will not be wholly complied with. The Court directs that the Commissioner's Court make immediate plans for full compliance within a reasonable time. A regional jail is a possible answer to the complete fulfillment of these requirements, but plans for a regional jail are not sufficient reason for the failure to implement all the statutory provisions for a "safe and suitable" jail as required by Article 5115.

2. The Commissioner's Court is directed to provide an outdoor area for exercise and a rehabilitative program of recreation. As a temporary arrangement it is suggested that the roof of the jail be remodeled to provide for such facilities, the possibility for which was suggested by the sheriff. In a permanent plan for new facilities, quarters should be provided for chapel services and educational programs.

3. The Commissioner's Court is directed to provide jail guards sufficient for security for jail facilities without the use of inmate assistance.

4. The permanent injunction heretofore issued relating to censorship of mail is affirmed and carried forward in this judgment. The sheriff is directed not to open or censor mail transmitted between inmates of the jail and the following persons: courts, prosecuting attorneys, probation and parole officers, governmental agencies, lawyers and the press.

5. The preliminary injunction, heretofore issued relating to the destruction of reading matter belonging to inmates, is made a permanent injunction, and the sheriff and other jail officials are enjoined from destroying law books, legal materials, legal documents, books, magazines and newspaper clippings provided such material is maintained in good condition and does not create a fire or health hazard.

6. While this Court will not interfere in the standards set up by the sheriff for inmates receiving magazines or books, it appears that the policy has not been adhered to, and the sheriff is directed to see that greater care is exercised in determining the books and

magazines made available to inmates so as to permit inmates to have reading material not prohibited and to restrict the receipt by inmates of prohibited material.

7. The sheriff is directed to make effective the new policy relating to rules of conduct of inmates. These rules must be communicated to the inmates apprising them of what conduct can subject them to discipline, the penalty for infraction, and the procedure by which such a determination will be made. Before any punishment for confinement of more than three days in solitary is inflicted, hearings should be held. In case of the appeal of any sentence the officer charging or sentencing the inmate should not be a member of the Board of Appeals.

8. The sheriff is directed not to allow persons to see prisoners except with the consent or request of the inmates. This has particular reference to "cop-out" men, who have had free access to the jail.

10. The sheriff is enjoined from using inmates as corridor bosses to enforce rules and preserve discipline.

11. The sheriff is directed not to use any cell of less than forty square feet, not to place more inmates in cells and tanks than those such facilities are designed to accommodate, nor to place anyone in a solitary cell unless it is provided with a bunk, water closet and a combination fountain and lavatory.

12. The sheriff is directed to have employees and inmates handling food examined by a licensed physician to detect the presence of communicable diseases as required by Article 705d of the Texas Penal Code.

Attorneys fees are denied. Costs are taxed against defendants.

While this opinion closes this case it may be reopened within a reasonable time on application of the plaintiffs contending that defendants are not making a diligent, good faith effort to comply with the order of this Court.

Sarah T. Hughes
United States District Judge

REFERENCES

1. Title 81, Article 5115, Texas Revised Civil Statutes Annotated.
2. Wilberson v. Utah, 99 U.S. 130, 136 (1878).

3. Louisiana *ex rel.* Francis v. Resweber, 329 U.S. 459, 470 (1947) (Frankfurter, J., concurring).
4. Trop v. Dulles, 356 U.S. 86, 101 (1958).
5. *See,* e.g. Wiltsie v. California Dep't of Corrections, 406 F.2d 515 (9th Cir. 1968); Jordan v. Fitzharris, 257 F. Supp. 674 (N.D. Cal. 1966); Talley v. Stephens, 247 F. Supp. 683 (E.D. Ark. 1965).
6. See Novak v. Beto, 453 F.2d 661, 675 (5th Cir. 1971) (Tuttle, J., concurring in part and dissenting in part).
7. *See,* e.g. Jackson v. Bishop, 401 F.2d 571 (8th Cir. 1968); Holt v. Sarver, 309 F. Supp. 362 (E.D. Ark. 1969), *aff'd,* 442 F.2d 304 (8th Cir. 1971).
8. Address by Chief Justice Warren E. Burger, National Conference on Corrections, Dec. 7, 1971.

SELECTED BIBLIOGRAPHY

BOOKS

Acton, H.B.: *The Philosophy of Punishment.* New York, St Martin, 1969.
American Correctional Association: *Manual of Correctional Standards.* 1966.
Alexander, Myrl E.: *Jail Administration.* Springfield, Thomas, 1957.
Carter, Robert M., et al.: *Correctional Institutions.* Philadelphia, Lippincott, 1972.
Clemmer, Donald: *The Prison Community.* New York, HR&W, 1958.
Cressey, Donald R.: *The Prison: Studies in Institutional Organization and Change.* New York, HR&W, 1961.
Fox, Vernon: *Introduction to Corrections.* Englewood Cliffs, P-H, 1972.
Johnson, Savitz Wolfgang: *The Sociology of Punishment and Corrections.* Somerset, Wiley, 1962.
Killinger, Cromwell: *Penology: The Evolution of Corrections in America.* West, 1973.
National Advisory Commission on Criminal Justice Standards and Goals: *Corrections.* Wash. D.C., 1973.
Sykes, Gresham M.: *The Society of Captives.* Princeton, Princeton U Pr, 1958.
Wolfgang and Rabinowitz: *The Criminal in Confinement.* New York, Basic, 1971.
Comfort, Alex: Institutions without sex. *Social Work,* 1967.
Fox, Vernon: Analysis of prison disciplinary problems. *J Crim L, 49*:321, 1958.
Gill, Howard B.: New prison discipline. *Fed Probation, 34*:29, 1970.
Goldart, I.: Corrections: The plight of reform. *U Med L.F., 1*:27, 1971.
Goldfard, and Signer: Redressing prisoner's grievances. *Geo Wash L. Rev, 5*:277, 1970.
Jacob: Prison discipline and inmate rights. *Harv Civ Lib L Rev, 5*:227, 1970.

Moore, Bruce: Prisoners are people. *Natural Resources J, 10*:869, 1970.
Paulsen, Conrad G.: Prison reform in the future. *Vill L Rev,* 16:1082, 1971.
Sneidman: Prisoners and medical treatment. *Am L Bull,* 4:450, 1968.
The Prison Journal, special issue on "Prisoner Incentive Systems." Spring-Summer, 1967.
A jam in the revolving door: A prisoner's right to rehabilitation. *Geo L J, 60*:225, 1971.
Beyond the ken of the courts: A critique of judicial refusal to review the complaints of convicts. *Yale L J, 72*:506, 1963.
Censorship of prisoner's mail and the Constitution. *ABAJ,* 56:1051, 1970.
Standard minimum rules for treatment of prisoners. *NY L J Int'l and Pol,* 2:314, 1969.
Symposium: Prison and prisoners. *Hast L J, 23*:4, 995-111.
The jail: Its operation and management. U.S. Bureau of Prisons, 1970.
Turn 'em loose towards a flexible corrections system. *So Cal L Rev,* 42:682, 1969.

APPENDICES

APPENDIX A

State of Illinois

MUNICIPAL JAIL AND LOCKUP STANDARDS

I. Legal Authority To Set Up Standards And Exercise Supervision Over Jails And Lockups

Illinois Revised Statutes, Chapter 127, Section 55a, paragraphs 5 and 6 amended, effective January 1, 1970. Section 55a.

1. The Department of Corrections shall have power:

(5) To establish for the operation of county and municipal jails and houses of correction and juvenile detention facilities minimum standards for the physical condition of such institutions and for the treatment of inmates with respect to their health and safety and security of the community and to make recommendations to such institutions to assure compliance with the requirements of such minimum standards. In no event, shall standards set by the Department exceed those established by the Federal Bureau of Prisons for county and municipal jails and houses of correction in which federal prisoners are incarcerated and any jail or house of correction inspected and approved by the Federal Bureau of Prisons shall be deemed to have the minimum standards set by the Department. In no event, shall standards set by the Department exceed those established by the United States Children's Bureau for juvenile detention facilities. At least once a year, the Department shall inspect each such facility for compliance with the standards established and the results of such inspection shall be made available by the Department for public inspection. If any detention or correctional facility does not comply with the standards established, the Director of Corrections shall give notice to the county board or the corporate authorities of the municipality, as the case may be,

of such noncompliance, specifying the particular standards that have not been met by such facility. If the facility is not in compliance with such standards when six months have elapsed from the giving of such notice, the Director of Corrections may petition the appropriate court for an order for the closing of that facility or for other appropriate relief.

(6) To provide consultation for the design, construction, programs and administration of detention and correctional facilities and services for children and adults operated by counties and municipalities and shall make studies and surveys of the programs and the administration of such facilities. Personnel of the Department shall be admitted to these facilities as required for such purposes. The Department may develop and administer programs of grant-in-aid for correctional services in cooperation with local agencies. The Department shall provide courses of training for the personnel of such institutions and conduct pilot projects in the institutions.

II. Legal Rights Of Accused While In Custody

Illinois Revised Statutes, Chapter 38-Criminal Law and Procedure
A. Section 103-2 Treatment While in Custody:

(a) On being taken into custody every person shall have the right to remain silent.

(b) No unlawful means of any kind shall be used to obtain a statement, admission or confession from any person in custody.

(c) Persons in custody shall be treated humanely and provided with proper food, shelter and, if required, medical treatment.
B. Section 103-3 Right to Communicate with Attorney and Family; Transfers:

(a) Persons who are arrested shall have the right to communicate with an attorney of their choice and a member of their family by making a reasonable number of telephone calls or in any other reasonable manner. Such communication shall be permitted within a reasonable time after arrival at the first place of custody.

(b) In the event the accused is transferred to a new place of custody, his right to communicate with an attorney and a member of his family is renewed.

C. Section 103-4 Right to Consult with Attorney:

Any person committed, imprisoned or restrained of his liberty for any cause whatever and whether or not such person is charged with an offense shall, except in cases of imminent danger of escape, be allowed to consult with any licensed attorney at law of this State whom such person may desire to see or consult alone and in private at the place of custody, as many times and for such period each time as is reasonable. When any such person is about to be moved beyond the limits of this State under any pretense whatever the person to be moved shall be entitled to a reasonable delay for the purpose of obtaining counsel and of availing himself of the laws of this State for the security of personal liberty.

D. Section 103-7 Posting Notice of Rights:

Every sheriff, chief of police or other person who is in charge of any jail, police station or other building where persons under arrest are held in custody pending investigation, bail or other criminal proceedings, shall post in every room, other than cells, of such buildings where persons are held in custody, in conspicuous places where it may be seen and read by persons in custody and others, a poster, printed in large type, containing a verbatim copy in the English language of the provisions of Sections 103-2, 103-3, 103-4, 109-1, 110-2, 110-4, and sub-parts (a) and (b) of Section 110-7 and 113-3 of this code. Each person who is in charge of any courthouse or other building in which any trial of an offense is conducted shall post in each room primarily used for such trials and in each room in which defendants are confined or wait, pending trial, in conspicuous places where it may be seen and read by persons in custody and others, a poster, printed in large type, containing a verbatim copy in the English language of the provisions of Sections 103-6, 113-1, 113-4 and 115-1 and the sub-parts (a) and (b) of Section 113-3 of this code. As amended by act approved Aug. 5, 1965. L1965, p.---, H.B. No. 1664.

III. Minimum Municipal Jail And Lockup Standards

A. The Primary Purpose of Lockups:

(1) The lockup is a security facility, usually operated by the

police department, for temporary detention of persons held for investigation pending disposition of their cases by the judiciary, or awaiting transfer to another institution. Usually the period of detention does not exceed forty-eight hours; persons who must be held longer are transferred to a county jail.

(2) No minor under fourteen years of age may be confined in a jail or place ordinarily used for the confinement of prisoners in a police station. Boys under seventeen and girls under eighteen years of age must be kept separate from confined adults and may not at any time be kept in the same cell, room, or yard with adults confined pursuant to the criminal law. Refer to Juvenile Court Act as revised by 76th General Assembly (Article 2, Section 2-8).

(3) No prisoner with a known history of mental disorder or mental defect, or who shows evidence of such condition, shall be housed in any municipal jail or lockup. In the event such type prisoner is received he shall be afforded protective custody and individualized supervision until such time as he is transferred to another facility. Such prisoner shall immediately be referred for appropriate professional study and diagnosis. If a finding of mental illness or mental disorder is made, the Chief of Police or the Chief Jailer shall immediately notify the appropriate authorities regarding the mental condition of the prisoner so that the transfer can be made.

B. Minimum Physical Standards:

   (1) Each lockup or jail must:
      a. Be built upon a durable foundation, and be of fire-resistant construction.
      b. Be well lighted, comfortably heated and ventilated.
      c. Have electrical conduits, fixtures, switches, and outlets outside the reach of prisoners, or of tamperproof construction.

(2) In no case shall the heating facilities be of such character as to constitute a fire hazard or jeopardize, in any way, the lives of those confined.

(3) The lockup shall be properly lighted so that adequate illumination for supervision and safe custody is guaranteed at all times.

(4) It is essential that there be complete segregation of male

and female prisoners—to assure adequate privacy. The women's quarters shall be completely separate from the men's quarters and in no event, shall male and female prisoners have physical, visual and audible contact with each other.

(5) Preferably no cells or detention rooms wherein persons are confined should be located in a basement. A basement is a story whose floorline is below grade at any entrance or exit and whose ceiling is not more than five (5) feet above grade at any such entrance or exit. Wherever cells or detention rooms are located in a basement they must be adjacent to the office of the jailer responsible for the supervision and care of the prisoners. This basement area must be provided with adequate heat, light, and forced air ventilation.

(6) No cells and detention rooms shall be located on upper floors unless elevator service is provided.

(7) All cells shall be designated for the use of one prisoner. Because of very little knowledge concerning the prisoner in the lockup situation, separation of inmates from each other is really vital.

(8) The minimum size of each cell shall be approximately six (6) feet wide by eight (8) feet long by eight (8) feet high.

(9) Each cell shall contain the following equipment:
    a. A rigidly constructed perforated, steel-bottomed metal bed firmly anchored to the floor or welded to the plate walls so as to prevent removal or the opportunity of a prisoner tearing the equipment loose.
    b. A prison-type washbowl with piped water.
    c. A prison-type toilet.
    d. A prison-type light controlled by the jailer is optional.

(10) The lockup shall be maintained at all times in a clean, sanitary and safe condition.

C. Prisoner Search:

(1) On arrival, at the place of detention, the prisoner shall be thoroughly searched for any contraband or articles with which he might injure himself or others, or mar the cells.

(2) Property rights of prisoners shall be protected by issuing them receipts with an accurate listing of all money and property

taken at the time of admission and by obtaining their receipts when property is returned to the prisoner or turned over to the Receiving Officer of another facility. All prisoners should be required to countersign the receipts for personal property, thereby eliminating the possibility of a dispute upon transfer or release.

D. Supervision:

(1) Twenty-four-hour supervision shall be maintained when prisoners are confined, and a personal inspection of the persons confined shall be made at least every hour. A record of such supervision, on appropriate forms, shall be maintained in ink, showing the time of visit by an officer, his signature, the apparent condition of each prisoner, and any relevant remarks.

(2) The supervision of female prisoners by male officers is extremely objectionable and undesirable. A matron or other qualified female employee shall provide proper supervision of female prisoners when any are confined in the lockup.

(3) Any prisoner who, upon admittance or while confined, is unconscious, injured, or shows signs of physical or mental distress shall be immediately examined by a physician—who shall have full power and authority to order his removal to a hospital if necessary. A record of all physicians' visits and treatment shall be kept.

(4) For the protection of the city officials, suspected inebriates should be examined by a physician before commitment— to determine intoxication or illness. An undetected skull fracture, diabetic coma, epilepsy or other diseases or illnesses often produce behavior resembling drunkenness.

(5) At no time shall an armed officer enter a cell where a prisoner is detained.

(6) At no time shall an officer enter a cell where a prisoner is detained without the presence of another officer.

E. Sanitation

(1) When occupied, the lockup shall be thoroughly cleaned daily. The jail officer should be made responsible for the cleanliness of the lockup. Preventive measures must be taken to preclude the presence of vermin. If vermin is present, immediate measures shall be taken to eradicate it.

Appendix A

(2) Toilet paper, soap, and paper towels shall be available, and a supply of paper drinking cups should be on hand unless lavatories in the cells are provided with drinking fountains. Shaving equipment and a comb should be made available (e.g. before going to court, discharge, etc.).

(3) Each prisoner detained overnight shall be provided with clean bedding if, in the opinion of the jail officer, it does not present a hazard to the inmate or the facility.

(4) If a prisoner is detained longer than seven calendar days, clean bedding shall be re-issued on at least a weekly basis.

(5) If a prisoner is to be detained in excess of seventy-two hours he shall be issued linen toweling. Such toweling shall be re-issued twice per week.

F. Food for Prisoners:

(1) All prisoners shall be fed three meals per day at the approximate times of breakfast, lunch and supper in sufficient quantity and of wholesome quality—at the cost of the municipality.

(2) Food should be given to a prisoner in his cell. Under no circumstances should he be taken to a restaurant.

(3) Good food, well served, is perhaps the most important factor in maintaining discipline and reasonable conduct among inmates. Conversely, insufficient, monotonous or impalatable food is a constant source of resentment and discontent which may at any time break into open violence.

G. Fire Hazards:

(1) Each lockup shall be equipped with approved fire extinguishers in each cell block or cell section, which must be inspected annually and tagged with the date of inspection and the identity of the fire inspector.

    a. Fire extinguishers shall be placed at strategic points, in a suitable receptacle, but where they will not be accessible to the prisoners or any unauthorized persons.

H. Emergeny Plan:

(1) Each lockup must have in writing its own specific plans to meet all emergencies—escapes or escape attempts, prisoner disturbances, fires, presence of contagious diseases, assaults on jail

officers, etc. These emergency plans should be developed in cooperation with the resources available from other agencies in the community. These emergency plans must be known by all personnel of the jail and be ready to go into operation immediately upon the recognition that a state of emergency exists.

I. Prisoner Records:

(1) The following minimum identification data shall be recorded for each person detained in the lockup:
    a. Name and aliases
    b. Address at time of arrest
    c. Date of birth, age
    e. Social Security number
    d. Race, sex, height, color of eyes and hair, tattoos, visible amputations
    f. Name, address, telephone number and relationship of nearest relative
    g. Marital status
    h. Date and time of confinement in lockup
    i. Charge on which arrested
    j. Arresting officer
    k. General physical conditions when confined
    l. Date examined by physician (if necessary)
    m. Disposition of case
    n. Date of release or transfer
    o. Remarks (unusual events).

(2) The Bureau will provide a sample uniform card to record this data on each prisoner.

J. Extraordinary Occurrences:

(1) All unusual incidents which involve, or endanger, the lives or physical welfare of jail officers or prisoners in the lockup must be reported to the Bureau of Detention Facilities and Jail Standards in Springfield in writing on a form supplied by the Bureau within 72 hours. It is advisable for the Police Department to keep one copy of such extraordinary occurrence report for its own records. Only one copy shall be sent to the Bureau.

(2) Extraordinary occurrences shall mean:

Appendix A 311

    a. Suicide or attempted suicide
    b. Homicide
    c. Death (other than suicide or homicide)
    d. Serious injury or illness (accidental, self or other inflicted, incurred subsequent to detention)
    e. Escape
    f. Attempted escapes
    g. Fire
    h. Riot
    i. Assaults on officers
    j. Other serious disturbances.

K. Lockup Population Reports:

(1) The Chief of Police, Chief Jailer, or any other responsible supervisor shall furnish the Bureau of Detention Facilities and Jail Standards on or before the seventh day of each month, the total number of adult males, adult females, juvenile males, and juvenile females received (booked) and released or transferred from the lockup during the previous calendar month on a form provided by the Bureau.

L. Discipline:

(1) Minor matters of discipline, where no danger of safety, property or life exists, shall be handled in such a manner as to attract as little attention as possible to the incident.

(2) Officers shall not strike or lay hands on a prisoner unless it be in self-defense, or unless it is necessary to prevent escape or serious injury to person or property, to quell a disturbance, or to effect detention. In such cases, only the amount of physical force necessary to accomplish the desired result is authorized.

(3) Each detention agency should have some type of restraining equipment available for use in emergencies and under the direction of competent medical authority. In such instances, full-time supervision should be provided and further action determined by the physician.

M. Specifications For Approved Construction And Equipment Of Cells:

(1) Heating: Any standard heating system is acceptable. Con-

trolled heating by forced air is preferred, providing the heat produced is ample to insure comfort during cold and damp weather and is reasonably controlled as to temperature. No heating equipment, such as radiators, shall be located in the cells. If radiators are necessary, they shall be located outside the cells and adequately shielded to prevent accidental injury.

(2) Ventilation: The system shall provide ventilation of each cell, so that any foul air or odors can be drawn off adequately. Tempered air throughout the entire police station, including the lockup or jail, is strongly recommended. It will result in greater efficiency from staff and less problems with prisoners.

(3) Lighting: Lights shall be located in the cell block corridor or vestibule. Only approved prison-type lights may be installed in the cells. Standard, safe fixtures are acceptable, preferably spot-type fixtures anchored in the cell room wall opposite the cells or suspended by conduit from the cell room ceiling and sufficiently out of reach of prisoners through the cell fronts. Illumination provided must be of sufficient intensity to clearly light up the cells for supervision purposes at all times. All lights shall be under outside switch control. Individual switch control is preferable.

(4) Emergency Electric Generator: This equipment should be available in the event of power failures. It can be powered by natural gas with built-in capacity to also run on gasoline. The generator equipment should be the automatic type employing a **transfer** switch which will activate the equipment within seconds after a power failure. It should be of sufficient capacity to activate necessary overhead lighting, communications equipment, heating and ventilating equipment, sump pumps, partial site lighting and gasoline pumps.

(5) Windows: None shall be in the cells. They are not required so long as both artificial illumination and ventilation in the cells are adequate. Where artificial ventilation is not provided, windows should be located on the outer cell block wall. The window areas should be equal to at least one-eighth of the floor space of the cell block served by the window and one half of the window should be able to be opened. The windows should preferably be of an approved detention type with suitable security screens to prevent unauthorized entry of persons or the smuggling of weapons or

contraband into the cells or cell block. They should be glazed with translucent glass.

(6) Cell Plumbing: Each cell must have a prison-type toilet and washbowl. Standard jail fixtures made of stainless steel or cast aluminum are acceptable. The toilets should be wall or floor-mounted, seatless, tankless and with push-button valves. The bowl must have piped water with push-button controls. Each jail should have adequate shower facilities with hot and cold running water.

(7) Cell Bunks: They shall be of metal construction permanently attached to the cell wall (without chains) or firmly anchored to the floor.
> a. The bunk edges should be turned either upwards or downwards so as not to represent a safety hazard.
> b. Bunks should be anchored through the cell walls, preferably back-to-back by means of anchor plates imbedded in the partition walls.

(8) Detention Facilities for Women and Juveniles: They may consist of a cell or detention-type room. If a detention room is provided it shall be equipped with approved prison-type toilet and washbowl and either an approved metal cot permanently anchored to the floor or a bunk of metal construction, permanently attached to the wall. If cells are provided they must have the same type of equipment as that specified for male prisoners. Sanitary conditions shall be maintained on a basis equal to other detention facilities.

(9) Cell Door and Fronts: Steel grille sliding doors, with snap-lock as well as key-lock, are preferable to swinging doors. Each door shall contain a food pass, approximately twelve (12) inches long and four (4) inches high. The rest of the cell front can be steel grille or solid masonry. If grille construction, the fronts must be not less than 7/8 inch steel bars, round or hexagonal, five (5) inches on centers

(10) Cell and Cell Block Corridor Walls: They can be either steel or reinforced masonry. Masonry may consist of cement block or pre-cast concrete. If masonry is used for the cell walls, it must be at least six (6) inches thick. For cheaper maintenance and easier cleaning, it is advisable to cover masonry surfaces with salt-glazed tile, which requires no painting, or other hard-finish material.

(11) Cell and Cell Block Corridor Ceilings: They can be steel or

masonry. Construction of either reinforced plaster or cement is more desirable and practical and should be painted, with fire resistant paint.

(12) Cell and Cell Block Floors: Concrete or cement construction, with protective surface sealer (epoxy coating), rather than paint, is the most preferable. Non-skid tile material can be used, but is not required. Cell floor should be pitched one or two inches above the corridor floor for drainage purposes, so that cells can be hosed down for cleaning purposes.

(13) Water Drains: They must not be located in the cells but in the cell block corridor floors. One drain should be provided for each two or three cells. Drain covers must be securely anchored so that prisoners cannot use them as assault weapons.

(14) Cell Block Entrance Door: It can be of hollow steel with air louvers on bottom and also a safety-glass observation panel, to shut off noise from the cell block. Otherwise, a grille door can be used. The door must be at least three (3) feet wide, and the space on either side of it must be unobstructed, for reasons of safe passage of both prisoners and police.

(15) Cell Block Corridors: They must be at least four (4) feet wide to permit the safe passage of prisoner and escorting officer(s).

(16) Visiting Area: Semi-private compartments should be provided for the prisoner to communicate with duly authorized visitors (attorneys, clergy, immediate family). The prisoner should be brought into the cubicle from the lockup side and the visitor enter from the public corridor side in view of the jail officer. It must be constructed with bullet-proof glass separating the prisoner from the visitor. Mechanical speaking devices shall be so constructed to prevent the passing of contraband from one cubicle to another. Hand-set telephones on the prisoner's side should not be considered. They could be used as weapons against the jail officer. The door leading into the prisoner side of the compartment must be a totally secure door, operable only by the jail officer.

N. Approval Of Jail And Lockup Construction Plans:

(1) The plans and specifications for the building of new jails and lockups or the renovation or revision of existing facilities must

given every reasonable opportunity to confer with their attorneys, but the jail officials should see that they are not fleeced or exploited by unscrupulous persons.
16. Regular visiting by the family and friends of the prisoners should be permitted under reasonable conditions and under supervision.

Appendix B

medical examination when admitted to jail.
8. Juveniles should not be held in jails, but if committed should be definitely segregated and well-supervised.
9. Prisoners with contagious diseases, hardened criminals, and the sexes should be segregated.
10. Women prisoners should be under the supervision of a matron at all times. No male employee should have keys to the women's quarters or be permitted to go there unless accompanied by a matron. Male prisoners should never be permitted to go to the women's quarters to bring food or for any other purpose.
11. Prisoners should be fed three times each day. The food should have the proper nutritive value and be prepared and served in a wholesome and palatable way. The eating utensils should be returned to the kitchen and washed with soap and scalding water after each meal.
12. Adequate bathing and toilet facilities should be available, and water, soap, towels, and toothbrushes should be supplied to prisoners. These are essential to the health of any human being —prisoners not excepted.
13. Convicted prisoners should be kept employed. An ingenious jail official can find many ways to occupy the prisoners working for the state or city or county, without interfering with private industry or free labor. They can work on salvaging government property; repair autos, trucks and other items; paint bridges; some of them can work on the highways under proper supervision; and perform other useful jobs. They should also be required to keep their own quarters and other sections of the jail clean. This work should be done under the supervision of an employee. Prisoners who have not been convicted should be given the opportunity to work within the jail confines if they are suitable and care to do so. Useful occupation stimulates self-respect; idleness breeds trouble and leads to more crime.
14. There should be good reading material available. Outdoor exercise should be required, and provisions made for education and religious instruction.
15. Prisoners' legal rights should be protected and they should be

APPENDIX B

Minimum Jail Standards
Jail Services, U.S. Bureau of Prisons*

1. A jail should be under the direct management and control of a person qualified by training and experience to supervise and control prisoners. As many persons as are necessary to provide constant supervision over the prisoners should be employed and be under authority of the head official. Salaries should be sufficient to attract persons of high caliber.
2. Jail officials should have a set of policies and regulations for the operation of the jail, for the employees and for the inmates.
3. The building should be structurally sound, secure, fire-resistant; properly heated, ventilated, and lighted. Windows should be screened. There should be a good locking system, and the devices should be in operating order.
4. All parts of the jail should be kept immaculately clean.
5. Kangaroo courts or similar inmate organizations should be prohibited. No prisoner should be allowed to have authority over any other prisoner. Employees should fulfill their own responsibilities and not turn them over to prisoners, any more than a hospital superintendent turns over his responsibilities to the patients.
6. Brutal treatment by employees or prisoners should be prohibited. No prisoner should be permitted special privileges. Trusties, so-called, should be under the supervision of employees.
7. A competent physician should be available to take care of the medical needs of the prisoners, and to give each prisoner a

---

*Courtesy of Jail Inspection Service, Federal Bureau of Prisons, Washington, D. C. 20537.

be approved by the Bureau of Detention Facilities and Jail Standards, Illinois Department of Corrections.

    a. The Bureau is concerned with all factors and aspects of the construction, maintenance, and operation of the detention facility which effect the safekeeping, care, and welfare of all persons detained in the cells.

    b. Two sets of drawings must be submitted, one of which will be retained for record purposes. Included should be architectural, heating and ventilating, plumbing and electrical sheets, and specifications for construction materials, equipment and furnishings.

    c. It is advisable to bring the preliminary drawings to the Bureau office for examination and discussion. This will better insure that the lockup plans will satisfactorily meet the standards and requirements in every respect.

APPENDIX C

TABLE OF CASES ON PRISONER LEGAL RIGHTS
AND JAIL CONDITIONS

Cases:
First Circuit—
 Rozecki v. Gaughan, 459 F.2d 6 (1st Cir. 1972).
 Conklin v. Hancock, 334 F. Supp. 1119 (D.N.H. 1971).
 Palmigiano v. Travisono, 317 F. Supp. 776 (D.R.I. 1970).
 Inmates of Suffolk County Jail v. Eisenstadt, Civ. Action No. 71-162-G (D. Mass. June 29, 1971).
 Second Circuit—
 Wilkinson v. Skinner, ——— F.2d ———, 11 Cir. L. Rptr. 2417 (2d Cir. June 28, 1972).
  Seale v. Manson, 326 F. Supp. 1375 (D. Conn. 1971).
  Freeley v. McGrath, 314 F. Supp. 679 (S.D.N.Y. 1970).
  Valvano v. McGrath, 325 F. Supp. 408 (E.D.N.Y. 1971).
  Davis v. Lindsay, 321 F. Supp. 1134 (S.D.N.Y. 1970).
  Rhem v. McGrath, 326 F. Supp. 681 (S.D.N.Y. 1970).
 Third Circuit—
 United States ex rel. Jones v. Rundle, 453 F.2d 147 (3rd Cir. 1971).
  Fidtler v. Hendricks, 317 F. Supp. 738 (E.D. Pa. 1970).
 Fourth Circuit—
 Collins v. Schoonfield, ——— F. Supp. ——— Civ. No. 71-500-K (D. Md. May 15, 1972).
 Fifth Circuit—
 Anderson v. Nosser, 456 F.2d 835 (5th Cir. 1972) (en banc).
 Hamilton v. Schiro, 338 F. Supp. 1016 (E.D. La. 1970).
 Taylor v. Sterrett, 344 F. Supp. 411, Civ. Action 4-5220-B (N.D. Tex. June 5, 1972).
 Sixth Circuit—

Jones v. Wittenberg, 330 F. Supp. 707 (N.D. Ohio 1971), aff'd sub nom. *Jones v. Metzger,* 456 F.2d 854 (6th Cir. 1972) *Jansson v. Grysen,* ——— F. Supp. ———, No. G-130-71 C.A. (W.D. Mich. June 1, 1972).

Seventh Circuit—

Inmates of Cook County Jail v. Tierney, No. 68 C 504 (N.D. Ill. Aug. 22, 1968).

Petersen,, 51 F.R.D. 540 (E.D. Wis. 1971).

Eight Circuit—

Moore v. Ciccone, 459 F.2d 574 (8th Cir. 1972).

Hamilton v. Love, 328 F. Supp. 1182 (E.D. Ark. 1971).

Garrison v. Hickam, ——— F. Supp. ———, No. 2280 (W.D. Mo. June 7, 1972).

Tyler v. Ciccone, 299 F. Supp. 685 (W.D. Mo. 1969).

Ninth Circuit—

Payne v. Whitmore, 325 F. Supp. 1191 (N.D. Cal. 1971).

Brenneman v. Madigan, 343 F. Supp. 128, 11 Cr. L. Rptr. 2248 (N.D. Cal. May 12, 1972).

Tenth Circuit—

Curley v. Gonzales, Civ. Nos. 8372, 8373 (D.N. Mex. Feb. 13, 1970).

State Court Decisions:

McCray v. Maryland, Misc. Pet. 4363 (Cir. Ct. Mont. Cty, Md. Nov. 11, 1971).

Comm. ex rel. Bryant v. Hendrick, 280 A.2d 110 (Pa. 1971).

Jackson v. Hendrick, No. 71-2437 (C.P. Phil. Pa., April 7, 1972).

Wayne County Jail Inmates v. Wayne County Bd. Comm'rs., No. 173217 (Cir. Ct. Wayne Cty., Mich. May 18, 1971).

Lowery v. Metropolitan Dade County, No. 71-1858 (Cir. Ct. 11th Dist. Dade Cty., Fla., Feb. 11, 1971).

In Re Cisson, (N.J. Super. Ct., Som. Cty. March 24, 1972).

DATE DUE